An Almighty God? Get Serious!

By Darlene Lamoureux

and

Trophies of Grace

By Karen Hanson

XULON PRESS

Xulon Press
555 Winderley Pl, Suite 225
Maitland, FL 32751
407.339.4217
www.xulonpress.com

© 2024 by Darlene Lamoureux

All rights reserved solely by the author. The author guarantees all contents are original and do not infringe upon the legal rights of any other person or work. No part of this book may be reproduced in any form without the permission of the author.

Due to the changing nature of the Internet, if there are any web addresses, links, or URLs included in this manuscript, these may have been altered and may no longer be accessible. The views and opinions shared in this book belong solely to the author and do not necessarily reflect those of the publisher. The publisher therefore disclaims responsibility for the views or opinions expressed within the work.

Unless otherwise indicated, Scripture quotations taken from The Holy Bible, New International Version®, NIV® Copyright © 1973, 1978, 1984, 2011 by Biblica, Inc.® Used with permission. All rights reserved worldwide.

Unless otherwise indicated, Scripture quotations taken from The Holy Bible, English Standard Version © 2001 Crossway Bibles, a publishing ministry of Good News Publishers. All rights reserved.

Unless otherwise indicated, Scripture quotations taken from the *Holy Bible,* New Living Translation, copyright © 1996, 2004, 2015 by Tyndale House Foundation. All rights reserved. Used by permission of Tyndale House Publishers, Carol Stream, Illinois 60188.

Unless otherwise indicated, Scripture quotations taken from the New King James Version®, Copyright© 1982, Thomas Nelson. All rights reserved.

Unless otherwise indicated, Scripture quotations taken from the New American Standard Bible (NASB). Copyright © 1960, 1962, 1963, 1968, 1971, 1972, 1973, 1975, 1977, 1995 by The Lockman Foundation. Used by permission. All rights reserved.

Unless otherwise indicated, Scripture quotations taken from the Word English Bible (WEB) – *public domain.*

Unless otherwise indicated, Scripture quotations taken from The Holy Bible, Berean Study Bible (BSB). Copyright ©2016, 2018 by Bible Hub. Used by Permission. All Rights Reserved Worldwide.

Paperback ISBN-13: 978-1-66289-691-0
Hard Cover ISBN-13: 978-1-66289-692-7
Ebook ISBN-13: 978-1-66289-693-4

Dedication

This book is dedicated to I AM WHO I AM.

"This is my name forever, and this is how I am to be remembered in every generation."
~Almighty God
Exodus 3:15b (BSB)

Endorsements for
An Almighty God? Get Serious!

I couldn't put it down! You know how you say that with a great book? I couldn't put it down.
~ Barbara Messing, West Hartford, CT

This is timely and well written, and I am proud of you for wanting to tell your story to all. I'm very proud of you and thankful that you are able and desirous of doing this. I know that you are one of the most God loving people that I know.
~ Roy Wedell, Jr., Judsonia, AR

SO much to digest but soul quenching would be my overall take. I meditate on a few chapters at a time. So far, …delightful …practical…FUNNY …insightful…extremely interesting… intellectual…informative and so good in every way!!!

Chapter 2, where you explain your vision of how Paul responds to the people in Athens hit a huge chord with me. It was SO encouraging…!

Chapters 3 through 9 went by so fast I was shocked. I was going to stop at Nine for tonight when the first sentence of Chapter 10 caught my eye, and you had me for the rest of that chapter!

I am already ready to pass it out to all my friends!!
~ Millie Skidmore, Round Rock, TX

Hey Sister! Truly enjoy your writing. Keep it going! The Lord is using your gift for communicating His Truth, Himself.

~ Matthew Brinckerhoff, Litchfield, CT

What a title! *An Almighty God? Get Serious!* If that doesn't perk up your ears, nothing will. I also love the purity of your soul shining through. It's beautiful.

~ Janie Warden, Amarillo, TX

Beautifully done, the telling of your experience. Bravo, Sister!

~ Nancy Petrokansky, Wolcott, CT

This is outstanding! I would think that it would intrigue any non-Christian looking for answers.

~ Nicholas LoRusso, Bethlehem, CT

Everyone should feel the peace, love, and intimate care only an Almighty God can offer, and anyone can have that upon coming to genuinely love God. We titled our stories with the intention to catch the eye of a variety of minds. Our hope is to share His appeal with believers, skeptics, and unbelievers because if our readers are tempted to look at what joy He offers, we will have accomplished our goal.

~ Darlene, DWLamoureux.com

Endorsements for *Trophies of Grace*

Trophies of Grace will challenge you as it draws you into the life of a troubled girl, a life that keeps getting worse until the story is flipped on its head by a miracle that only God can do. You will end up inspired and encouraged. A must read.
~ James Jordan, Springdale, AR

Wow Karen!! Amazing! I couldn't put it down each time I started! So well written and a very clear explanation of how the Lord works in our lives and changes us. I could feel your joy and desire to seek Him and learn of His ways through your words. Thank you for sharing your book with me!
~ Kim Ledingham, Livonia, MI

I finished reading your book. Amazing testimony!
Karen, I love the introduction of the book with the beautiful poem!
You expressed the way things happened to you so well through the pages! It was easy to see you in my mind, the struggles and trials you experienced! Beautiful ending as I also saw the pursuit of our living Lord in your life. He never gave up on you.
~ Olga M Tellez, Louisville, KY

Karen is an outstanding & fun storyteller of the unique miracles of her life and testimony of her salvation through Jesus Christ. This book is an easy read, delightful and intriguing. Enjoy!

~ Dorothy Nyako, Daytona Beach, FL

Trophies Of Grace will leave you in awe of The Great I Am (Yahweh). The author takes no glory or honor for herself but points to the one who redeemed and restored her broken life.

~ Michelle Jordan, Springdale, AR

I am absolutely amazed by *Trophies Of Grace*. This is an awesome story and personal testimony that will definitely encourage the lost and broken. I believe it will reveal to all of us, that God will meet us right where we are! "For by grace you have been saved through faith. And this is not your own doing; it is the gift of God" (Ephesians 2:8, ESV).

~ Tami Davis, St. Joseph, MO

An Almighty God?

Get Serious!

Table of Contents

Introduction xix
Chapter 1 Finding Peace 1
Chapter 2 Irrational Love 5
Chapter 3 The Gospel 10
Chapter 4 Seeking Answers 15
Chapter 5 Answers Right Under My Nose 20
Chapter 6 Surpassing Peace 23
Chapter 7 God's Assistants 26
Chapter 8 Hold Your Horses…and Turn Over The Reins 28
Chapter 9 I'm Not a Baby When My Father Is Near 34
Chapter 10 Where's the Almighty When You Need Him? 40
Chapter 11 God's Incredible Timing 49

**No End in Sight! Are We Living Expectantly,
or Merely Enduring? [Part 1]**

Chapter 12 Your Turn, What's Your Story? 61
Chapter 13 Your Turn, What's Your Take? 64

**No End in Sight! Are We Living Expectantly,
or Merely Enduring? [Part 2]**

Chapter 14 The Almighty God of *Possibility* 71
Chapter 15 The Almighty…God of Providence 76
Chapter 16 An All-*knowing* God 80

No End in Sight! Are We Living Expectantly, or Merely Enduring? [Part 3]

Chapter 17 Gift for the Bride 87
Chapter 18 Hidden Treasures......................... 94
Chapter 19 The Thing that Hinders Us 97

An Exceptional Husband

Chapter 20 What If Your Husband Is Far from Normal?
  [Godly and Faithful] 103
Chapter 21 What If Your Husband Is Far from Normal?
  [Adoring and Daring] 108
Chapter 22 What If Your Husband Is Far from Normal?
  [Ready and Willing] 113

Don't Be Shy, Share Some More! [Part 1]

Chapter 23 There's Strength in Joy! 125
Chapter 24 New Mercies............................ 131
Chapter 25 Thorns in The Flesh Are Battle Scars 137

Don't Be Shy, Share Some More! [Part 2]

Chapter 26 God's Perfect (and Perfecting) Panoply 145
Chapter 27 God Is Sooo Good...................... 148
Chapter 28 An Almighty God? Get Serious! 153
End Notes 307

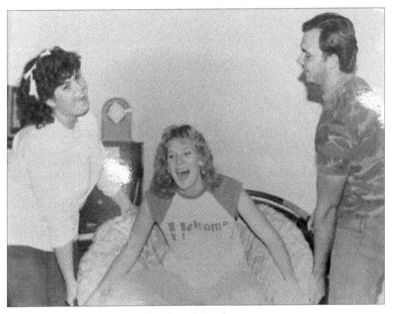

Lori and Darlene

"LORD, remind me how brief my time on earth will be. Remind me that my days are numbered— how fleeting my life is."
~Psalm 39:4

Introduction

"Paraplegic, quadriplegic, comatose, or dead." I remember looking at the faces around me to read their expressions. Was there angst? Fear?

Concern I saw, of course, but no one seemed overly wrought with worry – not even Lori, whose sleeve has always been prone to show her every emotion. So, I signed my consent, and put those horrific-sounding possibilities out of my mind. After all, the surgeon and his medical team were scrubbed and ready to perform this critical life-saving operation. What could I do at *this* juncture if things weren't going to turn out as planned? Besides, my soul was confident that God, whose creation I was in the first place, was also ready, and He would orchestrate this process from start to finish. If that process should take me home (to Heaven), I trusted Him with that, too – all of it was in God's hands.

If ever there were a time to have faith, it was now.

If someone had asked me earlier that April morning to predict what I'd be doing around…let's say two o'clock…, I certainly would not have guessed I'd be wondering whether this would be the last time I'd see my parents' faces, or my sister, or Lori!

I confess, I don't recall my exact words, or even all the thoughts that were going through my mind at the time, but I do remember talking to God my Creator, like I'd done tens of thousands of times before, and I was sure He could hear me. You can bet it wasn't one of those "thank You for the day and please be with me" prayers playing in my mind. No, this was a heartfelt, pleading, expectant prayer. I understood what the waiver said. ...*Or dead.* Somehow, I wasn't afraid of moving on, yet I *was* eager to spend more time here with the people I loved.

Spiritually, I was ready to go, but mentally, I wasn't prepared to say goodbye.

It turns out that the other side of that 13-hour neurosurgery saw me, alert and able to use the forearm and fingers of my right arm "to command." I clearly recall hearing my head nurse's grinning voice say, "*There* she is – she's awake!" I also remember hearing professional chatter about my movements, which were limited.

Lots of other conversations and events have unfolded since then, and as you can imagine, there are events I have forgotten. Some seem "lost," and then comes a word, or a sound, or a smell, and a flock of memories rushes back. What's even better, though, is that some of these memories are in writing.

My journal keeping lacks a lot to be desired, but I've always done a superb job of jotting down noteworthy details on random fragments of envelopes, cardboard packaging, and notebook paper, which are then "filed." So never fear, I do have a system, and when in doubt, I am willing to consult the documentation of others, if need be. In fact, just a year after this neurosurgery, I had the satisfaction of reading the surgeon's notes, which served to substantiate my pretty accurate(!) memory of some of the post-operation details. If you run across a photo of an "old- timey," *typed-directly-on-paper* note, that's my surgeon's record of my operation, which I've included for those of you who are interested.

Oh my, that explanation reminds me of when I was a little girl, and my grandmother would describe things from her horse-and-buggy days. It would seem that *I'm* the "back in the day" reciter now…. (*Really*??)

Anyway, I'm so glad for my recoveries! No…that's not a typo. I look back, and I see *multiple* blessings that you could put under the heading: <u>Recovered</u>. My life, my health, control of most of my motor skills, my voice, my vision, my sense of smell, my ability to walk, the fact that I can breathe on my own again…. I'm just as grateful, though, for the things I never *lost*: my family, my friends, my home, my sense of humor, my cognitive abilities, my job, my church family. In truth, the blessings are innumerable.

God has saved me in so many ways. Now – as a child of God – I've asked myself, how can *I* use the goodness I've experienced, personally, from His hand, in order to magnify His name? Could I help someone catch a glimpse of His beauty in their own life – someone who has, so far, been blind to it? I think maybe I can. I should say, rather, that through my sharing His goodness to me, God can help someone see His eminence.

I've been wanting to write a book about God for a long time now, and my main purpose is to bring glory to His name, since I love everything about Him (not saying I *understand* everything about Him…but *love* and *trust* Him). In my mind, He deserves all glory, honor, and praise. But in addition to that – or really, in harmonization with that – I hope that sharing some of the marvels from my own life might help open a few minds to "see" God.

My Christian friends and I often reminisce about the ways in which He has helped us through difficult situations, and invariably, one of us will interject the discussion with, "I just cannot understand how anyone can make it through life without relying on God." We are constantly finding new blessings from His hand and find such joy in knowing Him, as our loving Father, that we agree that life outside of Him would leave us wanting.

...EMPTY.

Even before David defeated Goliath, he felt this way. I don't know when, in relationship to that event that he penned "the Lord is my Shepherd; I shall not want (for anything)," but he most certainly knew God as his Guardian and Guide before he ever ran out onto that battlefield.

Would he have had the wherewithal to grab some stones from the brook, shout the giant warrior down, and run at that intimidating foe with all His might and only a sling, if he hadn't felt God's presence?

He didn't just shout something like "Say your prayers, buddy!!" or "God is great!" No, David yelled at the top of his young voice: "you come against me with sword and spear and javelin, but I come against you in the name of the LORD Almighty!"[1]

Another English translation gives a fuller expression to this youth's reverence for God's Name. David was boldly communicating the fact that his Lord – the LORD Almighty – was *the LORD of hosts, the God of the armies of Israel*, and he wasn't afraid to call this enemy of God's people out for arrogantly daring to taunt the Almighty. In fact, David went on to declare with absolute certainty, "This day the LORD will deliver you up into my hands...*that all the earth may know that there is a God*...and that the LORD does not deliver by sword or by spear; for the battle is the LORD's."[2]

I have learned this lesson over and over again throughout my life, and I have come to realize that our Almighty God does

NOT rely on humankind's puny little devices and ideas to get the job done. He's the One who has given us our knowledge and understanding, our strength and tenacity, our ability to achieve. He actually loves us in our everyday walk, and I don't see *why*. But He does, and He's active, and my own life is my witness.

Hopefully, by sharing some stories from my life, I can introduce someone to The Almighty God, who lives, and *gives* life. This book is basically a collection of Scripture, thoughts, quotes, and personal experiences. I hope you, the reader, will see what I see… the committed, dynamic love that our Creator demonstrates to each of us constantly, in the hopes that we – with our freedom to choose our own destinies – will choose *Him*.

Acknowledgements

First of all, I'm serious when I thank Almighty God! I found that completing a memoire like this can be difficult for quite a few reasons. In my case, for example, I wanted to edit out the things that didn't keep the focus on *Him*, and that meant leaving out some of my fond but less relevant memories. Too, I wanted to speak only the truth in love, and that meant leaving out some details that I wondered about. And finally-not-finally, I wanted to keep myself from appearing unconquerable on my own, since the point of my story here is to encourage others by showing how I (and others) overcome huge obstacles and bleak circumstances by the hand of an **almighty**, yet accessible, God.

I feel quite certain that the finished manuscript would never have seen the light of day had it not been for a God-sent mix of wonderful people and events coming to its rescue again and again. I thank all who have a part in helping me honor God with this book.

I want to thank my parents, Roy and Colleen Wedell, who brought me up to know the LORD of hosts and to appreciate His mighty power while still learning to love and revere His holy Name. Their steadfast nurturing of me and my siblings caused us all to trust, honor, and thirst for our Creator.

My sister Rhonda and my brother Roy have enriched my life in too many ways to count, and I'm so thankful to them for who they are. Each of them has contributed to my writing this in many ways.

Beck, my formidable, yet most constructive writing critic, has become more than a daughter and editing whiz to me – she's my true friend (and yes, she's cringing right now).

My son George has been invaluable to my efforts as my encourager, cheering me on in my efforts and propping up my dreams in front of me so I can see them more clearly. He even surprised me with his own (*gorgeous*) book cover concept (which the publisher was gracious to replicate as closely as possible). Makes my heart swell every time I think of it!

I thank my brothers and sisters in Christ throughout the earth, whether or not they have any knowledge of me or this book. I say this because just knowing that the Almighty loves each one and helps each one through hardships and pain, as He does me, spurred me on to remain faithful and write.

Importantly, this work is finished because of the influence of more friends and allies than I can adequately squeeze in here. Some served as a focus group and shared their reactions, for which I am very grateful. A few of them have a place in the narrative, and you'll see what I mean when you encounter them.

Gramma Rebecca (while living here) was like the grand Ma of our family's faith, putting in the hard work and preparation necessary to influence a few generations in the nurture and admonition of the Lord.

Her daughter Janie continues to shape the "fibers of my being" through faithfully demonstrating how to build up the broken with insightful encouragements, while willingly admitting her own shortcomings, and that's a skill I need to hone.

Brenda and Millie, my cousins, have energized me – generally with their love and positivity, and specifically with their gracious edification – as I've tried to convey my thoughts and memories.

I thank my husband George, who stays faithful to his promises as a family man.

And to cut short this unremitting list, I thank my new-found friend, sister, iron sharpener, and co-author, Karen, who skillfully spurred me on to "finish the job."

Chapter 1

Finding Peace

I just watched a beautiful sunrise. At first "all" I could see were the pinks and oranges – a rising mix that shone amid the light-tinted azure of this morning's sky. But even in the time it took me to visually scan that stunning canvas – from the strips of wispy white clouds to the leafy silhouettes in front of me, the sun had already recharged the autumn trees bordering the yard. Within moments my backyard was full of color.

What a gorgeous sight, and what a way to start a day!

I had simply gone out there for a few minutes to run my dogs – to give them a chance to get some fresh air, to run and play, and of course, to take care of business. But what began as an ordinary routine quickly turned into an unexpected memento of a higher presence…of a spirit and influence much greater than mine.

Probably, most of us have had a similar experience. Maybe lots of them. Do you recognize the spiritual aspect of life? Spend time in thoughtful worship?

Thoughtful worship…. This is my favorite – and most effective – form of meditation.

Lots of people, from many walks of life, have made meditation a regular part of their day. Some practice conscious breathing, which seems to help them focus on their breathing rather than the emotions that tend to run rampant through their minds. Others concentrate on the beauty around them, in an effort to clear their minds of other unwholesome, uncomfortable, or even harmful thoughts or concerns.

Still other individuals find it valuable to keep their thoughts on things they are grateful for. The idea behind the practice of meditating is usually connected to an effort to improve our mindset somehow – help us calm our minds, figure out our convictions, summon courage, improve an attitude, revive our calling to a mission, discover who we are.

As with anything people do, there are countless varieties of meditation, and each variation has its own set of techniques for achieving its purpose. Some approach their meditating through using words or phrases, others through visualization.

When *I* talk about meditation, I'm referring to that type of mental activity that includes thinking. You know what I mean when I say that, right? Reflecting, contemplating, reasoning, deliberating on your understanding of something, maybe also some theorizing and/or emotion. But always using intelligence at some level.

So, I'm not talking about thought*less*ness, which some meditation leaders encourage as "emptying the mind of all thoughts." I'm also not considering what is known as *transcendental meditation* (often called simply *TM*). TM uses a meaningless sound, or *mantra*, as the means by which a meditating person attempts to settle their mind down (e.g. that famously repeated "ommmm"). The aim is "to achieve a state of perfect stillness and consciousness" by focusing only on the mantra and letting thoughts "come and go, like the passive activity of watching a cloud float by."[3]

One thing that possibly all forms of meditation have in common is the goal of helping an individual calm his or her mind. I know my mind needs settling from day to day. How about yours – are there times you need some peace, and if so, do you meditate? Regularly?

I don't think there's an only way to do it, but I do believe there is a best way, and that's directly due to my belief in an almighty God – completely just, but mind-bogglingly loving and merciful.

Meditating, as mentioned in the Bible, always involves thought. Whether great or seemingly insignificant, every problem's solution starts with thought, and all of us, whether "great" or seemingly insignificant, have the God-given privilege and right to ponder our lives and reason our way through them.[4]

For me, meditating on God's Word each day readies my mind *and* my heart for the challenges and joys ahead. I love the Scriptures because I've found they offer something powerful to meet every one of my difficulties, and marvelous things to contemplate in my times of tranquility. Praising God's goodness helps me recognize the blessings in my life and fills my heart with deep joy – much more valuable to me than momentary happiness based on mere circumstance. Thanking Him causes me to reflect on His great, steadfast love–unceasing and merciful.[5] And reflecting on His love motivates me to love others. Empowers me to think proactively. Stirs me to action. Draws me ever closer to Him.

I need that draw. Because without that confidence-building and prompting to do something, I tend to become stationary. It's hard to move forward when I can so easily self- induce a feeling of disheartenment. Not to mention the very disempowering sense of "paralysis by analysis." Ever been there? It's during those times I find I have no choice but to meditate on my Creator and His will for me to live a good life. A good, fulfilling life with Him at the helm. Then I can move again, and with lots of confidence. And peace. The world's Creator is my mentor and my gauge, my inspiration and my guide. He's my peace of mind…my All in all.

Chapter 2

Irrational Love

We all seem to have something we value above all else. Sometimes we recognize it – especially when we have deliberately chosen to espouse this thing as our ideal, or even as a deity – and sometimes we do not even see that our behavior demonstrates our idolization of it. But chances are, each and every one of us spends a majority of our thought centered on *someone* or *something*.

To whom (or what) do *you* offer most of *your* time and devotion? An ideal? A spirit? A divine presence? Maybe a material object? Whatever it is, may I suggest, it is your god.

How did you learn about your deity – a book? A TV personality? A world-renowned guru?

I'll ask you candidly, do you ever wonder whether what you are exalting above your other priorities is really worth so much of your focus? Is this idol a real god?

The God?

We could spend time, until eternity, discussing all the types of gods and brands of religion in the world, but what good would it do? Where would we be in the end? Better off? Somehow, I don't think so. If history is our witness, we have to recognize our human inclination to argue with, judge, and condemn our philosophical opponents.

Even if we could debate every point peaceably and respectfully, it wouldn't make any position right if it were wrong, or wrong if it were right. Truth is truth.

If we seek truth, we'll find it, don't you think? I say this because if there's a truth, it will be revealed by virtue of that well-known process of elimination. Truth will stand when all falsehoods fail against it.

Sometimes it takes a lot of time for the truth to be seen, and I think that's when people start to give up on the truth and begin to settle for look-alikes.

I suppose we could easily be deceived by those look-alikes – or "false truths" – if we focused our minds on investigating *them*, rather than on just looking for the manifestations of Truth, itself. So, my suggestion for all of us, if I may? Keep our eyes open.

I pray, as I write everything here, that our eyes may be truly open, that each of our hearts will be enlightened, and that our minds will be able to comprehend the dimensions of God's love through Christ.

Isn't that cool? The dimensions[6] of God's love... Have you ever thought deeply about the love our originating, sustaining Savior has for *us*, His wayward (sometimes outright rebellious) nourishment-needing and provisions-hungry creation?

The Bible describes God's love in many different ways – so that any and all of us can grasp it. Yes, and also **treasure** it. So that He can reach each mind – each attitude, every intellectual level, all personal interests, each individual personality.... So that each of us can be filled, through obedient faith, with all the *fullness* of God. The love of God calls to all of us, no matter our current mindset.[7]

Irrational Love

For example, if you are a romantic, who craves world peace, perfect! God's love is totally looking to get you on board.[8] If your aesthetic is the pure beauty and harmony of nature, just open your eyes – the Scripture is full of visuals geared toward you![9] Are you intrigued by relationships? The Bible is rife with interpersonal narratives (the good, the bad, and the ugly).[10] You love animals? So does Jesus.[11]

You math whizzes out there will like the description the writer gives in his letter to the Ephesian church – he expresses the love of Christ in terms of width and length and depth and height, saying it's beyond knowledge.[12] Would that translate into *uncountable infinity on every dimensional plane*? If that doesn't tantalize your inner fundamental-theorem-of-calculus self, I'm not sure what will.

I think of Christ's apostle Paul, as he spoke to an audience in Athens some 2,000 years ago. Paul was always willing to meet anyone at his or her level of understanding, in order to help them see the truth in Christ Jesus,[13] and on this particular occasion, he had walked through parts of the city and had seen exhibited symbols of their religious devotion.

Unsurprisingly, he was moved to talk with the people there about Jesus,[14] who only a few years prior, had claimed repeatedly to offer serenity in God's presence, both during this temporal life,[15] *and* throughout an eternal life,[16] face to face[17] with the Almighty. God's incomparable gift, received through faith in Him (Christ Jesus), the Son.

As soon as he had an opportunity for it, Paul shared his message with his listeners:

> I see that in every way you are very religious. For as I walked around and examined your objects of worship, I even found an altar with this inscription:
>
> TO AN UNKNOWN GOD.
>
> Therefore what you worship as something unknown, I now proclaim to you.
>
> The God who made the world and everything in it is the Lord of heaven and earth and does not live in temples made by human hands. Nor is He served by human hands, as if He needed anything, because He Himself gives all men life and breath and everything else. From one man He made every nation of men, to inhabit the whole earth; and He determined their appointed times and the boundaries of their lands.
>
> God intended that they would seek Him and perhaps reach out for Him and find Him, though He is not far from each one of us. 'For in Him we live and move and have our being.'
>
> As some of your own poets have said, 'We are His offspring.' Therefore, being **offspring** of God, we should not think that the Divine Being is like gold or silver or stone, <u>an image **formed by man**</u>'s skill and imagination.
>
> Although God overlooked the ignorance of earlier times, He now commands all men everywhere to repent. For He has set a day when He will judge the world with justice

by the Man He has appointed. He has given proof of this to all men by raising Him from the dead.[18]

"God intended that they would seek Him…"
"…and perhaps reach out for Him…"

Now that's hope. An Almighty God – our all-powerful Creator…our *Father*, **betrayed by us** with our shameless rebellion against the sovereignty of His will, yet ~~willing to take us back~~, no, *pleading for us to love Him back*. The idea seems completely irrational.

Chapter 3

The Gospel

So, I've asked myself (and maybe this is your question, too), *is my hope in life founded on something real?*

My hope is built on faith in an Almighty God and on His unequaled and irreplaceable love. On Jesus' blood and righteousness. Obviously, I've come to a place where I am convinced my hope *is* based on reality, on truth.

What is your conviction? Are you firmly convinced about whether or not there is a living, breathing, intelligent, creative, almighty God? This is a question worth asking, isn't it?

Did an Almighty God raise His only begotten Son from the dead, or not? I can't, for the life of me, think of a more important question to ask. It's so important because on the answer to **that** question hinges everything else. *For the life of me* (and of *you*). If a supreme, omnipresent, invincible, all-powerful God exists, you and I are affected, whether we like it or not.

Help me think it through. If there is no God…

Or if there is a *god*, but this god is not *almighty*…

Or if there *is* an **Almighty God** – but He didn't, because of His great love for a lost world, give His only begotten Son to die for our sins in exactly the way that prophets had foretold in different ways, and at various times *in the past* (over *thousands of years*)…[19]

What am I to do with my faith that says God *is*,[20] and that He is *Almighty*,[21] and that He *did send His Son* to take away my (and others') sin and reconcile me (and others) to Himself[22] and help me (and others) live abundantly in His care, even throughout eternity?![23]

Abandon it? I'll *have* to–if I'm seeking the *Truth*, and *if* my faith is not that!

Please understand – I'm being extremely focused here, because *the hope so many others and I share and hold dear is at stake.* *Everything* I base my life on and center my daily thoughts around is in question.

It's actually sobering to consider this: let's just say for a moment that what I believe is correct – that the Almighty, unable to abide with sin, sent His Son to live on earth[24] because this was the only[25] way to save us from our sin.[26]

So, God did what was necessary, regardless of the cost to Himself, in order to free us from the slavery of sin,[27] and His reason for doing it was because He **loved** us,[28] pure and simple. Such a realization is both appalling and alleviating, right?

Part of that whole plan (as the Bible tells it), is that it was necessary for the Christ (God's Son, Jesus) to **suffer** some specific things,[29] **conquer death** by rising,[30] and then to **enter His glory**.[31] And since He rose from the dead and entered into glory – into the very presence of God, His followers can expect to rise from the dead and enter into the glorious presence of God, as promised.[32]

However, like Paul points out, if the only Son of the Almighty God *wasn't* **buried**,[33] and *didn't* **rise** again the third day,[34] *according to the prophecies written about Him,*[35] my faith is in vain! There is no good reason to hold onto it.

There's more, too. If Jesus wasn't then *seen* by those who knew Him best during His 3-year teaching ministry…[36]

Or if the risen Son wasn't also later seen by hundreds of other eyewitnesses who were believers of His message…[37]

Well really, if *any* of the given details (predicted or otherwise) were wrong, it could be reasoned that the Son's birth, life, death, burial, and resurrection were *not pre-planned* by God.[38] And THAT would spell disaster for the millions upon millions of people who hold fast to the faith. It's a sickening thought to think you might have *mistakenly* placed Jesus' salvation as **first priority** in your life.

I understand now what Paul was saying to the church in Corinth, when he wrote, "Now if Christ is preached, that he has been raised from the dead, how do some among you say that there is no resurrection of the dead? But if there is no resurrection of the dead, neither has Christ been raised. If Christ has not been raised, then our preaching is in vain and your faith also is in vain.

"Yes, we are also found false witnesses of God, because we testified about God that he raised up Christ, whom he didn't raise up if it is true that the dead are not raised. For if the dead aren't raised, neither has Christ been raised. If Christ has not been raised, your faith is vain; you are still in your sins.

"Then they also who are fallen asleep in Christ have perished. If we have only hoped in Christ in this life, we are of all men most pitiable."[39]

Of course, Paul could talk like that with good reason – I mean, he was brutalized again and again[40] for sharing his faith, and he just kept on sharing the good news[41] which he believed everyone should know.⁴² So it stands to reason he would feel hopeless and *stupid* if his faith were proven false.

In the same way, though, if I suspected my faith were not based on truth, then I would feel duped. I've been living a careful life that some might call boring. I'm not perfect, by any means (believe me!! My friends do) – but I've definitely met with negative consequences for some of the decisions I've made just trying to please God. That can feel a bit frustrating and foolish.

Additionally, I'm well aware that a lot of people already think me foolish for adopting the greatest commandments (according to Jesus) as my top moral code: loving God, my Creator, with *all* my heart, soul, mind, and strength…and loving my neighbor in the same way I love myself.⁴³ (Okay, I'm not always feeling the love. And ok, I often fall short of *doing*⁴⁴ the love because I'm not *feeling*⁴⁵ it…but I *try* to do as I know to do.⁴⁶) The neighbor-loving concept is easy to grasp and is even commonly touted by people of many walks of life, but putting so many resources into loving God just doesn't make a bit of sense to "my" (i.e. the *Bible's*) critics. Not only that, more than a few people know my behavior and attitude aren't always up to snuff.

So, it's not easy at times, to be sure, making choices contrary to what I'd rather make, or to what others think I should make, or to what my friends might sometimes ask me to make. Especially when I'd rather just go with the flow.

If I found out today that my faith was worthless, I would be in a desolate place. My daily life would no doubt undergo a radical change (once I were no longer out of action emotionally) – as I would need to figure out what should matter most to me in this new-to-me environment.

But if my faith were useless, I'd have to deny the precious salvation story, which for centuries has continued to give so many people so much hope. I'd have to declare the story of such an enormous (and undeserved) sacrifice by an Almighty God to be ridiculous – completely absurd. That I can't do.[47]

Never yet have I been convinced that my faith is useless. But more importantly, I find my faith both satisfying and <u>watertight</u>. In fact, rather than being doubtful about it, I am **confident** that I am a created being, made in my Creator's image. And, as a human – prone to fall short, I candidly believe in my need for a savior, without whom I could never hope to spend eternity with God.[48]

Yes, I believe the gospel message of John 3:16-17. And I believe the distressing details about my Savior's death – its terror and its requirement.[49] Like Paul, I'm not ashamed of the gospel, because it is the power God uses to save people from sin.[50]

The specifics of *our need* for, and *God's plan* for, our **salvation** are in the same book. And that book was shaped by God, Himself. I can't choose only the good things I like from the Bible and disregard the other stuff.[51]

Why not? Because the Bible claims it is *the* Word of *the* Almighty God, and history (not "only" the Bible) tells us that Jesus corroborated that claim.[52] So, for me, faith is an *either-or* thing, not a hodge-podge menu of faith items from which *I'll-take-a-little-of-this-and-some-of- that*. I just want the truth, the whole truth, and nothing but the Truth, so help me, God!

Which leads me to some questions....

Chapter 4

Seeking Answers

Truth. It's one of the most important words in our lives. People are always talking about "the truth" – claiming to know the truth, quarrelling about what's true, calling others who do not agree with them *liars*. But, what *is* truth? I mean, *really*. Does anyone really know?

Can anyone really know it? Does truth even exist?

The Bible says, point-blank: "the truth is in Jesus" (Ephesians 4:21). I believe that statement, and I take Jesus, Himself, at His word when He says, "**I am** the truth."[53]

Everything Jesus did while He lived on the earth confirmed what He said. Just think about the types of things He is documented to have done....[54] He healed sick people,[55] even raised some people from the dead.[56] Other people in the community (especially those sick or deceased persons' families and friends) *recognized* the healed and raised, *as their own*.[57] (That must have been astounding!)

Jesus drove out demons, or evil spirits, from individuals who were possessed.[58] He calmed storms[59] and miraculously fed thousands of hungry people at one time.[60] He walked on water.[61] He knew what people were thinking and sometimes "called them out" for their evil thoughts.[62]

He said something amazing to those people who believed in Him. I find it amazing because I am one of those people, and I can attest to the truth of what He said. He said, "If you hold to my teaching, you are really my disciples. Then you will know the truth, and the truth will set you free."[63]

I'll share a personal experience with trusting in truth – more aptly, you could say "trusting in God" – but the two are so closely connected (one and the same in *my* book [hahaha…get it?])….

Anyway, have you ever heard someone say, "Well…don't worry about it because nothing is too hard for God"? I have, and I believed it for years. Now, though, I know better, and I'm about to tell you why.

It was a Wednesday, over thirty years ago, when I finally followed the advice of friends and coworkers to see a doctor. *(Where did all that time go?)*

I'm thankful for their dogmatic prodding because without it, would I have made that appointment? I don't know. Probably eventually, but the outcomes may have been more ominous….

My journey toward better understanding the spiritual battle that is happening around us all the time – daily, hourly, moment by moment – got interesting when I was 25 and teaching preschool. While I really did love it, childhood education was not my ultimate goal, and this was somewhat of a transitional form of income until I could get my foot in the door somewhere "exciting" (not at all meaning the impending bout with my health).

I had been with School Time Child Development Center for a bit under two years, when I began to experience sporadic episodes of what I'll call "almost a blackout."

First, I would start to get this light-headed feeling, and then the noise around me – conversations…music…children

Seeking Answers

playing…a ringing phone – would become dimmer and dimmer until ultimately it would disappear.

At the same time that the sounds were fading, my vision would also grow dim. I can describe it as tunnel-vision, since it seemed as though darkness was closing in on me from all around. It's hard to describe, but I remember having a sense of having a heavy shade being pulled down over my eyes from the top, while simultaneously feeling like I was looking through a cardboard tube – much like peering through a paper towel roll big enough for both eyes – and the circumference kept shrinking. So, essentially, I lost my peripheral vision over a brief matter of nano-moments until all was finally dark. A few seconds later, everything would come back, and I'd be fine.

It was very strange, and you're probably wondering to yourself, "How in the world could you let something like that go without seeking medical help??" I don't really know the answer to that, myself, except that I know I'm not the only one in the crowd who disregards warning signs. People can be quite resilient, and like we can do so easily, I had ignored my symptoms over time, from the less intrusive, beginning signs until the monsoon of danger-level symptoms was "suddenly" in full-swing. I had unwisely learned to cope to the point of "where did THIS huge symptom come from?"

Anyway, I had become so used to these odd interruptions to my day, that I knew how to get quickly to a wall or something immovable and hold on until the "blackout" passed. Then it would be back to the activity at hand, as if nothing had happened.

Another bizarre thing that began to ring alarm bells, if ever so faintly, would happen on my drive home from work. I lived about 15 minutes away from my job. *Maybe* 20 with icy roads. But one day, it took me an hour and a half to get home! I got so incredibly drowsy that I had to pull off the road, into an empty lot (really, at this stage of sleepiness, anywhere would do). I turned off the engine, locked the doors, reclined my seat as far back as it would go, and fell into blissful sleep. Not just once, either. I don't remember whether that scene replayed twice, or five times, or ten. But it was enough to have become a pattern.

Right there – as I was writing that – a thought occurred to me. Aren't there people who go about their business, like nothing is amiss, even while their inner lives are shattered? They are hurting inside. Some of them feel betrayed by the people they love and admire the most. Some of them sense that something is terribly wrong with them, that other people view them as weird, and they don't know what to do to change that – "if there even *is* any way things can change." In fact, we probably *all* feel one or more of these things at some time or another.

We feel left out, or mistreated, or ugly, or unfortunate, or discriminated against, or alone, or guarded, or stupid.... The list goes on and on and on. But it's often easier to ignore the signs of emotional peril and to just carry on as *normal,* than it is to deal with the pain. Not *God's* normal, but what we have come to recognize as normal for *us*.

We people tend to figure things out in a skewed way, which leads, ultimately, over similar encounters and multiple seasons, to our persuading ourselves that this is "just how it is." I don't like that analysis of affairs, but it's what I see, even in my own life. Even while each of us has his or her own problems, few of us know how to successfully navigate through them all the way to the other side, where the problem will have been resolved and life can proceed somewhat predictably. It's really a job for a super-hero.

(Enter, the already present Almighty God...able and willing to do immeasurably more than any of us can even ask or imagine!)[64]

Okay, so back to those crazy symptoms. I saw my primary care provider, Dr. Scappaticci, who told me to lay off the caffeine (he said it much more nicely), watch my sugar intake, drink lots of water, get plenty of sleep, and one more thing (I remember there were five) – maybe don't drink alcohol? Or cut out a little salt? Could have even been to take care not to stand up suddenly? Whatever it was, I followed orders.

But the symptoms didn't subside. In fact, the episodes were happening more and more frequently. I saw Dr. Scappaticci a second time and explained to him that I felt I knew my body – that having lived with it for 25 years without anything remotely close to these symptoms, I knew these were footprints of something new and unfamiliar. They were different than anything I had experienced, and I was sure there was "something else" involved.

"We'll go about this systematically," he said, "I'm going to have you see an ophthalmologist. Here's a list – you'll need to choose one."

An ophthalmologist? I didn't know what that was. An *eye* doctor, of course, but how do you choose an ophthalmologist when you don't quite know what they do, and you don't know who anybody else uses for an ophthalmologist? So, not having any other resource at the moment, I looked at the list. There were quite a few names on the small paper, or maybe it just seemed like a lot to *me* because I had to select the one who would know how to attack my problem.

Oh, I couldn't believe it! Dr. Robinson was on the list! He was an ophthalmologist? I only knew him as the dad to two of my preschoolers.

It turns out, he was an excellent ophthalmologist.

Chapter 5

Answers Right Under My Nose

Dr. Robinson and I chitchatted about his children as he examined the backs of my eyes, and then he said I could just relax for a few minutes. He was going to take care of something, and he'd be back shortly. When he came back, it was to tell me he had scheduled an emergency CT scan. The swelling he had seen in my optic nerve probably indicated either an eye disease that affects primarily women or a brain tumor, and that my friend should drive me to the hospital immediately.

Well, Lori would end up driving me to many places in the coming months. The ER, the "rehab," the *Ice Cream Churn*, home, follow-up doctor visits, the church building. Later, I'd try acupuncture, and she'd drive me there.

But for now, it was to the hospital. A CT scan did reveal a tumor on my left occipital lobe, which plays a huge role in vision-related matters. The tumor was the size of a large grapefruit, and that helps clarify why I was having "blackouts" – the spinal fluid was trapped, unable to make the rounds as it should. Nothing like a grapefruit-sized obstruction to hinder circulation.

I can laugh about it now, of course, but at the time it wasn't funny. After the CT scan discovery, Lori and I were shown into a small, windowless conference room. This is where I would need to quickly (there wasn't much time) choose a neurosurgeon to perform the brain surgery. What? Again, I was given the task of selecting a specialist to defend my life. And again, I had no idea how to choose.

"What does a neurosurgeon do?" My words seemed to cut into the heavy air. I remember looking across the room at Dr. Robinson and Dr. Wasley, who was filling in for Dr. Scappaticci this night. The two of them were seated side by side at the end of the room, while Lori and I stood, still close to the small room's one door. We had been invited to sit with them (there was plenty of seating available), but I'd rather stand, and my stalwart friend stood with me.

A neurosurgeon, as it turns out, was who would be able to operate on the tumor and hopefully remove it.

"Well, I don't *know* any neurosurgeons—"

At once Dr. Robinson began to read aloud the names on the list he had in his hand, "There's Yale, in New Haven. There's So-and-So, in such-and-such a place. After "Yale, in New Haven," I perceived sound…what seemed like dozens of inconspicuous names and places.

Somewhere in the middle, I heard "…and Jonathan Ballon, in New Britain," and then there were more names, which turned into a meaningless stream of rambling by the time they reached my preoccupied mind. Then suddenly, the list came to an end, and it was time to choose. I was looking at Lori, and she and both doctors were looking at me, expectantly. What was I waiting for? Let's have a name. This is not what they said, it was what I heard. I remember feeling like I bore the enormous weight of electing my champion to settle my fate…a one-time chance. No do-overs, so I'd best choose wisely.

An ALMIGHTY God? Get Serious!

I prayed. Nobody else could hear me, but I knew God had. *Who should I choose, LORD?* I still didn't have a clue whom to choose, but since I clearly remembered that name in the middle of the list, I looked at the doctors and said, timidly, "I guess Jonathan Ballon in New Britain."

Chapter 6

Surpassing Peace

Once again, without hesitation, Dr. Robinson was on his feet, taking the lead through this clutter of unwanted little details. Immediately, it seemed, Dr. Ballon was walking into the small examination room in which Lori and I were now waiting. He had a commanding appearance – well-groomed, handsome, smelling of men's cologne, and ready, I remember, for action. It was very calming for both me and Lori, to be in his presence. I felt he could help me.

He, as Dr. Robinson had been, was forthright about any information I needed to be aware of. He did a few tests, engaging my eyes with a flashlight…. I told him I could see doubles of everything when looking hard to my left, and we both could tell my left eye would dance then, too. He asked me some questions, which must have provided him with what he needed to know, because he told us (Lori and me) that we (Dr. Ballon and I) would get an MRI and do some other things to assess how we could best take care of this tumor problem. He ordered medication to reduce swelling and said I could go home for now.

When I voiced my concern that I needed to go to work tomorrow because I was a preschool teacher, and I didn't want to leave everybody (coworkers and children) in the lurch, he gave me great advice that would impact a lot of my decision-making going forward. He told me I would be hearing lots of stories in coming days about relatives, friends, and acquaintances who also had brain tumors, as well as complications, feelings, and results from their experiences. I was to always keep in mind, he said, that there wasn't any tumor just like mine. Every person is different, making the related details unique to each patient, and I should take all of those stories with a grain of salt – better yet, politely refuse to even hear them.

I can hear Mama say, *that was some good advice, boy-howdy!*

The next day was remarkably like any other day at preschool. I loved "my" kids and felt energized and hopeful around them.

A normal *morning*, I should say. At snack time, Lisa and Laurice (the two Infant Teachers) and I were preparing the morning snack foods and drinks for the children when Liz, our Director (and Supervisor), joined us in the kitchen area.

Liz tossed a handful of popcorn into her mouth and asked, "So how did your doctor visit go yesterday?" She was smiling (as was typically the case – *it's wonderful to work for someone with a happy disposition!*), clearly expecting a good report.

I don't know why I hadn't thought beforehand how I would divulge the news. I guess I assumed everyone else would accept the diagnosis with the same sense of peace I had…. But I was wrong, of course. It's often harder to hear bad news about a friend than it is about yourself.

In any case, I just casually divulged, "Oh, I have a brain tumor."

We had the proverbial pin-drop moment, and I watched Liz's eyes grow very wide. Then she chastised me for joking about something like that. I assured her I wasn't joking, and her eyes welled with tears before she bolted out of the classroom, down the hall, and around the corner. I chased after her, calling

"Liz! Liz!" but to no avail. By the time I got to the corner where she had disappeared, I realized where she had gone.

The door to Mary's office (around the corner) was open, and Mary – the nursing facility's Director – was staring at Liz in disbelief. Mary had an amiable personality and had established affectionate bonds with her various department Directors, of which Liz was one. Although I hadn't heard their exchange, she had obviously gotten the scoop.

I don't recall much about the rest of that day, other than offering an ineffective "I'm in God's hands now, Liz." Ineffective because I shouldn't have said "now" when I understood that I had been in God's hands all along. Those words might have been more encouraging if she knew I didn't simply imagine God riding gallantly to the rescue when He saw my circumstances had turned bleak. It is reassuring to recognize that God knew those circumstances long before I did, and besides, He has been my refuge ever since I learned how to find a good hiding place as a playful child. I thank my parents for that spiritual acumen!

We are never too old to learn, however, and I have continued to learn a whole lot about casting **_all_** my care on Him and trusting in His care for me.[65]

Chapter 7

God's Assistants

Back home – whether it were that evening or another, I don't recall – I wrote a note on a small card to let Dr. Ballon know that I knew God had chosen his capable surgeon hands to perform my surgery and that, since that was the case, I wanted to thank him for being available. By the way, do you remember when I was in that little conference room and chose the only name I heard from a spoken list of neurosurgeons – *Jonathan Ballon in New Britain*?

I learned later that he was the only one available that day because the others who might have been called to take me as a patient were at a convention in Boston.

I'm grateful to have been allowed to choose my surgeon, because it made me feel like I had a say in the outcome of my treatment. But even more, I love the way this happened because my faith was bolstered ten-fold. What a treasure!

Part of my immediate treatment regimen for home included filling a prescription for a med to reduce the swelling that had occurred due to the blocked spinal fluid. The medication did its job, I guess, but scary things started happening in rapid succession. I felt very strange (I could try to describe it, but the minutia of it all would take "47" pages, and you still wouldn't be able to fully appreciate the feeling). Then I started to dry-heave, slumped in front of the toilet bowl. Lori kept calling my name, I remember, but I didn't feel up to responding.

She called her father, and before I knew it, I was in Ken's van, flying to the hospital. I would learn there, that the brain swelling had increased pressure inside my skull and required immediate attention.

Dr. Ballon materialized out of nowhere somehow (I jest – he was just always available when needed, which is simply amazing to me), and soon, he was guiding one of the exceptional neurosurgical students, a *Fellow* at UCONN Medical Center – also known as *John Dempsey Hospital* – through a procedure known as a ventriculostomy. I had to be awake for it, so Susan, who would prove to be my main nurse for about 3 weeks in ICU, held my hand and carried on little conversations with me to help me feel relaxed. She was good at it.

Using a hand drill, the two experts cut a small hole in my skull and inserted a plastic drain tube. Actually, they needed to bore a second one, as well, in order to establish the very best placement for the tube. This second hole they did as discreetly as possible, I'm sure, so as not to worry me. But being awake and all, I could tell… (bizarre, right?) The purpose of the procedure, of course, was to allow the built-up cerebrospinal fluid to drain from inside my brain, helping to relieve the pressure.

After the surgery, though, that fluid wouldn't flow. Not good news. Dr. Ballon was a bit perplexed because he wasn't sure what could be causing the stoppage.

Chapter 8

Hold Your Horses… and Turn Over the Reins

It sounded like a smart idea. The purpose of the shunt would be to direct excess spinal fluid away from my brain so it could not get a chance to build up again and cause my brain to swell, a dangerous condition called *hydrocephalus*.

Under normal conditions, our brains use that fluid for cushion and protection against injury, as well as to get the essential nutrients they need. Not only that, but spinal fluid also takes away waste products. It flows through the brain's ventricles to the base of the brain. The fluid then rinses the brain and spinal cord well before the blood reabsorbs it.[66] It's a beautiful design.

When this normal flow is disrupted, however, the buildup of fluid can create harmful pressure on the brain's tissues, which can do a lot of damage and keep the brain from working properly. The problem can be devastating. To fix it, doctors can surgically place a medical device (a shunt) inside one of the brain's ventricles to carry excess fluid away from the brain and get the flow and absorption of spinal fluid to be optimal.[67]

Once Dr. Ballon saw that the spinal fluid was not flowing out following my ventriculostomy, the shunt really became my only option. Even while he presented the "option" to me, and I made my appeal ("I'm going to talk to God about this because I *really* don't want a shunt"), somehow I felt calm. It's that peace that surpasses our human ability to understand it.[68]

I truly believed that all was in God's hands,[69] and that God considered me His child.[70] There was absolutely no doubt in my mind that God knew the situation inside and out, and He was using Doctor Ballon's vast knowledge and excellent capabilities to help me through this whole brain tumor ordeal. I could see, too, that my neurosurgeon was compassionate and had an admirable bedside manner. What could be more ideal here? You'd think a patient really couldn't ask for more.

Still, I felt discouraged by the prospect of having a permanent catheter – a shunt (even the word itself sounded appalling). I didn't like the idea of it requiring ongoing attention…possibly throughout the remainder of my life.

You may be wondering, like I am now, why I wasn't just *thankful* that there were options like using a shunt to help my body do what it could not do on its own. Youth played a big part, I'm sure (I was 25), but I just felt I wouldn't find things "acceptable" with a shunt in my life. I couldn't bring myself to entertain the idea.

I sometimes think back on my then attitude and, knowing I'm not alone in the attitude department, wonder why God listens to us. He wouldn't have to. As Master of the universe, He'd have been completely within His rights to have let me struggle with my petty sense of the way things "should be." He could have pointed out all the blessing He had poured out on me over the course of my life already, and then He could have reminded me that He is the Potter, and I am the clay.[71] And that lumps of clay don't design themselves. And that there's not a potter, world-wide, who has a protocol in place for letting clay lumps even express their grievances, much less have them resolved.

He could have asked me, like He asked Job, "Where were you when I laid the foundations of the earth? Tell me, if you know so much. Who determined its dimensions?"[72]

Wrecked! I know I wouldn't have anything to say.

"Where does light come from, and where does darkness go? Can you take each to its home? Do you know how to get there? But of course you know all this! For you were born before it was all created, and you are so very experienced!"[73]

The God I cry to could have said any of this and put me immediately in my proper place.

Instead, He invited me to *dare* approach His throne.[74] Incredibly, the Creator Himself invites anyone who will listen to Him through obedient faith to approach. And not only that, but as followers of Christ, we are told to make our requests *confidently* because He promises to hear us when we ask according to His will![75]

Furthermore, it's not our goodness that allows us the special privilege of prayer, but rather, it's that the Almighty God loved us enough to *sacrifice of Himself*[76] so we could obtain the right *to become* His children.[77] (He did the self-sacrificing before anyone had the right *to be called* His child – even while we were His *enemies!*)[78]

The thing that allows us the special privilege of obtaining His righteousness is the fact that, while *merely occupying* "earthen vessels,"[79] we are eternal souls *made in His own likeness!*[80] Choosing to live our lives in devotion to His likeness through faithful obedience, we will return to our Maker,[81] just as He promised, and live with Him forever.[82]

Believing this changes every perception I have regarding my own life. If I start thinking I'm "all that and then some," I tend to look at my hardships as blights, even plagues – undeserved, of course – and I become miserably discontented. But then…, **paradigm shift**! In less than a heartbeat, I can recall the fact that God loves us – loves *me* – and just by remembering it, I see things clearly again.

It's fitting that I echo David's sentiments – I am fearfully and wonderfully made.[83] My mind just can't wrap around God Almighty's power. His knowledge and wisdom are far too marvelous for me to comprehend.

Who I am, and what I want, pale in light of God's unmerited grace toward me. Suddenly, I feel overwhelmed by how loved I am. My fear turns to joy, and my pain loses its toxicity.

This is a taste of the abundant life Jesus talked about.[84] There's more abundance besides, as the word itself implies…. Abundant peace, abundant comfort, abundant patience, abundant faith, abundant love, abundant opportunity for serving others, abundant blessings of many kinds.[85] Some physical,[86] some material,[87] *all* spiritual.[88]

God is all-powerful. The Almighty is not blind, deaf, or disabled in any way, but *we* are – spiritually, without question – and if not also physically, then mentally, or financially, or relationally, or educationally, or something else. But the Almighty has got His eye on us, He's willing to listen to us, and because of Jesus He can reconcile us malfunctioning believers to Himself and make us perfect. Have you ever heard any better news?

The apostle Paul understood how great the news is, and he reminded his fellow believers whenever he could:

> For what we proclaim is not ourselves, but Jesus Christ as Lord, with ourselves as your servants for Jesus' sake. For God, who said, "Let light shine out of darkness," has shone in our hearts to give the light of the knowledge of the glory of God in the face of Jesus Christ. But we have this treasure in jars of clay, to show that the surpassing power belongs to God and not to us.
>
> We are afflicted in every way, but not crushed; perplexed, but not driven to despair; persecuted, but not forsaken; struck down, but not destroyed; always carrying in the body the death of Jesus, so that the life of Jesus may also be manifested in our bodies. For we who live are always being given over to death for Jesus' sake, so that the life of Jesus also may be manifested in our mortal flesh. So death is at work in us, but life in you.
>
> Since we have the same spirit of faith according to what has been written, "I believed, and so I spoke," we also believe, and so we also speak, knowing that he who raised the Lord Jesus will raise us also with Jesus and bring us with you into his presence. For it is all for your sake, so that as grace extends to more and more people it may increase thanksgiving, to the glory of God.
>
> So we do not lose heart. Though our outer self is wasting away, our inner self is being renewed day by day. For this light momentary affliction is preparing for us an eternal weight of glory beyond all comparison, as we look not to the things that are seen but to the things that are unseen. For the things that are seen are transient, but the things that are unseen are eternal.[89]

Amen! Some of the effects of my schwannoma challenge are ongoing, but not debilitating. With each medical dilemma, my first thought is to seek God's help, and that makes all the difference. Like the Bible verse so many Christians prove again and again: *I've learned to be content in whatever situation I'm* in. I know how to live in poverty or prosperity. No matter what the situation, I've learned the secret of how to live when I'm full or when I'm hungry, when I have too much or when I have too little. I can do everything through Christ who strengthens me.*[90]*

So, while I can't speak to Dr. Ballon's faith in God, I can tell you that when I made my bold announcement, he never skipped a beat.

"Okay, I understand that you feel that way. How about we do this: have that conversation with God, and I'll go ahead and line up a slot for us in the O.R. in case we need it. It's easier to cancel an appointment we decide we don't need than to need a timeslot and have to wait for an opening."

What a kind man. His reply was both comforting and wise. He wasn't coddling his ill-fated patient. This was genuine and much needed support.

I'm always amazed how God puts the right people in our lives to help us when we acknowledge our need. I'm even more amazed when I consider that He can use *me* in the same way![91]

Maybe my doctor wasn't even aware of how profound the relief was that his gesture handed my mind at that point. His quick inclusion of my choice of action made all the difference for my peace of mind. I felt some control of the storyline. This was a knowledgeable specialist, doing surgery to alleviate the pressure on my mind. Ironically, that might arguably have been as important an operation as the one to relieve the pressure on my brain!

Looking back at it, I have absolutely no doubt, whatsoever, that the entire "brain tumor experience" was masterfully orchestrated by God. Every detail was just too expedient, and that's the way my faithful, protecting, almighty Father in Heaven works.

Chapter 9

I'm Not a Baby When My Father Is Near

It was a schwannoma – a growth of Schwann cells on my facial nerve. Apparently, everybody's got 'em (…not growths, but Schwann cells). And they're all throughout the body, so a person could have a schwannoma on an arm or leg, etc. Tumors of this type are slow-growing and usually benign, but they can wreak a lot of havoc on the nerves they target.

Mine was exceptionally rare, though, I was told…I guess, because of its size (large grapefruit) and where it was, occupying a substantial portion of the left occipital lobe. Some of the nerves affected include the olfactory (sense of smell), optic and oculomotor nerves (eyesight), and the 5th cranial nerve (facial things – both sensory and motor, affecting biting, chewing, and feeling sensations). Not an award-winning neurology lesson, but you get the point, right? It was a rather nasty tumor.

But anyway, back to the drainage predicament…

What would become of that stubborn spinal fluid? I asked God for mercy and help. So thankful He listens! The answer came the very next day. Dr. Ballon contacted the operating room registrar and canceled the procedure he had scheduled.

At some time during the night the cerebrospinal fluid that had, until then, been trapped inside my head – unmoved, like standing water – began to flow freely!

How did it start to flow? I don't know. But what I do know is: no shunt! Typically, an excessive buildup like this can cause severe brain damage, or worse. So, again, I was thankful. Yet, the most important operation – the one to remove the tumor – was still looming….

Okay, well, the main surgery – a *craniectomy* – lasted 13 hours. Dr. Ballon would later quip that my surgery made a man of him. If you're a little curious about what a craniectomy entails, I'll tell you some of what I know, based on *mine*. As I understand it, my chin was virtually, if not literally, pressed up against my chest and held there for the procedure. You might be interested to know that my neck muscles, though very weak and tired for quite some time afterwards, healed remarkably well!

I am still stunned that surgeons can keep such steady hands and clear vision for what must seem like eons, in order to correct their patients' medical concerns. And in addition to that, neurosurgeons (who operate on the nervous system, including spine- and brain-related trauma) have to make sure all the "wires and plugs" line up perfectly so hopefully, there's no "interruption in service."

The days, weeks and years following my operation have shown Dr. Ballon's work to be exquisite, and he always showed me the upmost respect as his patient, as well, by keeping me informed about my condition and prognosis. I couldn't have asked for a better surgeon, and I'm eternally grateful I didn't have to.

Continuing on now, this surgery required the removal of part of my skull, in order to access the tumor, and "my" doctor had to cut through several layers of protective material, including he explained, the very thick and fibrous *dura mater*. You don't necessarily need to know that, but it's one of those medical terms that stuck with me, so there. Now you know it, too, for free!

One of the most heartening memories from my tumor experience (though there are many to choose from) is when Dr. Ballon told me he made a "pivotal choice" during the surgery, based on his knowledge of my personality. He had to decide what to do about some small fragments of the tumor that were a little too attached to me (my words, not his).

Because they were so intertwined with facial nerves, there was a high probability that those nerves would be damaged if he scraped the tumor stuff off. On the other hand, leaving the residuals there could mean chemotherapy and/or radiation following the surgery, and we all know those side-effects are not desirable. In fact, they can be devastating. What would you choose? It's definitely not a fun decision to have to make.

Would you be too surprised if I told you he chose to scrape the nerves? He decided to make a clean exit and get any and all tumor matter out of there – as much of it as possible. I am sooooo happy he did that! As a young woman (25 years old), I was able then to go about the business of healing, as I went about my business, living.

Dr. Ballon had reasoned (correctly) that I would rather deal with fewer health-related side effects, even if it could mean I deal with the more or less cosmetic effects of facial paralysis. In the end, my perception of my best life (under my new circumstances) excluded constant tests and check-ups. My Father in heaven already knew it. I believe He had the solution for me before I knew I had the problem.

The reason I said this part of the ordeal was *heartening* is that Dr. Ballon told me later that he had made that critical decision because of the card I had written him prior to the operation – which he had kept with him during surgery, in the pocket of his scrubs. Inside the card, he had found an unguarded glimpse of what I held dear – Almighty God.

Suffice it to say, the outcome was well worth it, but the secondary results of the surgery packed a wallop. When I awoke from surgery, the only thing I could control well was my right hand and forearm. To communicate, I relied on poor Marlene (my other regular and <u>*wonderful*</u> nurse in ICU) to interpret my laboriously slow sign-language alphabet spellings. On the occasion she spoke the wrong letter, my frustrated fingers would scream the intended one. "Noooooo! "g! g! g!" I suppose it was a positive thing for everyone involved that my speech was speechless.

And that Marlene was so patient and attentive.

Other aspects of my health that would prove difficult in the months ahead included the ability to perform run-of-the-mill tasks that we often take for granted. Blinking…swallowing…focusing (visually)…hearing…walking…and yes, breathing. Even heartrate. Taste, too.

Smelling. Feeling with my skin. I could probably write a short booklet's worth of one-word items, but we can leave it there. The important take-away from all this is, that if it hadn't been for the Almighty's compassion and care, I wouldn't be sharing this message today. Or, another way to say it was said by a man named Jeremiah, in about 587 B.C.:

I cry out, "My splendor is gone!
Everything I had hoped for from the LORD is lost!"
The thought of my suffering and homelessness is bitter beyond words.
I will never forget this awful time, as I grieve over my loss.
Yet I still dare to hope when I remember this:
The faithful love of the LORD never ends! His mercies never cease.
Great is his faithfulness;
his mercies begin afresh each morning.
I say to myself, "The LORD is my inheritance; therefore, I will hope in him!"
The LORD is good to those who depend on him, to those who search for him.
So it is good to wait quietly
for salvation from the LORD.[92]

Writing Samples, Pre-Craniectomy   **Letter Home, from ICU**

The ramifications of the brain surgery and all the peripherals connected to it have been incalculable, really.

It's funny, though, how when you're grateful, rather than fretful, you sometimes don't even notice when things get tricky.

You just do what you do, how you do it, and it's done. Of course, it's all done better when you're using the strength that only Christ Jesus – the author and perfector of your salvation – can give.[93]

Writing about challenges I've had over the years since the events has caused me to recall a few memories that might've been lost otherwise. Like when the physical/respiratory therapist told me he'd take me line dancing when I was back on my feet, or that Dr. Robinson, my ophthalmologist, admired my hockey stick incision because he was a big hockey fan. And like when Dr. Ballon accompanied me down the hall once as I was using a walker for the first or second time (this was after I had finished my 3-week ICU stay and had been moved to the 2nd floor). He wanted to make sure I had a realistic expectation of my prognosis, and he told me, "You are doing very well, making lots of progress. Keep in mind, though, that you are in the infancy stage of your recovery."

I didn't want to hear that, of course, since I wanted to be me again. But, true to form, he just smiled and nodded when I – recalling my heavenly Father's non-stop help – answered that no, I wasn't an infant. I was at least a toddler!

Operation (Craniectomy) Notes

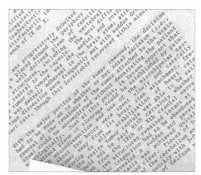

"Pivotal" Point

Chapter 10

Where's the Almighty When You Need Him?

Throwing your wheelchair's armrests over the side of a hill is not a very mature thing to do, I'll grant that. But how else can you express your anger and total frustration that you're allowed only one shower a week, you're not permitted to practice walking because of the rehab's liability issues, and you haven't got a voice because your left true vocal cord is paralyzed?

That happened on Dr. Ballon's 40th birthday. How do I know? He had a celebration to go to, but he had stopped by the rehab to see me first – found a shocked Lori and a despicable me in the parking lot. This visit wasn't quite what the doctor ordered…. He was turning 40; I was turning five. In retrospect, though, I'd say some elements of a lively party were there – a large venue… high energy…friends. Good times.

Why did I hurl those poor chair arms off the hillside? I'm not entirely sure, but revisiting that momentary impulse, I remember feeling a deep sense of frustration. I don't doubt that other emotions factored into my outburst, but the pressing ones that triggered my arm-flinging powers came from my feeling trapped. I was somewhere that was not my home, for who knew how long. But, even more, I was deprived of what I felt should be my basic rights. Rights to the normal, daily activities I had been accustomed to all my life.

I look back now and can see so many blessings I could have been thankful for, even at that very point in time, but I have to admit I didn't feel very thankful right then. Even so, and providentially, I had a sense, deep down, that I still had blessings to count and am glad to have previously hidden God's Word in my heart to sustain me in moments like this one.[94] Little else, after all, can trip me up like my feelings can.[95]

I remember recounting to Dr. Ballon the same grievances I had unloaded onto Lori just moments earlier. "They won't "let me take" (read, *they won't give me*) a shower except once a week! They won't let me exercise! They won't let me…" I didn't want *they* to be in charge of *me* anymore.

It isn't an easy thing to be at another's mercy. It's angering, frightening, and humbling – and I guess the more independent you've been, the more acutely you feel these insults. But on the same token, the more acutely you feel devalued, the more grateful you can be for your blessings, especially when you recognize that they're from the God who works everything for the good of those who love Him and are called according to His purpose.[96]

Mama and Daddy were good at reminding us, "Count your blessings! There are a lot of people who would love to have what you have." (Or similarly when we moaned about "our" things, "What are you complaining about? Some people don't even have food to eat.")

I've said those very things to my own children, but somehow, it's a hard concept to grasp, isn't it? Most of us have to experience hardship, before we can have *true* compassion for others, and I guess that's one of the most important reasons the Almighty allows believers to suffer – right next to 'so that we will learn to depend on Him….' He wants us to learn to offer genuine sympathy, caring support, and real aid to others.[97]

Now, I am a Texan, born and raised, as they say. And though I had lived four years in New Mexico during high school, I had only lived in the southwest. After college, I had followed my roommates (Lori was one of those) up to the northeast, to go where the money and opportunity seemed to be. Only for a *while*, though. Um… yeah, right.

Having a BA degree in French from Abilene Christian University and a full-time job that was paying my bills, I began to hatch my plan for the future. I would get a position as an interpreter for a large, international company and travel the world. Clothes, hair, romance, money, adventure – the whole nine yards.

So, after teaching for about 2 years at the preschool, I began to submit my resume to several well-known corporations in Bristol, CT. I was a shoo-in, I thought. But that's exactly when I began to have those black-out episodes I told you about. Bing, bang, boom, and my dreams of traveling the world as an interpreter were gone. I couldn't walk, couldn't talk, couldn't smile, pucker, or frown, couldn't even raise a playful eyebrow. I might have written Jeremiah's lament – my splendor was gone, and everything I had hoped for from the LORD was lost!

But since then….

Since then, I've discovered the fast lane isn't *my* lane. I prefer home and family and stability. I do admit, stability tends to be elusive in some regards. However, where I lack stability in areas of my life, the steadfast love of the Lord sustains me. I know by faith and experience that the Almighty's got my back.

To underscore the fact, I just want to point out that if I had run off to Europe or somewhere exotic, I wouldn't have met my assiduous husband, George, or given birth to my children – George, a.k.a. *G3* (long story…just know we had three Georges and a Georgia, all in the same family…) and my precious Rachel (oops, just a minor postpartum slip of the lips), er, Becca Lou. (The truth of the matter is that her birth certificate says *Rebecca*, and there's no "Lou." But when it just rolls off the tongue, exactitude doesn't matter. Right, Becca Lou? …Beck?... Right??). Anyway, they make my life full! Wonderful, educational, and fun!

Our Little Family

I've also had the privilege of being part of some fabulous ministries. As a matter of fact, an opportunity "fell into my lap," once, to serve as interpreter for a missionary in Haiti. This was a one-week stint, with six weeks' worth of stories! (Unless I leave out the insignificant details. It's all a matter of preference. Do you want brevity, or attention to detail? Some of my friends can testify – through gritted teeth – of my propensity for the latter…. Hey, they'll thank me down the road for helping them learn patience.)

I was advised to bring very lightweight clothing (a couple of trouble-free dresses made of cotton proved ideal)–not only to survive the heat of the equator, but also to make room in my suitcase for yummy treats for the Haitian children I would encounter. Then, at the end of my trip, the clothes could be left behind for a few people who could use them.

The plan to go started as a simple announcement at church service one Sunday *(or possibly Wednesday?)*. The preacher explained that Freda, who had helped her husband with the planting of our congregation eighteen years earlier, was in Haiti doing some mission work and could use an itinerant companion/interpreter. Jim (our preacher) mentioned the names of two single gals with no small children – Ruth's and mine. Neither of us spoke Haitian Creole, but Ruth (now 99 years old, as of this publishing!) had been friends with Freda since the early days of our congregation[98] and liked to travel. I didn't know Freda personally, but I had recently completed my bachelor's degree in French. Given that Haitians are educated in standard French, it made good sense for me to be the one to join Freda there.

It was kind of a group decision, as I remember. Besides that, Ruth just might've taken into account that, while *she* had been active in the Lord's work for decades already, here was a young, inexperienced woman who could learn a lot by doing. Who knows, older women in the church can be biblically deliberate that way. *(Maybe I'll ask her!!)*

I can't recall Jim's words, but he asked me something right then, like, "would you be up for going if you are able to take some time from work?" In a surreal moment, I said yes, and as soon as service was dismissed, an encouraging number of church members began to file toward me, to express their support. Before I could process what was happening, I was surrounded by well-wishers, and my coat pockets were brimming with dollar bills–singles, fives, tens, twenties.... I was amazed at the enthusiasm and support these believers had for doing the Lord's work. And I deduced that I was actually going!

From that point, I had a week to get ready for the trip, and I would be there (in Haiti) a week. There was a lot to do, and I had a full-time job, but if the Almighty is the author of an opportunity, He'll make sure all the details get worked out.[99] Long story, short, everything worked **perfectly**! The travel was well-orchestrated by the church leaders and the money count entrusted to me was precisely right for the job ahead.[100]

I had to okay the plans with my employer the next day at work. My boss, Liz (same boss, same Liz), was fully supportive of my going, though understandably a little stunned at the special request. Especially at such short notice.

The church gave me a printed, stapled set of papers loaded with travel information and a checklist of things to do and buy for the trip. When I called the clinic where I could get the prescribed shots (polio, *ouch*!) and pills to ward off diarrhea and malaria (...and typhoid?), I found out it was open only until 5, or was it 4. Whichever, I didn't normally get out of work until then, but Liz graciously let me leave early.

The clinic was not nearby, and I had never been to it before. GPS? Bah! (For real?) I don't think most of us had even heard of that yet, which meant grabbing a sheet of paper and scribbling down directions, always with landmarks and turns.

We're talking the mid '90s – a GPS was as foreign as a UFO. DVD players weren't even around yet! In fact, you weren't likely to know many acronyms, unless you were working a crossword puzzle. Hard to wrap your mind around, right?

Anyway, amazingly, I whizzed through green lights the whole way there and *eeked* into the parking lot, managing to run in the door without a minute to spare. The travel doctor was very accommodating, and he advised me to allow about 7 days before leaving the country.

Whew, another *barely-made-it* detail! The coming days would witness many of those, and I could plainly see God's handiwork through those circumstances, as they played out.

I was constantly noticing God's orchestration as I got a passport, took the appropriate medical precautions, stocked up on prepackaged foods, and procured items for personal hygiene, etc. His guardianship was clear, too, as I boarded – without a shred of fear (well, maybe a *little* shred, but it was manageable) – that tiny crop-duster (okay, not really, but it was a **_small_** plane), knowing it was to take 17 other (non-English speaking) people and me across that enormous ocean.

I felt His peace as we landed on a large slab of concrete somewhere near Cap Haitien – and even moments later, when I suddenly realized I didn't know how to get to Freda or even how to contact her. Cell phones weren't yet a thing, and even landlines were a rarity there. Reception was almost non-existent. Are you curious as to how we connected? Here's what happened.

I'm sure I thanked the pilot upon stepping off the plane, but I can't honestly remember. I do remember looking around me and seeing dirt fields enclosed by a very long wire fence. The plane, my fellow passengers, and I were inside that fence. For some reason, when my mind flashes back to it, I see a few chickens meandering through the area, but my rational brain doesn't want me to think there might have been chickens in the landing space....

Regardless, there was a small, partially covered stand – something like a food booth you might find at a fair (can't remember whether that was inside or outside the fence) – where a bunch of people were speaking Creole. Assuming this was the check-in desk, I went straight to it. Also, there wasn't anywhere else to go.

The man behind the desk was friendly enough, though he didn't know how he could help me. Don't ask me about the particulars of that conversation, because at this point, you know as much about it as I do. There was a little waiting area with chairs, so I did the airport thing to do and sat down. I took out my spiral notebook, and I wrote a letter to my parents. Of course, I couldn't send it, but it made me feel better.

Sometime later, I approached the man behind the desk again, to…I don't know, see if anything had changed. Suddenly, a teen-aged guy – a Haitian – heard me trying to communicate my plight and came up to us. After a short exchange with the desk clerk, he then greeted me with a huge smile, picked up my suitcase, and confidently beckoned me to follow him. I was so relieved to be following someone somewhere. It felt like progress.

He led me to a jeep full of friendly people who welcomed me aboard. Who were they? Happily, one or more of them spoke English. I think they were all men, but I can't recall. I also can't remember whether any of them were Haitian, but I discovered they were with a mission-oriented organization, there with a work assignment, and they knew where the orphanage was! I added yet another *thank You, Father,* to the constant prayer/devotional flowing from my heart to God's.

I can identify with anyone reading this and thinking I was so naïve and foolish to get in the jeep. Especially if you watch shows like *NCIS* or *Law & Order*. My only defense is that this was a work for the almighty God, and to be honest, I don't think it occurred to me to fear these people. Perhaps the Holy Spirit was "written all over them" because I sensed intuitively that they were godly workers. Actually, a better way to put it is that I felt that our spirits connected.

The Almighty didn't just create a universe and then step away. He's always where you need Him.

Chapter 11

God's Incredible Timing

Another thing about Him is His timing. The way God harmonizes His life-giving purpose with our (sometimes deadly) comings and goings is flawless.

Thinking about the deep-rooted difficulties people have endured in the nation of Haiti causes me to consider God's timing. He keeps faithfully pursuing the hearts of those He has created in His own image. Hopefully, you'll see significance in the details I'm about to share!

Haiti has been a country of unrest for most of its existence, and so many people living there are continuously plagued with violence, hunger, and spiritual apprehension. The political climate is a big part of the problem, and the nation struggles for stability. Many in the country do not know the God of creation, though they are very religious, and these conditions serve as somewhat of a backdrop for my story.

Prior to my traveling there in 1994, this impoverished nation had already experienced decades of calamity due to vicious gangs and cruel dictatorships. The powers controlling the small country still continue, even today, to change as various factions try their hand at hostile takeovers,[101] so, as you can imagine, Haiti is rife with inner turmoil, both spiritually and physically.

As it happened, in the Fall of that year (1994), the small nation saw a semblance of orderliness. Without pretending to understand the obscure, internal workings of the corresponding political events, I'll just say that American troops had built a strong presence on the island only a few months before I arrived, and with that presence came a general impression of security and stability (as well as brand-new opportunities for mission work.)[102]

Did I know any of this at the time? Didn't even have an inkling. But then, I didn't need to – this mission was God's thing. He's the one in charge of all the jots and tittles. Besides that, I'm willing to bet that my knowing might very well have made me afraid, which could have changed my resolve to do the Lord's work.... *quite* possibly..., so I'm thankful the Lord held that from me at the time.

As you might know, mission work comes in many shapes and forms, and because sincere followers of Jesus Christ understand that people also suffer with spiritual needs, they tailor their ministries to address both spiritual and physical difficulties.[103] They recognize that suffering excessively in either way can lead to death... or life. Christian missionaries who love their neighbors as themselves and minister to them do it because it's completely comforting and **liberating** for the person who welcomes *salvation* from death and accepts God's gift of *eternal* life through Jesus.[104]

And that liberation in Christ Jesus tastes sweeter each time the person now walking *in newness of life* recalls that it is truly the Almighty's compassionate solution to our sin problem (speaking from experience).[105] So, along with supplying food, clean water, clothes, shelter, and work opportunities to people in distress, a lot of evangelism tends to take place in situations where strife and hardship abound.[106]

True disciples have hearts for service that lead them to wherever they believe they can do the most good, and, like Jesus advises His disciples to do, they've already counted the cost.[107] As they faithfully follow their Lord, they go to great pains to actively love their neighbor. Their mission work isn't always overseas, either....

Ms. Thurman taught my mother about Jesus with such loving kindness that young Mama kept attending her 3rd grade Bible class, even while no one else in Mama's family went to services with her.

I'm forever thankful for Ms. Thurman's hometown evangelism, and likewise, that someone ministered to my Great Aunt Martha (on my dad's side), who invited Gramma Rebecca to church service, who then grabbed onto that offering of eternal salvation and made sure the rest of her family got exposure to Christ.

My own relationship with God is a direct result of the enduring faithfulness of my parents and their continuing familial ministry. Not only that, but my sister Rhonda and brother Roy also grew up in the Lord and continue to be a source of spiritual strength for me as I see them remain faithful in those inevitable dark nights of pain or hardship along their own journeys. I guess we all minister to each other in countless ways...and it's all to God's glory, isn't it.[108] Amazing.

So, back to Haiti! Inspiringly, there are many believers – some I've heard of, but most I've not– who have served there for years, regardless of the politics. They've offered shelter, food, clothing, and health-related care. They've coached Haitian citizens on how to create avenues of work, to support themselves and their families. And, most importantly, they've shared the gospel of Jesus Christ, teaching them from God's Word how to have their sins forgiven and be reconciled to God during the nonending(!) stream of eternity, through obedient faith.[109]

> *What good is it, my brothers, if someone says he has faith but does not have works? Can that faith save him? If a brother or sister is poorly clothed and lacking in daily food, and one of you says to them, "Go in peace, be warmed and filled," without giving them the things needed for the body, what good is that? So also faith by itself, if it does not have works, is dead.*
>
> *But someone will say, "You have faith and I have works." Show me your faith apart from your works, and I will show you my faith by my works. You believe that God is one; you do well. Even the demons believe—and shudder!*

Those words, from the second chapter of *James*, verses 14-19 (ESV) are easily said, yet so often hard to do! (Thankfully, practice makes easier!!)

With so many Scriptures to coincide with that one, the Bible couldn't be clearer, that God works to spread His gospel through the good works and teaching of believers, who serve His creation in faith.[110] The wisdom which birthed the church, that institution which Christ established to do His will in the world, just can't be overstated. Through the love exhibited by the church, people of any social status, in any economy, throughout any region (as well as the inhabitants of the spiritual realm) can recognize the Almighty's power and wisdom.[111]

I love the church. Again, here is God's own Word on the subject. "His intent was that now, through the church, **the manifold**

wisdom of God should be made known to the rulers and authorities in the heavenly realms, according to his eternal purpose that he accomplished in Christ Jesus our Lord."[112]

Freda and the other missionaries I had joined were pleased to be able to lodge at a Christian orphanage and work from there. I was a new visitor, but the young people living there welcomed me immediately. I don't even think they needed any "warm up time" (as my friend, Karen B., calls it). That, alone, was a testimony to the loving experience they certainly enjoyed with the Christians they had encountered before meeting *me* – there was a little fascination with my blonde, wavy hair going on, also. ;) The kids were precious, and even if we hadn't been in the country with some specific plans, it would have been worth the plethora of shots and medicinal precautions, etc., just to spend time with them.

I don't know all there is to know about Freda's agenda while there, but there was an exciting effort underway in Cap Haitien to build a school for preachers of the Gospel, and she played a role or two "somewhere" in all that. We saw the early beginnings of the school building which, I believe, also now serves as housing for the preachers-in-training. At present, the *Center for Biblical Training* has been actively teaching students for 27 years.[113]

God Almighty always blesses the endeavors of believers acting as His hands and feet – as His eyes, ears, and mouth,[114] because His purpose is to draw all people to Himself,[115] for reconciliation. Here's what the Bible says:

> *So we have stopped evaluating others from a human point of view. At one time we thought of Christ merely from a human point of view. How differently we know him now! This means that anyone who belongs to Christ has become a new person. The old life is gone; a new life has begun!*
>
> *And all of this is a gift from God, who brought us back to himself through Christ. And God has given us this task of reconciling people to him. For God was in Christ, reconciling the world to himself, no longer counting people's sins against them. And he gave us this wonderful message of reconciliation. So we are Christ's ambassadors; God is making his appeal through us. We speak for Christ when we plead, "Come back to God!" For God made Christ, who never sinned, to be the offering for our sin, so that we could be made right with God through Christ.*[116]

Freda hoped, as well, to help Haitians learn to cultivate and sell sunflower seeds, so they would have a worthy, dependable source of income. She worked hard, and I watched her continue to step through new doors as they were being opened so she could help in other ways.

Case in point, one day she told me she wanted to talk to an official from Port-au-Prince, who was in town, regarding the road(s) being built by American soldiers at the time. Her request, if I recall accurately, was for the soldiers to be allowed to build – or at least prepare the way for – a road leading toward the new school. Though I did meet the official, he spoke English quite well, so Freda didn't really end up needing my interpretation skills for that.

Another important mission, of course, was to support the orphanage's schoolteachers in their work. Freda wanted to make sure the children learned that they could create artwork to sell. Another valuable type of income. Once I was privileged to help out in the classroom by giving a small lesson with some art materials and sharing some ideas about a supplemental project. That was fun and a blessing to me. I enjoyed interacting with the class and having the opportunity to use my French.

The school children had such a gracious attitude! Before I left Haiti, they gave me a demonstration of their fast won love: some paintings and several intricately designed, homemade *oeuvres d'art*. Those gifts serve to remind me of the beautiful people in a beautiful land, and the diligent work of our Lord's body.

The Haitian culture is distinctive, and I often, still, recall certain disconnected memories.

For instance, it seems to me that there were a couple of banana trees in the middle of the orphanage grounds. Once, we were playing basketball there, in the center, when it suddenly began to rain – no, downpour – with no forewarning. I think I was the only one surprised. The kids enjoyed it for the blessing it was.

It didn't take long for my lightweight denim dress to dry, either, once the sun came out again. Another blessing!

The means of public transportation…which was almost nonexistent…was fascinating. I had the extraordinary occasion once to ride in a tap-tap. What's that, you ask? Well, a **tap-tap** is both the truck you rest your tootsies in as you traverse the countryside, and the method for hailing this taxi of sorts.

How to hail a cab in Cap Haitien:[117]

    a. Walk toward your destination until you hear a truck coming

    b. Turn around and look at it and smile and wave
    c. As it goes slowly by you, tap on it a couple of times
    d. When it stops, climb up and join the other privileged travelers in the truck bed
    e. Be friendly and smile a lot
    f. Rest your tootsies[118]

Tap-taps are a great concept and a wonderful alternative to walking when you're tired and you've still got a long way ahead of you. I would love to have been able to talk to the very first entrepreneur, whom I imagine to have been an owner of a pick-up truck (unlike most Haitians then), who realized he (most likely he) could use it to help others reach their destination while also earning a few dollars to feed his family.... Okay, that might fall into the "revised history" category, but even so, it's nice to imagine!

Nowadays, tap-taps are painted (and maybe some were then), with bright colors and images, but I recall a very old, very used, very small Toyota that did have some of its *original* paint. Hey, whatever helps me rest my tootsies! I was very thankful. Besides that, the people in the tap-tap with me and their chatter were colorful enough for a very interesting ride to my destination. I'm thankful for that whole experience.

And now? **The rest of the story.** (Did you mistake me for a radio personality there for a minute?) – Freda and I roomed together at the orphanage that week, so she, being the motherly type, asked me all about myself. What were my career plans, if any? Did I want to get married? Did I talk to God about these things? I enjoyed these and other talks with Freda enough to ignore the voodoo drums in the background and the rats scratching through our luggage.

God's Incredible Timing

So, I told her about my educational background and medical history, the career plans gone awry, my desire to get married and raise some children, and my deep love for God. She pointed out a Bible verse that has guided and comforted me ever since. She happened to have a plastic plaque with that verse molded into it, which she gave me for an encouraging reminder, and which I kept inside the mirror-medicine cabinet once back home. *Delight thyself in the LORD, and he shall give thee the desires of thine heart* ~ Psalm 37:4 (adapted from the KJV).

That was December 1994. One month later, in January, I met my husband to be. We talked every night on the phone for at least a couple of weeks, and we had our first date in February – a little Valentine's Day dinner at the church building. We sat at a table with Tony and Carrie, whose friendliness and genuine care were a real blessing. Actually, the whole church family welcomed "my" George right away, and that is just another testimony for me of God's love, this time, extended through His spiritual body.

Et voila! Stories of clothes, hair, romance, money, and adventure. God was with me there, too. He's everywhere.

Now, back to the part about nothing being too hard for God. Like I said before, I used to believe that. But now I KNOW it. Better!

No End in Sight!
Are We Living Expectantly, or Merely Enduring?
[Part 1]

Chapter 12

Your Turn, What's Your Story?

So, what about *your* story? What things have *you* experienced, and what things has God done in *your* life so far?

This is opinion – based on deductive reasoning and faith – but I believe that *all* of us have stories to tell about God's activity in our lives. Here's more opinion: most people don't even know they have a story. Every one of us has had experiences that make us stop and say "hmmm," right? Why is it, then, that some of us notice so easily the providence of God, and others of us can't see Him moving at all?

Personally, I'm puzzled about this. *Incredible* things happen (sometimes against a very common backdrop) which end up being an advantage (to *us*, to *someone we know*, or possibly even to *someone we've never met*), and many times *even believers* don't think to give God any credit for those extraordinary circumstances. Just think about those times when there was an assortment of *disconnected or rare* events (*all, without which* you could not have benefited). You know the times I'm talking about. Are you not left stunned?

I see it often in my own life, where I end up better off because of seemingly random (sometimes even undesirable) events! I'm willing to bet that you've experienced something remarkable, too, and your happy results have left you in wonder. Have you considered God's hand in the blessing? It's my real hope that you don't try to explain it away as coincidence or simply a bewildering occurrence.

It's actually easier for me to credit *God's* supernatural activity through a mundane situation, than to chalk that kind of thing up to mere *chance*. (I'm saying, *it makes more sense* to me to believe in the extraordinary work of an intelligent, almighty Creator.) To use my daughter's turn of phrase… ("you've got to do some elaborate mental gymnastics") to come up with some of these CHANCE theories.

The stars lined up… Really? And their natural alignment makes special things happen, why?

Please understand, this is not me making fun. This is me trying to use all that's at my disposal to make sense of things. Science doesn't explain a correlation between stars lining up and good things happening in a person's life, and that's okay. But neither does common sense. It takes <u>*faith*</u> to believe in that correspondence. You see?

Even if I could surrender my faith to a totally random idea (like the example I just used), I would not want to be depending on a random force (in this case, the stars) for my blessings.

Where's the hope in that?

Imagine. *"This is wonderful! Aww, how long do I have to wait until the next alignment?"* or, *"Ooh, I hope something good happens <u>next</u> time, too."* Or, conversely, *"How long do I have before I've got to endure something like* this *again?"*

Can someone petition the stars with any degree of certainty? That they'll hear? That they're autonomous? Capable? Willing? That they have a say in when or how they line up?

Am I belaboring the subject? Hopefully not. It's an important reality to grasp: what we believe determines how we react to events in our day, big and small.

Quite often, we attempt to solve our problems by first turning back to our belief system. We look at the situation; our minds hypothesize about it; and then we act, based on our understanding (belief). So, to me, what each person believes is paramount to their wellbeing.

Now, back to your story. How would you describe it? What do you believe about it?

Has your story seen you soaking in the high life? Friends in high places, money coming easy, excitement around every corner...?

No? Maybe you consider your life mediocre, with you going to work every day and having the chance for a little fun now and again....

Or perhaps in your opinion, life is merely existence. And hardship. You reckon that some people make their lives out to be like a fairytale...like, there's just no way!

Could even be that none of these scenarios suffice. You are acutely aware of the unseen, and readily attribute every good thing in your life to the Father of the heavenly lights. That's priceless, isn't it!

No matter what, we've all seen some of those moments like what we've been thinking about, right? I've got to suggest, then, based on gospel truth, that no matter where on the spectrum you feel your life fits best, you've got a story of Almighty God's activity in there. And when you put all those memories (good, bad, and neutral) alongside God's written Word, you find it!

Chapter 13

Your Turn, What's Your Take?

Can we revisit something for a few minutes? Going back to our thoughts having such an enormous impact on how we go about life, I find it chilling what people have come to believe about their origin. Not only that, but I also find it perplexing when I consider everything I have learned about the arguments of both evolutionists and creationists, I am astonished that there is even a debate going on.

A perfect example of <u>a lot</u> of conditions syncing together to make something possible is... Earth. Do you realize that *every single one of a multitude of conditions is absolutely perfect* for life – which is why we can have life on this planet?

Consider these facts:

- ✓ The Earth is at <u>the ideal distance from the sun</u> for it to have <u>the perfect temperature</u> range to sustain life.
- ✓ The Earth is made up of materials of the right kind and with the right properties for it to have <u>the perfect temperatures and pressures</u>.
- ✓ The Earth has <u>*ALL of the components which are necessary to sustain*</u> us and the rest of nature.

Your Turn, What's Your Take?

Perfect temperature range, liquid water, magnetic fields…. There are many, many more, but those qualities alone are remarkable enough to make the point I'm trying to make–that without a design, this physical place we call home would not have all the parameters in place to provide for life as we know it.

A **MAJOR** question for me, then, is where did the design come from? My mind simply cannot accept the nebulous *self-construction* notion postulated by the *Theory of Evolution* (i.e. that theory riding on the initial spontaneous combustion[119] of ("non-existent") fuel and oxygen, followed by natural selection[120] + randomized genetic drift over periods of time which, by the way, CANNOT be honestly calculated).

It makes so much more sense to accept the concept of a logically designed world created by an intelligent inventor. Honestly, how many of us would argue that the first cell phones came together by chance? Isn't it **rational** to *assume* that an inventor used intelligence to engineer their creation? And I find it equally **rational** not to work *against* logic in order to come up with an alternative hypothesis. What are *your* thoughts on that?

Some people like to imagine other life forms that could necessitate other types of requirements to live… alternate air, different nutrients, unfamiliar fields, mysterious forms of transportation…. Some do this because it's fun to be creative (Hmm, wouldn't creativity and imagination be imparted to us if we were made in the image of a Creator? Just thinking...). Yet, others do so in an effort to dissuade people from believing in a Creator.

I'm guessing some people truly believe, even deep down, that such a scenario exists. Without a doubt, the notion of *something coming from nothing* is a captivating concept. I'm thinking, though. What conditions could allow life to come about randomly (i.e. **<u>LIFE</u>** *(let this sink in)* to come into existence from

NONLIFE), and (importantly) have those conditions ever been observed? Nothing in observable nature points toward the idea of living beings, or "lifeforms," self-constructing over time, with elaborate, highly sophisticated, and exquisitely detailed anatomical systems to allow them to function properly. So personally, I've got to take a pass on such a storyline. It looks, sounds, and smells counterfeit to me. To my knowledge, neither science nor common sense can support the narrative.

And you? What's your take on these things?

I just want to add, that to give an idea like that one even a suggestion of credibility, someone would first have to invent an additional "theory," which could offer those necessary conditions we just thought about. More creativity. More false narrative. And why?

Here's where I am thankful for both science and biblical scripture because *both* will come to our rescue!

True science is, by definition, the practice of making **observations** about our world, drawing **conclusions** about those observations, and then **recording** *those* conclusions. Be careful of falling for pseudo-science, which can't be observed (*think, for example, 10 to the 6 hundred thousand trillionth. What!?*).

And the Bible is, by definition, the written word of the Almighty God, who created heaven and earth and every physical thing on the earth, including humankind in the very image of God. He did not give us a convoluted, difficult-to-navigate, damning matrix of mystique – impossible to figure out without the help of gurus. His aim was never to confuse His creation and cause us grief and watch us flounder, only to then punish us for not being successful in toeing the line.

Au contraire, scripture tells us He wants us to be in relationship with Him!

Your Turn, What's Your Take?

I readily confess that I can't cite all the logic behind how I can put my faith in an almighty Creator any more than I can contradict all the reasons why I cannot put my faith in alternate theories. Really, though, who can? I guess that's the nature of faith, right?

We had to come from somewhere. Either we were created by a Designer, or we weren't. If we say we weren't, then we are saying we do not have a Creator and everything came into existence by chance, evolving over time. Both statements can't be true, so which will you choose to believe? (Either way, you are making a decision based on faith.)

All right now, being TOTALLY honest with yourself, which is it?

Almighty God *and* Direct Support Provider?

Maybe it's just a weird concept to some, the idea of God (as the Creator of the *whole* world) reaching down to help us. I've realized something, though. The same people who can't see God's intervention in their own lives might possibly see it in *your* life, or in *my* life. Jesus taught this powerful reality all along. He said, "Let your light shine before others, so that they may see your good works and give glory to your Father who is in heaven."[121]

Of *course* He did. It's part of His Plan – to draw everyone to Him.

No End in Sight!
Are We Living Expectantly, or Merely Enduring?
[Part 2]

Chapter 14

The Almighty God of Possibility

"With God all things are possible."[122]
This is a mysterious truth! What's that old saying – *the truth is stranger than fiction*? Well, if we trust the Bible as God's written Word and (this next piece is key) **go _to_ _it_** for understanding, we learn that God works in our lives, no matter who we are or what we've done – whether we recognize Him as LORD or not. Jesus said that our Father in Heaven "causes his sun to rise on the evil *and* the good and sends rain on the righteous *and* the unrighteous."[123]

Many of us grew up thinking God blesses the just and curses the unjust. Our shared question tends to be, *is it…**possible**…for God to bless the **bad** guys??*

The answer is yes – at least according to Jesus. And not only that… it's possible for *us* bad guys to bless the *other* bad guys (if we want to look at things honestly). Let's face it. We're not always nice to others, nor are others always nice to us. Sometimes we even find ourselves with real enemies. Can we bless them? Yes, we can. When we are willing,[124] God makes a way.[125]

All right, so if you're already a believer in the Almighty God, I've got a question for you.

Have you come close enough to Him to stop limiting yourself with that (detrimental) one-dimensional view of His love and righteousness?

No doubt, as a believer you acknowledge that God's love is so very deep that He was able to give His only begotten Son so that you shouldn't perish, but that, instead, you could live eternally with Him. And hopefully, you recognize His claim on your life to the point that you stay focused on His will each day and strive to please Him by doing what you've read is right in *His* eyes. But then, do you find yourself hoping that you're righteous enough? Isn't that curious? I get it. I've been there.

For many years I felt I had a pretty good handle on God's plan of salvation and reasoned that I was in good standing with Him because of my obedience to the gospel and my willingness to repent again and again, as needed. Putting it simply, my (subconscious) understanding of His righteousness was too complex.

I thought that my messing up meant doing "make-up work." You know, like when you miss some time from school, and your teacher cares enough to allow you to do some make-up work so your grade won't suffer? While I did know that my salvation wasn't based on merit, and I deliberately rejected the balancing-scale method of righteousness, I still managed to operate on a phony reprimand system that said I could once again enjoy my relationship with God without feeling the guilty weight of the disappointment, anger, or grief I had caused Him... once I somehow *undid* the ramifications of my sin. Whoa! And woe!!

That interpretation of righteousness isn't *God's* righteousness at all.[126] The righteousness afforded to us by The Almighty is a matter of the heart. It's all about His endowing our attitudes with mercy and justice, and God's righteousness is *how* we are capable of loving and forgiving one another in the same way He loves and forgives us.[127] The righteousness of God influences everything we think and do, and it affects our entire connection with our all-powerful Father in Heaven.

Just look at how little children accept forgiveness. Why? Because Jesus is pleased with the humble faith of children, as we learn in the Bible (Mark 10:14-15). Do they fret about making up for their misdeed? I think not. They immediately relax and look to their parent or other caregiver for next steps. Their trust isn't in their own ability or authority to make things right, but they listen to their forgiver. The one forgiving is the one who can proffer fresh hope.

It's alarming, isn't it? To live with spiritual reservations…. I think what it really boils down to is that those are actually reservations regarding our *faith*. Not believing down to the bones that God can make all things possible… well, just isn't living by faith at all. It's living by "wishery" … mere wishful thinking. This kind of faith is, in reality, a very subtle spiritual delusion and can't please God because it doesn't get us closer to Him.[128]

What it can do, though? It can trick us into thinking we can somehow procure the uprightness, and thus worthiness, He demands.

No wonder Christians forget their hope…. Instead of adding to our faith the qualities that will keep our faith effective and productive, we focus on things that *this world* deems righteous, and we forget we've been **cleansed** (…um, *hello!!!*) from our past sins.[129] It's easy to get back into the rut of DIY righteousness. Have you ever slipped into that rut?

Believe me, I've done the *log-roll, slip-n-slide, pirouette-and-bob* trick in my attempt to keep my head above the muck, and I've found it exhausting and simply a waste of energy.

That old routine is no fun and has absolutely zero effectiveness. I'm more aware now, though, that we can't expect natural solutions to work for supernatural problems.

On the other hand, when we have believed that which God the Spirit has taught through God the Son and through the inspired writings about Him, we begin to comprehend the things that once were hidden from our minds.[130] Likewise, when we have chosen to love God back (remember? *He loved us first!*),[131] we find ourselves being delighted to know Him – can you fathom it? We can actually *know* our Creator, which means, we can have a *relationship* with Him!

Now we're back in familiar territory – *relationships* are something we all have experience with. For instance, we understand this: when we know and love someone comfortably, we discover how much we want to please that special person, right? We don't have to *force* ourselves to want to please this one whom we love, we just *want* to.

So common sense tells us that it's the same, in our relationship with God. When we love Him, *we* want what *He* wants. And get this – as we allow Him to use our lives for His purpose (of helping others come to love God, too), we can trust that The Almighty is working everything out for our good.[132] We can't get a win-win better than that!

When you share your life with others, every so often, you can expect to be on the receiving end of some naysaying. This seems to be true, no matter what it is you're sharing, but especially if you're sharing something about your experiences with God in Christ Jesus. It's all right, though. You are blessed.[133] Keep enduring.[134] You're in good company.[135] And remember, Jesus said they're not just rejecting you; they're rejecting Him.[136]

Doubtless, stories about Almighty God's supposed intervention in your life could sound laughable to your listeners. The same stories could even be a bit unnerving to them. The idea of a supernatural being who knows what's going on down here isn't new, but One who *cares* about you – and enough to *sacrifice His own blood to rescue you* from a world that holds you captive in sin? Unheard of!

Except in Christ Jesus, that is! His is the only spiritual story that begins with God as *Creator*, continues with God as *Sustainer/Teacher/Guide*, climaxes with God as *Sacrificial Lamb* and culminates with God as *Victor/Eternal Bridegroom*.

Chapter 15

The Almighty: God of Providence

The point is, you'll find that, no matter what, people will not always agree with you. Particularly when the narrative you share praises a God who is supposed to be in control of things down here. You claim He sees everything, is good, and knows how to fix things. He's powerful enough to do it, you say. So why *doesn't* He?

People can't figure out why a loving God would ever allow any injustice to happen – especially *terrible* things, like violence, abuse, neglect, injustice, physical disease, excruciating or chronic pain, natural disasters (and other kinds of catastrophes), loneliness, depression, mental illness, and heartbreaking deaths. And this is a short list. How could a good divine being – an *Almighty* God – tolerate this?

Some years ago, someone close to me said, "Yeh, okay. God was with you. Mm-hmm, yeh. Right...."

"Yes, of *course* He was," I answered. I'm pretty sure my voice sounded agitated. The sarcasm in his tone was clear, and I admittedly didn't have much patience, but it's hard for me to remain clear-headed when people speak flippantly about The

Almighty. God doesn't need my protection – I understand, but RAAAUURRRRRGH! (I felt a little hot under the collar....)

This critic went on, "If there was an almighty god, and he loves everybody *so* much, then why did he let my mother die from such a horrible disease?! She never hurt anyone! And why did he let you – a young woman in the prime of her life – almost die from a brain tumor?!

Okay, whew! This was something I could manage – even welcome. Legitimate questions.

I'll be honest, to say, *I don't know*. But I **do** know (by faith) that if God allows anything to be, He's got a reason. And I believe that His reason is *always* for our benefit somehow. So I've learned over time to *look for the benefits*.

Suffering can actually help us secure benefits for ourselves like *belief-building, faith- strengthening*, and a *compelling incentive for finding hope*.[137] Hope is a good thing, and yes, it's not at all unusual for hope to emerge from the ashes of misery. Likewise, joy often follows in the wake of our suffering and sorrow, too, because God is the author of hope and joy.[138] He's there with us as we cling to Him for aid and refuge.[139]

And let's never forget the peace – God's peace – that comforts and sustains our hearts in the middle of any ruckus.[140] In fact, it's the peace of God – the peace only He can provide – that makes the difference between suffering miserably and just suffering. Think about *that* if you will. It is possible to suffer, without being miserable!

God's gracious, merciful, consoling peace is a gift. Peace of mind, even while the body is not at peace.

My own experience affirms it. I've had headaches where I felt like my brain would rupture. Biting pain in places I don't even recall, though it required morphine to alleviate it. Practicing sitting up, with my torso as upright as possible, while mentally urging my weakened neck muscles and inflamed nerves to cooperate and hold my head vertically. I didn't even know whether the day would come when the gain would be worth the pain.

Not saying plenty of others don't have it worse. But did I suffer? I did. But did I feel a sense of peace, still? Yes. I did. I knew the Almighty was right there, holding me up – guarding my heart and my mind in Christ Jesus.

If painful experience leads us to self-reflect…or if our longing for relief allows us to love others more compassionately…or if the sorrow we feel because of our sin draws us, ultimately, toward earnestly seeking our God, then The Almighty has been able to accomplish His purpose through our suffering.[141] And this is why James tells Christians to "count it all joy when you fall into various trials."[142]

Here's an illustration of God's providence through my own unpleasant experience.

Remember Lori, who had transported feeble me all over our post-neurosurgery world… to doctor visits and other places like the movie theater, the ice cream shop, and the acupuncturist's? Well, her educational background in social work prepared her well – as you will see – for her role in helping me overcome my own sudden, unforeseen circumstances.[143]

Lori was also only 25 years old, so her experience was also on the youthful side, but it would prove invaluable to me on many levels.[144] As a social worker, she had been involved with the elderly and the common issues they face – which are very much like many of the issues I have had to contend with. (Ahem! Let me throw out a quick *who knew?* here….

I believe this beneficial combination of preparation and timing was not mere coincidence.

The Almighty: God of Providence

I don't have all the answers – I live by faith. Even so, I am convinced that the Creator God, Himself, was clearly *involved* – orchestrating all kinds of little details, to *minimize the harmful* effects and *optimize the teachable* moments of this crisis.

I *will* say that even after 45+ years of studying God's existence, power, glory, justice, mercy, and love, I still can't fully wrap my mind around what I'm about to tell you, though I've seen His extravagant, engaged love exemplified countless times, in countless ways.

Chapter 16

An All-*knowing* God

My parents were 1200 miles away, at home, when they received that phone call. And my sister, who was raising three children under extremely difficult circumstances, still managed to come up with my parents to see me. Many others, including – but not limited to – nurses, doctors, coworkers, families, housekeeping employees, volunteers, preschool children…were in their places, doing their thing, and God used who they were, where they were, what they did or didn't do, and my relationship to each one, to accomplish His purpose for me.[145] I'm continually amazed.

Maybe even more unfathomable, to *my* mind, is that this Almighty God, who for His own reasons, lined up these details to work things out for *my* good, also – at the same time – arranged the necessary details to work things out for *others'* good! Inconceivable, His working.

For example, I'm convinced He supplied Lori with the competency she needed to help me, even while He provided her with serenity as she worked through her own sense of loss. I might have died, and her friend would have been physically gone. I might have lived, and her friend could have been mentally gone. For all she *actually* knew, I would never be independent again – though she was adamant in her *trust* that my health would return to normal again. Her trust didn't keep me alive or cognitively capable; God did that. But her trust kept *her* consoled and able to navigate muddy waters – a blessing for her *and* me! God did that, too.

I'll give you an illustration. The skilled-nursing-just-turned-rehab facility my insurance approved for me would not permit me to get up out of my chair without a physical therapist by my side. You'll find that to be an understandable rule in principle, of course, and I did too…at first. But my PT time was limited to short sessions, and those were not very frequent, and since the whole point of my being there was supposed to be to rehabilitate myself, I felt increasingly frustrated with each new day. Those wheelchair arms I managed to pull off and chuck over the side of the hill attest to that!

I can't recall now how long the physical therapy sessions were – or how often – but I do remember very clearly that it seemed I was seeing the *cognitive* therapist every time I turned around. (That would be a figurative *turning around*, by the way. Actually, turning around was a physical challenge I craved to meet.)

Though I was on the traumatic brain injury unit, cognitive therapy was the one service I had little need of because the part of my brain that had suffered the most damage was not my frontal lobe. That lobe of the brain is like its control panel, designed to preside over things like personality and the ability to communicate. It controls vital cognitive skills like emotional expression, problem solving, memory, language, and some other functions.[146] So because I was performing like a person without brain injury on their tests, it really seems like a no-brainer (I know, bad pun) as to why I became a frequent guest for cognition-related observation.[147] I was something of an anomaly.

I think it was sometimes *more than once a day* that someone would come to my room and wheel me in for a cognitive assessment. Did I know the date? Where was I and why? Could I please read this and answer some questions? What colors did I see in the pictures?

These assessment exercises were all valuable tools and had great purpose, I do understand, and the therapists were all nice and often complimented me. I remember one of them was amazed that I could balance a checkbook without "carrying the ones" on paper, and she exclaimed, "You can balance a checkbook better than I can!" Looking back, I see God encouraging me through even these frustrations.

Still, feelings don't equate to understanding, do they! In particular, in a time of distress. At that time of my distress, I didn't see the benefits of those cognitive assessments. I was feeling like a research specimen more than like a person who was there for recovery support, and I was extremely frustrated. My physical, occupational, and at least one of my cognitive therapists were young enough to be fresh out of school. That's fine, but the problem was, I felt I was capable of reaching benchmarks that evidently had not been envisioned as reasonable for me.

If they'd said, "Darlene, let's get your body working as best we can. At the same time, our research would really benefit others. Could we do some cognitive exercises with you, so we can improve our knowledge base?" I would have jumped at the chance (metaphorically): "*Absolutely*! Just tell me what to do." But I'm wandering into a whole new topic, so let's get back…. We were talking about God's incredibly exact orchestration of things, to accomplish His purposes.

From the first day I took that troubling gurney ride through the corridor of the TBI unit, looking upon the unexpressive, sometimes vacant, eyes of my hall mates, I was determined that, if God allowed, I was going to leave by July 1st. That would give me only one month to get from an emaciated 5'11" young woman of 108 lbs, who had conquered the formidable 20' long parallel bars at John Dempsey, yet was still unable to stand without a walker…to a person able to convince the facility personnel I could survive *out there*.

It felt like Dr. R**** was accustomed to putting nails into the proverbial coffin. Was he examining me, a *person* – or an appliance? He did manage, as he took off his examination gloves, to ask me what seemed to be a rote post-inspection question: *So, do you have an idea of when you'd like to leave here?*

It wasn't the *question* that was discouraging. In fact, I *wanted* to talk all about that(only, read *whisper*, since with my left true vocal cord paralyzed, I had no voice). It was his response to my reply that set my teeth on edge. First, a chuckle, then, *"July 1st, eh,"* followed by a scarcely disguised smirk. *"January 1st, maybe, but **not July**."*

Thank God for Lori. Lori was my faithful friend, visiting me every weekday after she left work, and I'll venture to admit she probably got an earful of my grievances each time. She was a great sounding board, and I knew without a doubt that she absolutely had my best interests in mind at all times. I trusted whatever she said concerning my patient-hood, and so when she told me to dry my tears, hold onto the handles of my wheelchair, "march down that hall to the social work department and insist on talking to Margie," I did.

Margie speedily talked me into letting her push me back to my room, where we could talk. I felt that confronting the administrative office people in that way was a good step (*haha*) because it showed them my determination in wanting to recover my physical competencies. I wasn't "just" the patient in Room 321 (or whatever) anymore. At least, I *felt* more empowered.

Thankfully, though, the lifeblood of my hope was never in the abilities and confidence of my doctors, nurses, therapists, or even friends. Instead, my most basic hope was then – and still is today – in the undeniable power of the Almighty God who created the heavens and the earth, the cosmos and all of its intricacies, the deepest parts of outer space and the deepest parts of inner man. One prophet (who lived about 600 years before Jesus came to earth) voiced it perfectly:

"But this I call to mind, and therefore I have hope:

"The *steadfast* love of the Lord *never ceases*; his *mercies never come to an end*; they are *new every morning*; great is your faithfulness. 'The Lord is my portion,' says my soul, 'therefore I will hope in him.' The Lord is good to *those who wait for him*, to the soul *who seeks him*. It is good that one should *wait quietly for the salvation of the Lord*."[148]

Then, centuries later, Jesus said this: *"Everything is possible for one who believes."*[149]

Astonishing, right?

Oh, …you'll probably be interested to know that I left there to go home **a few days *prior*** to my July 1st goal date! My soul got a glimpse of God's personal attention and medical supremacy on **June** 26th – the day Lori and I *walked* to her car. Freedom at last! That was a good day.

Almighty God strengthened me, to endure. And He made everything worth the wait. Just sayin'.

No End in Sight!
Are We Living Expectantly, or Merely Enduring?
[Part 3]

Chapter 17

Gift for the Bride

Speaking of the wait being worthwhile...what are *you* waiting for? Are you, like me, waiting for this?

Then the angel showed me a river of the water of life, as clear as crystal, flowing from the throne of God and of the Lamb down the middle of the main street of the city. On either side of the river stood a tree of life, bearing twelve kinds of fruit and yielding a fresh crop for each month. And the leaves of the tree are for the healing of the nations.

No longer will there be any curse. The throne of God and of the Lamb will be within the city, and His servants will worship Him. They will see His face, and His name will be on their foreheads.[150] *[...]*

"Behold, I am coming soon, and My reward is with Me, to give to each one according to what he has done. I am the Alpha and the Omega, the First and the Last, the Beginning and the End."

<u>Blessed are those who wash their robes, so that they may have the right to</u> *the tree of life and may enter the city by its gates.* *But outside are the dogs, the sorcerers, the sexually immoral, the murderers, the idolaters, and everyone who loves and practices falsehood.*

"I, Jesus, have sent My angel to give you this testimony for the churches. I am the Root and the Offspring of David, the bright Morning Star."[151]

Oh, I want to be there! Can you imagine? To be able to look Jesus in the eyes without any shame or remorse?

This realization (that eternal life is *gulp* **eternal**, and that The Almighty didn't send His only Son lightly) became the catalyst for me to actually write and publish an account of how God has seen me through my own set of dangers, drudgeries, and hardships. He's been preparing me, all the while, like he has prepared His countless other children, each for the role He's given us – in order "to further the faith" of the church "and their [our] knowledge of the truth that leads to godliness...."[152]

Of course, while my personal journey to the faith is unique to *me*, the faith I proclaim is not. It's the same faith that the apostles taught, as presented in the Bible. Paul shared the very same faith through his letters to the church groups he had planted around the Aegean Sea. (Actually, there is only *one* faith[153] because there is only one truth)[154]

But why is it important to share this faith? There are a lot of people who would prefer not to hear anything about biblical faith.[155] They think it's offensive – out of line – to spread the teachings that Jesus is the Savior of people. They don't like the idea of sin, period, and do not take kindly to anyone suggesting that their lives are not entirely their own.[156] That there will be a day when they will have to give an account for the way they chose to live their lives.[157] That there will be *eternal* consequences.[158]

The answer, of course, is HOPE. The hope of eternal life gives believers (which includes me) confidence that we *have* eternal life.[159] This eternal life is what God (who does not lie) made certain before He even created the world.[160] He gives it to us freely. And it's clear:

"'Everyone who calls on the name of the LORD will be saved.' But how can they call on him to save them unless they believe in him? And how can they believe in him if they have never heard about him? And how can they hear about him unless someone tells them?"[161]

Sharing that hope with people is any Christian's responsibility[162] – especially with all those <u>who *are looking for* God and *ask* us</u> about the hope we have.[163] Believers are told, "Be ready to spread the word whether or not the time is right. Point out errors, warn people, and encourage them. Be very patient when you teach."[164] God, Himself, pleads with seekers:

The Spirit and the bride say, **"Come!"** *Let the one who hears say,* **"Come!"** *And let the one who is thirsty* **come,** *and the one who desires the water of life drink freely."*[165]

According to the Scriptures, then, those thirsting for life with God are invited to come to Him and drink. I understand that the Father Himself loved us enough to send Jesus, and I firmly believe that without Jesus, this wonderful, stunning invitation could never have been extended.[166]

But this is worth mentioning – did you notice in this verse that it is "the bride" who, in partnership with the Spirit, is sending out invitations?

And, as *I* understand it, the **bride** in Scripture consistently refers to the **church** of Christ[167] (the church that Christ Himself built upon that immoveable rock of the gospel truth – that He is the Messiah, the Son of the living God....).[168]

Other passages in Scripture explain more fully, so we can recognize the symbolism.[169] "The bride," then, is a symbol for *the bride of Christ*. Who is the bride of Christ? The church.[170]

I absolutely marvel about the way God reveals Himself through the written Word.

Sometimes He shows His character through the way He interacts with His people. There are instances where He displays His righteous anger in response to their disobedience,[171] and at times He demonstrates His merciful kindness because, in godly sorrow, they repent.[172]

The Almighty God grieves, weeps, administers justice, bestows mercy, and pleads our cause for us on our behalf.[173] He invites us to cast all our cares on Him because He cares for us.[174] And one of the most relevant things He does for us as we journey through this earthly life is teach.[175] He simplifies and illuminates the things He wants us to understand – what we need to know to be saved and then, to live good lives.

Many of us are familiar with the way Jesus taught. Through parables. *Analogies*, as some of us would call these "earthly stories with a heavenly meaning" – stories about earthly themes, to communicate profound heavenly truths. They're like the spoken version of the visual aids teachers use to help learners understand something better.

For example, we learn from Scripture that the LORD God – Jehovah – is *ONE* God. We read a lot about the Father, and we understand that He begat (more on this word[176]) His Son Jesus, and there is a Holy Spirit, as well, who fills a distinct role. Yet, the words used in Scripture to describe these three specified persons indicate that They are one and the same! What should we make of this?

The name the Hebrews used when talking about the Creator "God" was *Elohim*[177] (sounds like Eh-loh-heem' – or sometimes people say "Eh-loh'-him") and it's a plural noun (i.e. *gods*, but with a capital G.... I don't feel right spelling "God*s*" because it wouldn't be understood in conventional English – there is one true G̲od in the Bible, and His name is God, capitalized).

It's easier to understand when you think of our own language so let's look at an example.

In English, we say "boats" (plural noun) when we're talking about more than one boat. And to explain to you that there was some floatin' going on by those boats, I would tell you, "Those boats are floating." But, in the Hebrew language, when they talked about something *Elohim* did (remember, it's a plural subject: [G]od̲s̲), they used a singular verb. Those grammar forms don't match up. Appropriately, if you heard me say, "Those boats is floating away!" you'd be tempted to go sign me up for the earliest scheduled grammar class (*or*, alternatively, you'd wonder what part of Texas I done got schooled in. But that's my little secret.... ;*D*).

So, why does the Bible use the plural *Elohim* with the singular word for "created"? After all, wouldn't an almighty God hold the standard for His written word to be perfect, without error?

Well, I looked into this a little deeper, as if I were not aware that the most important explanation is that our magnificent Creator is one God, comprised of three individual persons who are so united as to be One in spirit and purpose and essence.[178] You may have heard one of these terms: "trinity," or "triune God." Neither of these terms are found in the Bible, but they are probably the best words we created persons can come up with to describe who God is, knowing He speaks of Himself in His Word as being three distinct Persons while at the same time claiming to be One God.

While it may look and feel like a conundrum, faith overcomes the problem. Here's the best explanation I found. When you hear it, I think you're going to agree that it makes total sense.

The plural name for God (*Elohim*) not only denotes more than one aspect, or person, or part of God, but it also captures the essence of all the powers, capabilities, and influences God possesses. It speaks to us of the three persons of God: Father, Son, and Holy Spirit, and their uniquely singular presence in one Being. The unified persons of the Godhead each used His distinct attributes to create the world, and together they are (He is) still sustaining it.[179]

All the powers and faculties required to bring the heavens and earth into being are His, and when we see them manifested in what He does in our own, daily lives, they communicate to us who God IS.[180]

The following analogy can't do justice to Him by any stretch of the imagination, but consider this if you will. One bodybuilding strongman can lift a lot of weight. But *two* strongmen can lift a lot more weight. *Three* can lift a lot more, still – more than I dare to envision. But can you even begin to imagine how much weight they could lift if ALL the strongmen in the entire world united?? That's intense strength and power!

Now maybe we can get somewhat of an idea about *Elohim*. His command of power is far greater than the union of all others' powers combined. And with good reason...all power on, above, below, within, and beyond the earth is organically derived from Him. God the Father, God the Son, God the Holy Spirit. The LORD God. All-powerful. The Almighty God.

This is a rousing mystery, wouldn't you say? *Elohim* personifies mystery, but here's another great mystery: Christians – we who walk with Him by faith today – will see Him face to face one day, and the Almighty's presence won't be a mystery anymore![181]

Right now, while we are living here on earth, our minds are restricted, it would seem, by our organic brains with their physical lobes and synapses.... Is it any wonder we have trouble wrapping our tiny minds around the spiritual, ever-present, all-knowing, almighty *Elohim*? I, for one, can't quite grasp the whole concept. Even three of me would not have the power to get it.

But I do understand *gifts*. And Eternal Life for all who are in Christ Jesus – for His church..., for His bride[182].... You know what? *That's* a gift!

Chapter 18

Hidden Treasures

That Day is coming! But, until then, we have the Scriptures to explain the mystery of our salvation, with parables and analogies to make things clearer. Many times, as well, the Holy Spirit guided the writers (of the letters and accounts which are now bound together as our Bible) to express in plain speech what was what. The apostle Paul explained that "all the treasures of wisdom and knowledge" are hidden in Jesus Christ.[183]

The Father reserves the right (and wisely so) to keep some things to Himself.[184] For instance, the Father is the only one who knows exactly *when* He has appointed for Jesus, the Son, to come back.[185] Even the angels in heaven – and Jesus Himself do not know![186] But the Almighty Father knows, and *Elohim* warns us throughout the New Testament, in every feasible way,[187] to be ready, because He wants us to be <u>united with Him</u>,[188] so we can be with Him <u>forever</u>.[189]

This union with Christ, itself, is a mystery. Can we understand it? Is this one of the secrets God reserves for Himself alone?

No, it's certainly not. The Holy Spirit has divulged all kinds of pertinent information to us in Scripture[190] so we, who want to, can understand.[191] Christ Jesus is depicted in the Bible as a devoted husband – a much loved bridegroom.[192] Even in the Old Testament message, God compares His love for His people to a husband's love for his wife.[193] The analogy, which serves as a wonderful visual aid for us, demonstrates the elaborate, celebratory, and incredibly self-sacrificing love God, in the form of Christ,[194] so willingly bestows upon the people who choose to love Him back, who agree to be faithful to Him. As His one and only.[195]

The Bible is rife with marriage illustrations. This is a hot topic, though – one that Bible adherents often do not want to broach when talking to people who have sharply different views on men and their (quote, unquote) *love* for the wives they once promised to cherish. More than a few women are bitter because of certain men whose attitudes or behaviors have had detrimental effects on themselves or others.

People are understandably opposed to the spousal rhetoric of the Bible. Especially when it comes to describing the love of God. The woman whose husband cheated on her…the guy whose dad left his mom high and dry…the arrogant abuser…the man who is not sure *how* to be a husband because his role model wasn't there half the time while he was growing up…. It just doesn't make much sense to them for the God who is purported to love sacrificially to be compared to the type of low-caliber person they've encountered in action, first-hand. The general consensus among a good portion of the population is, *husbands!? They're either violent or deadbeats. Who needs them??* For many the answer to that is, **women** don't.

Let's go back to the loyal devotion of God's sacrificial, protective love for the church. What, pray tell, does this have to do with the marriage relationship, we might wonder? Well, let's see!

God says: "Husbands, love your wives, just as Christ loved the church and gave Himself up for her."[196] If God has perfect wisdom, and He has equated the husband-to-wife relationship with the Creator's[197] relationship to His bride, the church, there must be some parallels between the two relationships worth examining. This is that mysterious unity bond that we, as Christians, have with our Lord! And marvelously, the Holy Spirit has chosen to reveal the crucial secret to us through beautiful pictorial language the whole world *should* be able to understand.

Okay…so why don't we get it? Why is it that so few of us comprehend the parallel between eternal salvation and the marriage relationship?

Could it be that we have become so proud, and have developed such a disregard for God's will, that we no longer can hear His voice? That we no longer know where to find the answers He gives? That we have lost our greatest treasure?

Chapter 19

The Thing that Hinders Us

We people have really messed things up. We think and act as though we created (or *are creating*) ourselves. Like we belong to ourselves and can therefore make all the rules.[198] It's baffling, though, as I think about it, because for some of us, the number one rule is that there *are* no rules. Does that make sense to *you*?

Even if God could be taken out of the equation, *no rules* makes no sense. It's an order-less state of affairs called **anarchy**, and you'll be hard-pressed to find any good ever having come as a result of such disorder. Anarchy leads to chaos, confusion, and unrest at every turn. This is definitely not the way of Almighty God.[199]

If we can learn from the mistakes of the Ancient Israelites, we can see our own problem in two statements from Isaiah: "This people draw near with their words and honor Me with their lip service, but they remove their hearts far from Me, and their reverence for Me consists of tradition learned by rote."[200]

The authority of our Creator can be plainly recognized.[201] Some of us see His majesty in the creation and are willing to acknowledge His rules. But every one of us is still imperfect.[202] Even with the words "The Lord is my Shepherd"[203] still in our mouths, we turn from the path He's leading us up – yes, the one with inconceivable treasures at the end of it (and priceless benefits along the way).[204] Amazingly, for some reason, we keep our eyes fixed, not on Jesus, but on finding immediate gratification, down a pathway not authorized by the One who made us.[205] Down a path of our own choosing. (We can assert our *"God-given" prerogative*, after all. Right?)

In Scripture, this tragic, self-directed journey is described as *a corruption of… a deception about…a wandering from…and a falling away from* – God's perfect instruction.[206] Matthew 16:24-26[207] relates a time when Jesus told his apostles candidly about the critical importance of sticking to God's Way:

Then Jesus told His disciples, **"*If anyone wants to come after Me, he must deny himself and take up his cross and follow Me. For whoever wants to save his life will lose it, but whoever loses his life for My sake will find it. What will it profit a man if he gains the whole world, yet forfeits his soul? Or what can a man give in exchange for his soul?*"**

If we take Jesus at His word, we have some fixing to do – a <u>lot</u> of fixing. And we are just not capable of cleaning up our mess.[208]

Almighty God, who made us, sees the problem, and knows how to get us out of the mess[209] before it destroys us,[210] and He has given us the secret's code![211] Isn't He merciful? He *could* let us rot in our own mire, but instead, because He loves us, He has given us all things along with His Son.[212]

"By his divine power, God has given us everything we need for living a godly life. We have received all of this by coming to know him, the one who called us to himself by means of his marvelous glory and excellence. And because of his glory and excellence, he has given us great and precious promises. These are the promises that enable you to share his divine nature and escape the world's corruption caused by human desires."[213]

Isn't The LORD beautiful?

"*In view of all this, make every effort to respond to God's promises. Supplement your faith with a generous provision of moral excellence, and moral excellence with knowledge, and knowledge with self-control, and self-control with patient endurance, and patient endurance with godliness, and godliness with brotherly affection, and brotherly affection with love for everyone.*

"<u>*The more you grow like this, the more productive and useful you will be in your knowledge of our Lord Jesus Christ.*</u>"[214]

But how can we actually put such a lofty plan into action? It's hard – if even doable.

After all, most people would probably love to be able to "be good" like that. How do we add all these wonderful virtues to our lives when we can't even see past the next looming problem? It can feel like God is asking too much.

I just want to remind you – like I remind myself – that God, though His standards for us are high, has never, and will never say "do this" and then leave us on our own to figure it out. That's precisely why He came down to live with us two thousand years ago, in the form of Jesus,[215] and that's exactly why He offers to come live with us now.[216]

One way The Almighty God takes part in our daily lives is by offering His Holy Spirit to us,[217] to remind us of Whose we are,[218] and assure us of our salvation.[219] By the power of the Spirit living in us,[220] we are able to bear good fruit, *against* which "there is no law."[221] Sweet, delightful, nutritious fruit:

- **love**[222] (which helps us produce all the other fruit!),
- **joy**[223] (can't beat it, nor squelch it),
- **peace**[224] (beyond any human understanding),[225]

- **patience**[226] (available, even at the end of your last nerve) ....
- Want to be **kinder?**[227] The Spirit of God in you will help you treat your neighbor at least as well as you treat yourself.[228]
- Need some **goodness?**[229] Put Christ Jesus on in baptism – the Spirit comes along![230] Can't get any gooder than that!
- Looking to become more **faithful?**[231]
- To be **gentle?**[232]
- Struggling with **self-control?**[233]
  (We've been given ample resources, haven't we!)[234]
- God's divine power, glory, and excellence[235]
- His great and precious promises[236]
- Knowledge of our Lord Jesus Christ[237]

Yet, few of us really stop to consider the fascinating parallel between eternal life with The Almighty and the marriage relationship. This is very unfortunate, since *the earthly husband-wife relationship is possibly the most brilliant likeness to God's desired union with His people that we have*! Maybe the reason we don't replicate the pattern well is that we don't grasp the value of a *marriage like it **should** be*. How can we emulate what we don't see?

Thankfully, The Great Teacher offers a great internship. Even when those of us who are married haven't gotten it right yet, we still have the tools and instruction manual available to us. Life will be better using them. I'm talking to myself, too, when I say, "Let's do this!"

An Exceptional Husband

Chapter 20

What If Your Husband Is Far from Normal? [Godly and Faithful]

"If I was going to marry somebody, I'd think I would at least hear him say 'I love you' first."

This was the cheeky reply Lori gave Herb, exactly 45 days after meeting him. Her soon-to-be fiancé had just said something bold about marriage, and she was a bit surprised – though not alarmed. So, on October 17th, this loyal friend I've been telling you about got her first peek into what would become a setting for the Lord to showcase His beautiful marriage blueprint.

OK, here's where it gets good! *Literally*.

Herb is a *good* husband. Nobody can rationally deny it. He takes his commitments seriously – his promise to love Lori as himself.[238] No, let me correct what I just said. Herb loves Lori *more than* his own life. He is *that* husband who is willing to give himself up for his wife.[239] The husband this earthly world doesn't recognize. Most of the human population doesn't even know that kind of husband exists.

And the funny thing is, Herb's not alone. God has many followers – men who love and obey His Word. Who love and protect and care for their wives because of the deep love they have for their Savior. I know several of these men, personally. If my mom were still here, she'd immediately tell you my dad is up there at the top of the list. (She wouldn't have to tell *me*, though, because I saw his humble, devoted husband-ness for myself as I grew up in their home.)

So I, for one, commend Herb and the other husbands standing resolutely with him in the godly marriage arena, because they are indeed outstanding in the field. More exactly, *they are out there in the field, standing with Jesus.* These men work *daily* to maintain a mindset like the one Christ Jesus had as he chose to stay that difficult course which had been predefined by God. And in this world we're in, that's not normal.

How do they remain faithful to their commitments? The same way Jesus stayed faithful to his. They look to the Father for guidance, strength, and refuge. And once they know what God desires of them, they comply. They willingly put the needs of their wives before their own, and God blesses them for it.

Godly wives take their roles seriously, too. Lori is one who does. So was Mama. Wives like this love and cherish their husbands and treat them kindly, serving their men as "helpmeets," in keeping with their Creator's beautiful and matchless standard[240] (and humbly proud of the opportunity to do so).[241]

The point of view that those men and women seem to share is based on the fact that the entire creation was made of both male and female,[242] and that both genders have been precious to God, and interdependent from the beginning.[243] They don't see themselves as greater than their counterparts, but rather, are thankful to be part of such a harmonious team.[244] They recognize that God Himself designed *men and women to **balance** one another*. To live agreeably as companions.²⁴⁵

In a healthy relationship, each has a distinct role to play, and both husband and wife behave in ways that are mutually beneficial, whether that means cooking, cleaning, earning income, raising children, praying, giving, or even – just not complaining about their marriage to other people. They understand that they belong to one another.²⁴⁶

Isn't it fascinating that some couples seem meant for each other, while others have to struggle with all their might to live in the same house? I've mulled over this a lot over the years. Why do some husbands and wives get along so extremely well, and others barely get along at all?

How is it that some married couples find each other more attractive as time goes on, while others get tired of their spouses after an unpredictable allotment of time and start searching for replacements – or at least, for freedom from their current… predicament? Many times, it seems, an individual leaves the marriage because of dissatisfaction with the current state of the relationship.

Could it be that spouses become so restless because they've never entrusted their marital union to the Creator, who, in the beginning, established the *purpose* and *essential attributes* of what He deems a **sacred** partnership? We commonly fail to respect the terms and provisions that God, Himself, put in place for the married couple's good.²⁴⁷ It's not at all unusual for us today to view them as customizable regulations – or worse, as pointless inconveniences, which exist only as holdovers from an outdated system.

I also wonder why we habitually fail to recognize the success of those partners who accept the biblical specifications for marriage. It would seem a smart thing to do, to actually seek out people with relationships like that if we're looking to improve (or plan) our own.

If we claim the Scriptures concerning marriage are God's all-around directions for joining flawed halves, why are we so blind as to miss the way that His blueprint mysteriously guides a couple into becoming *an indivisible whole,* a living entity, sustained by love? Paradoxical, isn't it!

So, *God* established the grounds for a lifetime commitment and built protective stipulations into its very foundations. Why? To provide *happiness* within its borders, and to preserve the couple's *commitment* to each other. God created male and female bodies and souls to complement each other in such a way that they become "one flesh" in marriage.

Is denying God's sovereignty in the marriage what creates the disconnect between two people whose lives were intended for unity? Yes, I think so. It seems to me that in learning what God wants for marriage and striving to reach those God-given goals, a couple is bound to enjoy a healthy, successful relationship, but it's not going to happen without some effort.

Generalizing a bit, from personal experience… it's not easy to follow God's perfect will for us without sneaking a little of our own attitudes into the mix. And that's why it's so important to enter the marriage relationship while emulating the attitude of Christ Jesus.[248]

Mindsets anchored in the world and seeking a neutralized fellowship can form marriage unions, but I believe that those types of relationships cannot compete well with marriages between God-centered hearts that are seeking the bond of unity. It's possible that the one will eventually achieve **independent synchrony**, while it's guaranteed that the other will continue to grow in **_interdependent harmony_**. Can you sense the distinction between the two?

Well, thankfully, we can learn from others' mistakes. I hope, also, that we will learn from others' successes! So, again, I'll refer to Herb and Lori.

Lori and Herb

Chapter 21

What If Your Husband Is Far from Normal? [Adoring and Daring]

If you spend any time with Lori, it won't be long before you'll hear something about Herb's wonderfulness. Usually, it's in the context of something he did recently to help her. Lori spends much of her time these days in her powerchair, overcoming ever-present challenges for her physical limitations. Who of us (here on earth) knew, 29 years ago, when Herb said, "I promise to protect," that the "*probable MS*" diagnosis Lori received in her twenties would become "*exacerbating-remitting multiple sclerosis*" in her thirties, and then, within another ten years, would develop into "*secondary progressive multiple sclerosis*" (SPMS)?

Herb certainly didn't know. Yet, he exemplifies the husband who loves his wife "*just as Christ loved the church and gave himself up for her.*"[249] Anything Lori needs (and just about everything she just wants, too), Herb will do, give, or get for her. He serves as Lori's hands and feet, providing care and support for her at every level. He loves God first, and God enables him to love Lori like he should. He's one of God's visual aids to this world. His example shows us what the New Testament marriage lesson looks like in action. Isn't his heart beautiful? Some cultures would "admire" his feet, for all the work they do to present that liberating message. To quote God's Word: *How beautiful are the feet of messengers who bring good news!*[250]

Lori just thinks he's beautiful, period.

"He's so cute! I can't help it, he's just sooooo cute." (These words still roll off her tongue as easily and frequently today as they did 29 years ago. And what's more, she still means them.) Lori would think Herb hung the moon if she didn't already know that the feat had been The Almighty's doing.

She's well-acquainted with The Almighty's accomplishments, though. Of course she is. Look at what He's brought her through already. The LORD is her first love, as well, and He's why she can accept her diagnosis and her need for Herb's assistance. She sometimes says, "God is so good. He knew 29 years ago where we'd be, and He has provided us with everything we need."

Another thought she frequently expresses is, "I've been so blessed. I wish other people could feel the joy I feel. I always ask God to turn my mess into a message." I know enough regarding her story to fill another book, but a brief overview might be best for now!

Lori has a tender heart. Like with all of us, her heart can be other things, too. Stubborn. Fearful. Selfish. Fickle. (Stay with me, LOL! If you'll remember, I grouped us all together in this.) So, she's not perfect. Not yet. But, through faith, she's moving in that direction. The one thing her heart is, ALWAYS? Thankful.

Anyway, as a social worker, she worked closely alongside other professionals in several multi-bed nursing homes, where just about every one of her colleagues found her other-worldly sense of decorum to be amusing. She didn't swear or use foul language, and…was she really waiting until she was married!? This was great joke material! As a matter of fact, these were terrific talking points during the variable lulls throughout the day.

It wasn't especially fun to listen to the curious questions and sometimes less-than-modest comments. The latter were intended, of course, simply to get a reaction from their well-liked coworker. Everyone knew this open-book colleague would not respond moodily to their mischief, but that rather, they could anticipate that delightful look of total disbelief on her face. And that was just too good to pass up – which ensured that gently delivered "teasing" happened regularly. She was good-natured, and these were her friends, so on it went. From time to time, someone in the facility would know of someone who would be a great match for Lori, and she would be encouraged to give a blind date the old college try.

Until one day, Lori fell in love. When I say "one day" she fell in love, I mean, in reality, *several* days. Okay, there were several *weeks* there, while she and Herb went through the focused, relationship-building process of getting to know each other, but it's quite possibly the case, that the actual falling in love happened – for each of them – within a week or two.

How do I know? I was there (so to speak), from *The Introduction* on day one, to *The Marriage Proposal* on day 77. As a matter of fact, it was I who concluded from Herb's dependable correspondence, filled with regular references to personal minutiae (like his son's tarantula, Spidey), that these steady communications were, undeniably, love letters.

Before she was convinced of that, my modest, single friend had merely been thrilled that he took the time to write her! Lori returned his letters, and inevitably, it turned into a regular correspondence through which they opened up their lives to each other, without the faltering speech and awkward body language that can so easily get in the way of people's impressions of each other. In time, though, I stopped being invited to read the letters!

It was September 2nd that they met, still in the beginning stages of the Fall season. Besides the crisp air and brilliant New England foliage, I don't know which has contributed more to her fondness of the season… the local fairs, the farmers markets, the luring charm of bright pumpkins, the dried corn stalks, the colorful mums in neighborhood-yards, …or just what, but I do know that Fall has been Lori's favorite time of the year ever since before I met her.

Even before the hugely celebrated *Pumpkin Spice Latte* appeared on the scene, it was Lori's practice to bundle up in a cable knit turtleneck, grab a cup of coffee, and take a drive with her closest friends, through the northwest hills of New England – to scope out the changing leaves on Route 63, or 7, or another rural road.

Lori's leaf-peeping tours usually combined driving along scenic foliage routes with trips to Mystic Seaport… Gillette Castle… Boston's famed Freedom Trail… the Essex Steam Train… Plimoth Plantation…. In fact, my own "nutmeggar-hood" very likely found its naissance in some of those day trips. I have Lori to thank; she never neglected to admire the glory of New England and its Fall.

So when you learn of her providential, Fall-time romance, you'll understand how it was an absolute blessing in so many ways.

Darlene and Lori, leaf peepin'

Chapter 22

What If Your Husband Is Far from Normal? [Ready and Willing]

Her initial attraction to Herb was immediate, despite the fact that she declined his first two invitations to get together – the first, to enjoy roasted marshmallows and Christian fellowship at the campfire devotional on Friday night, and the other, to take a walk through Two Lights State Park on Saturday. I think Lori refused the first invitation because of … we'll call her Molly, for privacy's sake. Molly had her eye on Herb and tended to be wherever he went. Lori didn't want to be a third wheel.

Two Lights Park was out of the question, because L.L. Bean overshadowed it (and you *know* that's hard to do… to overshadow two lights….).

Why were we even at that Singles' Retreat weekend, anyway? Wasn't it Lori, who had vowed (almost) never to attend one of those "things" for singles again? (Yes. It was.)

Suddenly, one day, though, she said, "Let's go. I'll drive!" Molly – one of the single people in our congregation – rode with us, and off we went.

You want to know why Herb was there?

Because he agreed to help his congregation with a ministry. Each year, many from the independent congregations who are local to New England come together at a campground for uplifting and relaxing fellowship. Believers who share certain commonalities get to enjoy a bit of fun together and meet like-minded individuals. Providentially, a lot of lifelong friendships have had their beginnings at events like these. There are Men's retreats, Ladies' retreats, Singles' retreats, and Couples' retreats, to list a few.

It turns out, the church in Manchester, NH was the sponsoring congregation for that year's Singles' Retreat in Maine and accordingly, had the responsibility of supplying enough food for four days. Someone in charge of the food aspect had asked Herb (who was a member of that congregation) if he would help, and he said *yes*.

There are some unexpected intricacies to this story – like the fact that Herb was offered, also at that time, a break from his too-long plight of underemployment! An opportunity for a job had finally opened up for him to earn some income. True, he was only guaranteed the weekend, yet opportunities like this were few and far between in Herb's related world of work that year. Even so, it was the same weekend as the retreat, and that longed-for opportunity now competed with Herb's time commitment. What to do?

Trustworthy Herb chose to help his church family "carry their load" that weekend (just a quick witticism – *wink*).[251] He helped pack the food into his SUV and then delivered it to the campground where Lori's curious and unexpected whim would soon deliver her, Molly, and yours truly.

Herb was newly a single man, having been married for 17 years, with the last ten or so being absolutely miserable. His wife had rejected him for obeying the gospel of Christ. His accepting Jesus as his Lord and Savior, repenting of his sins, and putting on Christ in baptism somehow revolted her.[252] Having lost her respect, Herb's efforts to restore their marriage were self-defeating.

They had two little boys, and especially for their sakes, Herb tried hard to keep the family intact. God blessed him during those difficult years, with the opportunity to spend much valuable time with his sons as their Scout leader, teaching them many nature-centered survival skills and a positive work ethic. While Herb recognized those priceless blessings, he began to understand that his marriage could not survive the deep schism between his faith in God and his wife's sharp disapproval of it.

The brokenness of his family relationships seemed unbearable. His wife spoke to Herb derisively and actively influenced the children away from their father's example, which broke his heart. Several extremely unfair events occurred before Herb, in due course, considered that he couldn't continue like this. Something had to change.

After countless pleas to his church family to pray for him in what had become an insufferable situation, receiving prayerful encouragement from the congregation, yet still finding no relief at home, Herb decided his Christian life caused more grief than he could endure. His wife would eventually sue him for divorce, but two years before that happened, Herb decided he should leave the church. He felt completely alone and neglected by God.

Of course, Herb was never completely alone, as we can see in retrospect, and he wasn't neglected by God. He had a brother-in-Christ in his local church family, who persuaded him not to turn his back on God. "Herb, I know it's hard. But don't leave God. God will never leave *you*."

I'm thinking of two Bible passages right now.

> *No temptation has overtaken you except what is common to mankind. And God is faithful; he will not let you be tempted beyond what you can bear. But when you are tempted, he will also provide a way out so that you can endure it.*[253]
>
> *Who shall separate us from the love of Christ? Shall trouble or distress or persecution or famine or nakedness or danger or sword? As it is written:*
>
> *"For Your sake we face death all day long; we are considered as sheep to be slaughtered."*
>
> *No, in all these things we are more than conquerors through Him who loved us. For I am convinced that neither death nor life, neither angels nor principalities, neither the present nor the future, nor any powers, neither height nor depth, nor anything else in all creation, will be able to separate us from the love of God that is in Christ Jesus our Lord.*[254]

Did you just gasp? If so, you're not alone. Some of the things revealed to us through the Word are head-spinning. Read those scriptures again, and tell me if you can, what could possibly outshine **that** kind of assurance?

I never stopped to think of this before, but I see, now, intriguing *timing* going on in this phase of their yet-to-be-connected storylines: three quarters of the way through Herb's own personal nightmare was when Lori first started having sporadic symptoms of what her doctor would identify as *Probable MS* (excruciating, tear-rendering pain in an arm, short-lived numbness in various places, temporary weakness in her hand...).

"Probable MS." Plus, she was almost 1200 miles away from home, at college in West Texas (beautiful, but tumbleweed region, not colorful-leaves territory), pining for the Fall season and missing **terribly** its vibrant foliage. That was just a parallel I saw – do with it what you will.

So, …seventeen years of marriage. Most of it felt to Herb like fruitless hard labor. But he took the advice of his Christian brother and clung to the hope he had in Christ Jesus.

"If any of you wants to be my follower, you must give up your own way, take up your cross, and follow me. If you try to hang on to your life, you will lose it. But if you give up your life for my sake and for the sake of the Good News, you will save it."[255]

What!

Jesus never asked of His followers what He was not willing to do, Himself, right? It's true, His instructions – so unconventional – can seem too hard to our dubious minds, yet they're viable, having stood the tests of time and universality…. Countless Christians can testify to this truth.

Few would deny that sometimes traumatic circumstances get even more harrowing before they get better. Herb's did. His wife essentially ended that marriage contract by having him physically removed from his own home – despite having no legally defensible reason – with his young sons as witnesses. By the time his divorce was finalized in the early months of 1994, his life had gotten even more convoluted. Due to some industry-related reasons, his employer was not, at least for the foreseeable future, a source of steady income for him.

Circling back to the singles' retreat weekend I began to tell you about… a work opportunity had just opened up for Herb, remember? Only, he agreed to use his vehicle to transport all that food for the sponsoring church, instead. So, long story, short – Herb and Lori showed up at a Christian singles' retreat at the beginning of Lori's favorite season, just seven or eight months after Herb became "a free man." Coincidence? I think not. And you?

Their romance was truly a whirlwind, with Lori hopping into her Chevy Blazer every possible chance she got, to drive the three hours to Nashua, so she could spend time with this guy she started referring to as "My Herb" after only a few weeks of knowing him. They made plans together. The Fall Singles' Weekend in Manchester later in the month, and the Singles' Day at our home congregation in Waterbury on October 8th.

I have it, from a reliable source, that their first kiss was the day after the Singles' Day in Waterbury, and that they exchanged declarations of love a short eight days later. Just a month after *that*, in November, Herb proposed to her spontaneously – even without the stunning ring he had purchased immediately following those verbal expressions the month before. No sweat, though! That ring was easily accessible, and after all, four weeks was long enough for it to be stowed in a safety deposit box…..

An immediate "yes" on the 18th and an unexpected ring on her finger the 19th sealed the deal. The extraordinary, lifelong marathon was underway!

You might laugh when you hear this part. It's a little peculiar. Lori and Herb told "everyone" (family and some friends) about their plans to get married. I think originally they were setting plans for early the next year, but getting all the invitees' schedules to match up was looking far from workable, so they decided instead to elope in late December, taking me as their witness. (To put things into perspective for you, this was a few weeks after my return from Haiti.)

Anyway, this brand-new couple invited the members of Lori's family to come along if they'd like. With no going back, there we all were... an eloping bride and groom and their supportive entourage, having made the three-hour trek to New Hampshire to see them exchange vows.

Yes, it *was* an elopement, but a *social* one – accommodated by loved ones, and with enough of the essential elements of a customary wedding that Lori is still refreshed by the memories. We all dressed up, and Lori wore white and carried a bouquet. Their vows of total commitment were spoken before God, family, friends, and a minister.

Moreover, not only was a videographer present, but there were *two* – a detail that only enhanced Lori's already confident sense of God's endorsement...especially considering that at that time, hardly anyone knew much about the more fancy cameras out on the market. Thankfully, Lori's dad and I each had a small video camera and took it to the wedding! Lori's cousin Michael operated mine since I was in the wedding party. {Teehee}

The newlyweds followed up their brief ceremony with a sitting for professional pictures, and later they enjoyed their wedding cake together, which they had delivered to their room in Nashua.

It's now been almost three decades – enough time for two people to know where they stand with each other. Are they sorely disillusioned about lost aspirations? Do they gratefully embrace their providential future? Or, are they somewhere in between?

I can answer that for you. Lori and Herb live 35 minutes down the road from me, we talk on the phone almost daily, and *su Dios es mi Dios*. In other words, I've got the low-down.

Herb loves Lori, and Lori loves Herb. They understand love to be an active verb (like God defines it), not a malleable concept (like we tend to theorize into oblivion). For them, the axiom has been precisely accurate: *"Friendship multiplies joy and divides grief."*

Each of them appreciates their relationship as a gift from God because they believe what the Bible reveals about The Almighty: *Every good gift and every perfect gift is from above, coming down from the Father of lights, with whom there is no variation or shadow due to change.*[256]

Speaking of gifts from the Father... Herb and his sons, Justin and Matt, have been given the precious gift of more time to be involved in each other's lives. Teenagers when they met Lori, they got along well with her right from the starting gate – a blessing that can't be overstated. What amazing ways God has used to restore Herb's ability to delight first-hand in his children's well-being!

The LORD has increased his fervor for life in other significant ways, as well. At the tippy top of that list, of course, is when Lori gave birth to Grace! This lovely go-getter is just finishing up her first four years at university, and if the Lord wills, Grace will soon be entering her graduate studies. Can you hear their proud hearts beating? Or catch a glimpse of how thankful Lori and Herb are for having this beautiful daughter in their lives?

So…

What if your spouse is not normal? Be thankful!!

Love for every season

Matt, Grace, and Justin

(**Important note to the reader**: My daughter is just as wonderful. Just sayin.)

Our wonderful daughters, Beck and Grace, with 1½ years between them

Don't Be Shy, Share Some More! [Part 1]

Chapter 23

There's Strength in Joy!

Have you noticed that our minds do interesting things when introduced to strange ideas? If so, you'll appreciate why I thought what I did, when a few years ago, I saw a young man tenaciously making his way along the edge of the road,. The first thought I had was that his stride reminded me of a zombie. You know, from one of the countless productions based on phantastic events (e.g. From Hollywood's *apocalypse* genre) …

And secondly, I saw that he was moving a lot like I did about three months after my brain surgery. Back at that time, I compared my uneven, sometimes lurching stagger to that of "a drunken sailor," but in today's environment, *zombie* gets the point across.

There were some conspicuous differences, though, between this young man's gait and my own…. My leg didn't drag behind me. Rather, it flew way up, ahead of me. As soon as I would try to lift it to take a step forward, it was like my whole left leg had a mind of its own and would take off, as if it wanted to fly. I found my struggle to walk dreadful and very frustrating, Strangely enough, at the same time, I knew deep down that I didn't have it all that bad.

My gait most definitely got better with time and effort. The recuperation from paralysis requires nerves to regenerate, muscles to strengthen, and motor skills to be redeveloped. I thank God for His mercy in causing (most of) the synapses, motor neurons, sensory perceptions, and large muscle groups assigned to me to heal. (Plus whatever else might be part of that inventory....)

Consider for a moment, if you will, how you would feel in a public place...a movie theater...walking like a zombie with an animated leg – although the zombie *culture* was not yet "alive" (LOL). Can you feel the gaze of onlookers as you try to ignore the bright blue feeding tube taped to your paralyzed cheek so it wouldn't dangle and swing from your nose?

That was me. Lori remembers. She's the one who almost literally dragged me out of the ~~nursing home~~ "rehab facility," so I could do "ordinary" things and practice my walking.

Was the experience enjoyable? No! Was it joy-able? Absolutely. My almighty Father and one of my Christian sisters were with me.

Moreover, I was being enabled to apply some too long abandoned skills (like walking) and to rehearse some relearned competencies (like holding a paper ticket without crushing it to smithereens). I can honestly tell you, I would not trade that experience.

Doesn't James say, "*Consider it pure joy, my brothers and sisters, whenever you face trials of many kinds*"?[257] Now why would anybody speak such nonsense!? That would be the automatic first reaction, I bet, upon hearing that advice. At least, for those who don't know Christ *and the* **power of His rising**.

In the natural realm, finding joy while experiencing pain or heartache sure does appear to be an absurd idea. Well, to be fair, those are opposite ends of the stick. I'm still going to say it, though – it's a fact. If we keep in step with our good Shepherd Jesus (who claimed what only an almighty God could: *"Before Abraham came into existence, I AM"*),[258] we walk full of joy, even in the midst of hardship. He strengthens our faith wherever we go.

So, that's why James explains how we can consider it joy when we face all kinds of adversities: *because you know that* **the testing of your faith produces perseverance.** *Let perseverance finish its work* **so that you may be mature and complete, not lacking anything**.[259]

Not lacking *ANY* thing?! Right. Nothing at all.[260] We can dare to sing with David: *we "shall not want."*[261]

Marsha doesn't have a soulmate and feels like she'll die without a companion to share her life with! Gary just can't live without the latest and greatest gadget because he believes he needs others' approval to live a worthwhile life. Kevin's mother has cancer – how can he go on if she doesn't survive? Governments threaten millions of people in terrible ways, every day.

Young children wake up to an empty stomach, after a restless night of hunger. *Where is the joy* to fit those situations!?

Clearly, there can be no joy in evil.

What about Diana's brother, shot dead by a random shooter? John's nephew, kidnapped and trafficked? We are aware of horrific evils taking place in people's lives. We see, hear of, or feel the complex effects of heartbreak and calamity. Sometimes we share their misery, but more often, we can only mourn on their behalf.

Jesus did that. Mourn with them that mourn. **He still does**. The difference, I suppose, is that two thousand years ago, any people around Jesus Christ could *physically* witness his love and support since He was wearing his human flesh around and walking among them.[262] Things are different now, in the sense that *these* days, since Jesus is in Heaven, at His Father's right hand,[263] His love and support are invisible to the natural eye and thus, largely rejected as ridiculousness. And if not considered absurd, then skillfully ignored.

We know the story of His *own* suffering. But do we?

Ridiculed relentlessly, threatened with harm, lied to, disbelieved, betrayed by friends, falsely accused, taken captive, mistreated by people in authority, whipped and beaten gruesomely, feeling the excruciating thrusts of thorns into his scalp, seeing His mom's mental anguish as she watched Him, helpless, hang on a coarse, roughly hewn cross.

It was Jesus' mother who was helpless there, not Jesus. His hands and feet were stabbed with nails, literally affixing His body to the positioned posts, but those nails – mere pieces of iron – were not what held Him there. It was His love. At any time, He could have ordered angelic "BOOTS ON THE **GROUND**!" He had the power and authority to snap that cross in two – no! to obliterate it into nothingness. There wasn't a soldier, ever in existence, anywhere, who could match His strength. Not a governing authority with an irrefutable right to sentence Him. But He *loved* us all.

So He stayed.

How is it that Jesus was able to forgive His very real, very dangerous, very hate-filled enemies?[264] And why had He been able to say, "Your will be done, Father, not mine," when He was so keenly aware of what atrocities would be set into motion before the evening was over?[265] We catch a glimpse of Jesus' success when we read *"Because of the **joy awaiting** him, he **endured the cross, disregarding its shame.**"*[266]

As the Son of God, He understood well the plan for our salvation. As the Son of Man, He willingly submitted to the Father's decrees to get the job done. *He set His hope fully on the joy that was waiting for Him,* and He was able to endure all that.

Can *we* endure our heartaches and injustices? Can we submit to God, and find hope in the joy of fellowship and eternal life with our Savior, who is our Peace? God's written Word says we can.

> *"Therefore, since we also have such a great cloud of witnesses surrounding us, <u>let's rid ourselves of every obstacle and the sin which so easily entangles us,</u> and <u>let's run with endurance the race that is set before us,</u> **looking only at Jesus**, the originator and perfecter of the faith, who for the joy set before Him endured the cross, despising the shame, and has sat down at the right hand of the throne of God.*
>
> *"For consider Him who has endured such hostility by sinners against Himself, **so that you will not grow weary and lose heart.**"*[267]

We, also, have joy awaiting us – once we submit to God! No matter what happens in our lives, if we belong to Christ Jesus, we have that knowledge that He has a place reserved for us when our work here is done. Again, straight from God's Word:

> *Think back on those early days when you first learned about Christ. Remember how you remained faithful even*

> *though it meant terrible suffering. Sometimes you were exposed to public ridicule and were beaten, and sometimes you helped others who were suffering the same things. You suffered along with those who were thrown into jail, and when all you owned was taken from you, you accepted it with joy.* **You knew there were better things waiting for you that will last forever.**
>
> *So do not throw away this confident trust in the Lord. Remember the great reward it brings you! Patient endurance is what you need now, so that you will continue to do God's will.* **Then you will receive all that he has promised.**
>
> *"For in just a little while,* **the Coming One will come** *and not delay."*[268]

I might not have been thinking, while sporting my neon-blue nasogastric tube and carefully balancing myself at the movie ticket counter, "Joy awaits me – I've got this!" But I *was* trusting God, relying on His decisions to bring me through. I know that faith is what set my mind at rest during every stage of my brain tumor ordeal. Rather than *I got this*, it's gotta be, *I can do anything I need to do* **with God's help.**[269]

Chapter 24

New Mercies

Unfortunately, my attitude can get pretty gnarly at times, and I'm not proud of those times at all. In fact, I receive *countless* blessings from God's hand, and I regret that my heart can be flat-out unappreciative. Can you relate? Nevertheless, I've learned that whenever I realize a wrong direction my heart has taken, I can repent, right there, on the spot. And then my joy returns. (Because I know He is faithful and just and will forgive me my sins and cleanse me from all unrighteousness.)[270]

Nice arrangement, isn't it! He's so merciful.

Well, like Paul, who gave a list of his sufferings, to show God's faithfulness,[271] I'd like to share some of the tough spots I myself have endured, to show you God's faithfulness in my own situation…and to remind you that we are lovingly told to <u>cast all our anxiety on Him because He cares for us</u>.[272]

So here are a few random events, which (depending on one's point of view) could be seen as reasons for despair or, as opportunities for faith and joy in the midst of uncertainty. Take it from me, every one of them is a reason for me to *praise God, from whom all blessings flow* (as the song goes).[273] They're here in no particular order. In fact, they are, for the most part, WAAAY out of chronological order. I just jotted them down as their memories occurred to me…

> On the Wednesday afternoon that found me at the hospital for an emergency CT scan, for example, a very compassionate Dr. Robinson called my parents and gently broke the news to them about the brain tumor; then he gave me the phone to finish the conversation.... None of us knew the right words to say, but because of our shared faith in our Creator's sovereign power over our lives, my parents and I avoided the hysterical route.
> My parents and sister (with young children in tow) drove up from Alabama. It was a very long drive, and there was a goodly assortment of work schedules, childcare concerns, and family responsibilities to consider, but "it worked out" so they could all travel together for the surgery. I remember seeing them around me immediately pre-op, and it refreshed my spirit when I woke up afterwards to see their faces again – all in a row near the foot of my bed! I wonder how often we realize what a pure blessing it is, simply to know that people we love are present with us. Do we have to be in the hospital, or somehow otherwise incapacitated, to glean strength and courage from their being present with us? Of course not, most of us would probably say their love matters *all* the time. Their physical presence sure does make it sweeter, though, doesn't it! **Especially** when we are down and out.
> Here's a random memory. Mama slept next to my hospital bed, in a Geri-chair. I have no idea whether that was only one night or every night she was in New England, and it doesn't matter because I *knew* she was there when I needed her, and *now* – over 30 years later – I know she was there when I needed her. The End. :)

➢ I have a recurring flashback from that time (when Mama was spending the night in a chair next to me). I don't know how long after the "major" operation (craniectomy) this was, but using my one working hand and arm, I recall banging angrily against the metal bed rail with my "saliva sucker" (a tool like the dentist uses to clear your mouth of unwanted liquid). *WHY was she ignoring me??* My poor, probably exhausted, Mama was trying to get some sleep, and I, in a me-first-and-NOW moment, went ballistic with that hard plastic straw on the only clang-able item nearby. I remember immediately feeling ashamed when I saw her jump awake, ready to serve. I don't believe I let my remorse show, though, since I also remember feeling entitled for some reason…. In my defense, all I wanted was…well, I can't even remember now. (Some defense, hunh?) To tell the truth, I think it was simply her attention I wanted. *I was awake now, and why wasn't **she**?!* Momentary as it was, I gave into a rude and inconsiderate attitude, and it came out in my sucker swing! That couldn't have been a pleasant experience for Mama. The blessing here? She still loved me. And she stayed by my side (literally) when I needed her most.

➢ A favorite memory about Mama during this period, was the time she came up to me, leaned over the bedrail, and laughed to me, privately, in her low, soothing voice, "I got you something silly." She had purchased a fun item from the hospital gift shop, possibly when they moved me from ICU to the 2nd floor. If you aren't familiar with my mother's natural enthusiasm for creative play, her choice of gifts might give you pause. But you can't know the instant reassurance she handed me with that quilt batting-stuffed person with the Velcro on his "clasped" hands and the loop sewed on the back of his shirt! Mama's "something silly" was a repurposing of what would typically be an adorable 24" (or so) wall-hanging for a young child's room…now it was the finishing touch for her 25-year-old child's hospital bedside!

➤ Shortly before I transferred from the hospital to a place for rehab, Dr. Ballon had somewhat of a "prepare-the-patient" conversation with me, to ensure that I understood the road ahead would be long, and that my recovery possibly might not be what I would hope. I told Dr. Ballon that I believed God made my body, to begin with, and so He certainly knew how to fix it. He said, "Ah! You have a good mechanic, then." That was no small encouragement, just let me say. Dr. Ballon spoke some life into me right then, and I've never forgotten those words.

➤ Necessary though it was, to save my life, the surgery to remove the tumor left me with significant paralysis – including paralysis of my left vocal cord. It was stuck open, and this meant that I was at a high risk for aspiration and had to be fed by way of a tube passed through my nose. After what seemed like an eternity, I was scheduled for a *barium swallow* (a procedure where a doctor could see a video of my swallowing – a bite of glowing food and a drink of fluorescent liquid – to determine whether my swallowing mechanics were doing their job)! I passed the *second* test, not the first, and though the verdict was *yes, I could eat by mouth now*, I wasn't yet "out of the woods." Food, and especially liquid, could enter my airway when I swallowed, causing me to cough and sputter. The nurses' biggest fear was that I could easily choke. (I still have coughing episodes today if that weakened epiglottis of mine lets stuff into my windpipe.) Well, Lori took this swallow-test success as the go-ahead for a trip to *The Ice Cream Churn*. I felt some trepidation about being away from my nurses, but wow, was that ice cream good!

➢ Up to this point – I'd say roughly 6 or 7 weeks (which felt like 6 or 7 lifetimes) – I had received all my nourishment via that nasogastric tube, and at times, intravenously. The reality that I could enjoy eating food by mouth again was HUGE!!! That ice cream I told you about was phenomenal! At the same time, though, I felt a HUGE disappointment. No matter how hard I tried, I could not fit the *half* Maraschino cherry on my spoon into my mouth – another setback. This time it was due to the paralysis in my face. I remember crying and realizing I didn't know what the future held. Regardless of the recent euphoria earlier on, that ended up feeling like a bad day.

➢ I remember that the nurses back in the ICU used to take me out of bed "for a few minutes" so my sheets could be changed. Did you know "a few" minutes can sometimes mean 20, 30, or even 45? Looking back, I view this little timing kerfuffle as a remedial part of God's strategic treatment plan for me. It was an unbelievably uncomfortable core workout. Frankly, if I had been consulted first, I'm not sure I would have chosen this regimen for myself. However, it turned out to be a crucial part of my physical therapy, to strengthen and retrain my torso and neck muscles so I'd be able to sit up straight, hold up my head, and eventually stand on my own. I remember calling the nurses often – so often that those rascals (who were truly excellent) started telling me they would be back shortly, and that if I needed them, I should use the call bell, but then, after about 5 *wearisome* minutes (if I made it that long), I'd be grasping for that call bell, and it would be ju-u-u-ust out of my reach. {What! Where was everyone?? When would those sheet-changing people arrive???}

> I was never really left unattended, of course, and I sensed it. Even though I couldn't turn to see them, it was easy to assume that someone was checking in on me. I felt... well, if you've ever felt boiling mad and grateful at the same time, *you* know. Doesn't make sense, right? At least, not at surface level. Anyway, struggling to sit there, and needing a distraction, I would feel *so* happy to have company, like the cleaning woman who would empty the trash can and clean the sink. And it might be *impossible* to describe the excitement I would feel when someone would finally come in to change those neolithic sheets. That was my clue I could get back in bed. Like I said, it sure made me mad at times, but does it make me mad today, *as I **sit** here* and think about it? No, it does not. :)

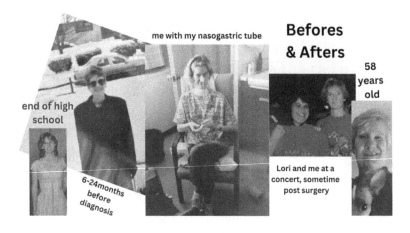

Befores & Afters

me with my nasogastric tube

end of high school

6-24 months before diagnosis

58 years old

Lori and me at a concert, sometime post surgery

Chapter 25

Thorns in the Flesh Are Battle Scars

Our afflictions can be painful! The apostle Paul likened one of his to a "thorn in the flesh." Great analogy, isn't it! And you know what? Where there are thorns, there are oftentimes roses…. Let's look for the roses. But never stop there. Keep looking until you find the Creator!

- ➢ A wonderful volunteer named Sue shaved my legs one time and then took me outside for some sunshine and fresh air in a Geri-chair (which is more doable than a wheelchair when you can't control your sitting & balance muscles). Kindness is listed in *Galatians* 5 as a fruit of the Spirit, and "the great outdoors" really is **good** to behold! I'd say I was blessed by my Creator through Sue that day.
- ➢ Once I was able to sit up without falling over into a slump, I could do some more extensive physical and occupational therapies. Steve was a fantastic therapist. Whenever he came into the room, I knew in advance that whatever we did during the session would be purposeful to my recovery. Even though his increasingly

complex exercises were challenging and difficult, I never remember wishing he'd "*leave* now, already." Au contraire! Here was the inviter who encouraged my soul with the "promise" to take me line dancing when I was ready. He wouldn't have gone *anywhere* "now already" if THIS patient could have arranged his schedule. Steve was the one who clapped rhythmically on my back once or twice, to help my collapsed lung regain its *je-ne-sais- quoi*…. He's the guy who noticed, and celebrated – even before I did – when I automatically and successfully dived down with that recovering, paralysis-afflicted hand, <u>catching</u> the slick bar of soap I had been laboriously turning around and around in it! Steve was the vivacious cheerleader, health specialist, and coach – prudently placed by the Almighty at the forefront of my post-tumor refurbishment. I know I thanked him countless times, but I can't recall how exactly…quite probably with the ASL sign, as I couldn't speak.

➤ I found out what it's like not to have a voice for a whole year (*plus*). The paralysis of one of my vocal cords made it impossible for me to produce normal sounds in order to speak. There was a procedure that could be done, to improve my prospects of using (at least a rendition of) my voice, but we first had to wait long enough for any affiliated nerves to regenerate before attempting to surgically manipulate my voice box. I had to wait one full year for this procedure, called *thyroplasty*. As a memory refresher – my brain surgery was in April 1991, meaning I wouldn't be able to have my voice back until at least April of '92. Lonnnng wait! Finally, May 1992 came around, and I was booked for my highly anticipated solution. Lori and I went to celebrate at the hometown diner, *Bill and Sam's*, on the way to the hospital, *so* excited that the long-awaited day had finally arrived! One tiny swallow of coffee later, it occurred suddenly to me! My whole vocal implant surgery would now have to be rescheduled! It was as abrupt a jolt of disbelief for Lori as it was for me. Our hearts sank... why didn't we double-think our plans, and how in the world could we have forgotten the no drink rule?? Fast-forward...our foolish mistakes didn't foul up The Almighty's plans for me.[274] I received a seriously strong dose of patience, which boosted my immunity to discouragement.[275] PLUS, I still have a future and a hope![276]

➢ The neurological challenges in the beginning days of my post-brain-surgery experience were indefinably difficult! Not only did I now have physical disabilities I had never even imagined could exist, but no one could know whether these new, harsh realities would be part of my life forever (well... "forever" in the *temporal* sense). It wasn't fun.

➢ There was the time, for example, after I was back home in our shared condo rent in Waterbury, when Lori drove me to my first appointment for outpatient physical therapy. The building was located, unnervingly, just down the *busy* main street from where I worked in Bristol as a preschool teacher. I think I was able to get myself out of the car, but from there, Lori had to come to my side and ever so carefully try to stay upright herself, as she guided me awkwardly around, to the front door. Did you notice, she guided me *around* to the door? Why not just straight to the door, you wonder? Were we parked behind, or on a different side, of the building? No, Lori had found a prime spot, and her car was resting only about 40 feet (my best guess, in retrospect) from the entrance. But my left leg absolutely refused to cooperate. It went its own way! I felt *so* frustrated trying to walk a straight line while in reality meandering around the parking lot. I wanted to cry and scream but only one tear duct would participate in crying, and I had no voice to scream with. As if to pour salt into my already raw heart-wound, when I looked at Lori for comfort and empowerment, all I saw was her shocked look of disbelief and fear. If somebody had shot me in that moment, I don't think it would have added much if any more agony.

NOW – maybe because I've "read the later chapters," so to speak, and can now visualize things through a comedic lens – I look back on some of these moments and find them quite funny. In fact, Lori and I have had a good number of belly laughs over the years about them! And I would even go so far as to guess that, by God's grace, we can actually laugh about the *majority* of our hardships. Maybe not always right away, but often, we are afforded the opportunity down the road. *Time heals a broken heart.*

Sorry – the em*PHA*sis there was on the wrong sy*LLA*ble! **God uses time** to heal broken hearts. Time, after all, is His creation.[277]

Here's another thing I believe to be true: absolutely no one can fathom the incredible grace of God! In addition to His grace in saving us from our sin and accepting us back to Himself through Jesus, God adds grace upon grace to the people who take Him at His word and obey what He has said. True, He gives sunshine and rain to everyone, regardless of their religiosity.[278] But there's more to it than that. His children call on Him for help, and He gives it – whether that be physical, mental, financial, emotional, relationship-based, or what. It's His choice, though, remember, how He chooses to help. I might think it's in my best interest for Him to do *a* to solve my problem, while He can see around the corner (figuratively speaking) and decides to do *b*. My ability to "rejoice in the Lord always"[279] depends on how well I've learned to say, *let it be, Lord – whatever You know to be best.*[280]

Well, life goes on, and I don't know whether – when we go to meet God face to face – we will have a memory of the earthly turbulence that He used in order to grow us, or not. But either way life will be grand because the Bible tells me there's going to be a day when we won't even consider our worst troubles as significant...not when we've entered God's place of joy, where sorrow is not allowed![281]

If that's the case, it makes good sense to appreciate what we can from our problems while we're here dealing with them. We can choose to use them – to build our strength, hone our patience, strengthen our resolve.

Of course, problems are tools in the hands of our enemy (the devil), as well – to drag us down and ruin our hope in the Almighty.[282] They're a means by which our adversary can try a power grab! **But. God.**[283]

But God can take those exact same difficulties and use them as instruments to grow us up in Him. Almighty God turns it all around. HaHA! Somewhere along the way, our hurts go from being both egregious weapons and crippling wounds to – first, soil **enrichers**. Then, mere battle scars!!

*Don't Be Shy,
Share Some More!
[Part 2]*

Chapter 26

God's Perfect (and Perfecting) Panoply

The Almighty gave us protective armor, too, didn't He! Would you go out to battle without putting on your armor first? Of course not. Neither would I! So, we've got to put it ALL on – isn't that what Paul tells us to do?[284]

That *belt of truth,* for example…is there any way, without it, that we could keep ourselves from being conformed to this world,[285] or – even better – to *renew* our minds to think God's way? Jesus says God's word is truth.[286]

Let's wrap truth around us, so it can provide all the functional benefits of a belt! Belts serve a lot more purposes than we generally think about, you know…especially the fascinating purposes of belts worn in Jesus' day…read up on it when you get a chance! You won't be disappointed, and you might garnish your understanding of the apostle Paul's very first directive, concerning the armor of God.

Essentially, the Almighty knows exactly what we need (collectively, and as individuals), and He offers everything we need, in every place, at all times. *Truth*…the power of faith in His Son's death, burial, and resurrection, completely surrounding us….[287]

Righteousness...an impervious breastplate to cover our hearts and safeguard the promises we've stored there. Righteousness is from God Himself, and so are the incentives for us to pursue it! God's "great and precious promises" provoke our hearts to get, and stay, right with Him.... *And* allow our encumbered selves to actually participate in His own, divine nature![288]

Our helmet of *salvation* keeps our minds guarded from the enemy's attacks of doubt and unworthiness.[289] Our feet can be dressed and *ready to take this wonderful message* to others. There we have it – we're covered head to foot!

Hold up that God-given shield – the power of our *faith* to deflect Satan's weapons! And, most powerful of all, as we make our way through each battle, may we learn how to rightly handle[290] *God's Word*, which is very much alive (and *active*).[291] With this extremely sharp sword, we test the spirits we encounter, to see whether they're from God.[292]

We're promised that as we do the things which cause us to grow in the knowledge of God and of Jesus our Lord, God will give us more and more grace and peace.[293] We'll give more thought to the good, not the bad.[294] We learn continuously, to imitate God in *all* we do![295]

To love the Almighty God with all our hearts...with all our minds...with all of our strength – with our entire being! And our neighbors? We learn to love them with the same care with which we love ourselves.[296]

Does it sound like a lot? Too much? I guess it sure can sound that way (all laid out like that), but these practices are completely doable because God is with us. *Truthfully*. Remember what the Spirit says? With God, all things are possible,[297] and Christ Himself gives us the strength.[298]

Besides, this isn't a checklist, it's simply a description of a great way of life, which occurs inherently, as we live to please God, and are growing spiritually mature with Christ Jesus in charge.[299]

"In view of all this, make every effort to respond to God's promises. Supplement your faith with a generous provision of moral excellence, and moral excellence with knowledge, and knowledge with self-control, and self-control with patient endurance, and patient endurance with godliness, and godliness with brotherly affection, and brotherly affection with love for everyone. The more you grow like this, the more productive and useful you will be in your knowledge of our Lord Jesus Christ." ~2 Peter 1:5-8, NLT

Chapter 27

God Is Sooo Good

The flashback memories of this season of my life are countless, but here are a few bullet points for you. There aren't a lot of details included – ***down with edits! down with edits!*** – which might leave you scratching your head about some of them. Feel free to ignore those, as you'll still recognize the essence of the share! (I won't cry, as long as I don't find out.)

- ❖ Visitors; cards; notes; flowers (couldn't keep in ICU room); classical music CDs from Lori's mom Lois who, with her husband Ken, had 2-3 years earlier graciously taken me – a newly graduated arrival with a case of Wanderlust – into their home so this southwesterner could get established in the far-flung land of New England; Marty Stewart music (something about a train)
- ❖ Couldn't swallow; Craved Banana pudding and my friends using that as hope and motivation
- ❖ Before diagnosis/physical changes agreed to a date with a guy on first and only bar scene ***Thankful*** that "fun" upcoming date (his Boston and my Texan accents) not happening, due to my hospitalization and newly acquired deficiencies:
  - ➢ Inability to speak
  - ➢ Decreased sensation

- Loss of balance
- Mild memory loss
- Vision changes
- Walking problems
- Muscle weakness

❖ Dr. R**** had plans to place a gastric tube into my stomach, to replace the naso-gastric feeding tube that had been in my nose for more than 5 weeks. The NG tube usually temporary (less than 6 weeks) because can shift and puncture lung; sometimes replaced by a more permanent G tube in stomach; Lori advised me against. <u>THANKFUL</u>

❖ Deafness in one ear

❖ Eye could not fully close, the cornea had to be protected from drying out (prescription eye drops or gel), tape shut at night, eye patch to keep safe from wind and cold; sun glasses; corneal tear right over pupil; decreased sensation; feels irritated and dry when really inflamed; tear gland not work, not drain well (ongoing problem)
  - One doctor wanted to sew shut at outside corner
  - One doctor wanted to sew in a piece of gold to weigh lid down at night
  - My having ability and autonomy to refuse those non-solutions – ***thankful***

❖ Very shortly after going back to work, extreme facial pain on left side, with excessive tearing in left eye and disproportionate activity of left salivary gland inside my mouth to point of pain

❖ Perceptual line down center of body from neck down; presenting modified sensory patterns: temperature, pressure, pain

- ❖ Left side facial paralysis and weakness/restricted mobility/paralysis on left side,: muscle memory wasn't there, and forgot how (the mechanics) to walk, retrained hand, arm, leg, foot, torso, neck
- ❖ On 2nd floor hospital, Liz brought me notebooks and pens so I could communicate with my visitors!
- ❖ Speech therapist's one and only visit to condo, and her comment about singing that still encourages me
- ❖ Vocal chord paralysis of left true vocal chord
  - ➢ No voice (roommate with voicebox removed, writing notes)
  - ➢ Year without a voice, whisper or used all energy to speak with voice that sounded like Darth Vader
    - Close college friend called me and I had to "yell" (to project voice to audible level), sounded monstrous, Peter in shock, have reconnected over email and via FB since
    - Went back to work as preschool teacher immediately after leaving the rehab (5 weeks after surgery)
    - My preschoolers so in tune with me, and God with us, wonderful days anyway
  - • Walking like a drunken sailor
  - • My neck red from very swollen larynx – looked like a man's Adam's apple
- ❖ Experienced the truth of the principle of Eph 4:29 in action
  - ➢ Pink color of my irritated eyelid, Liz asked me if I used eye shadow on it, I said no, as though that weren't preposterous, just curious as to why she asked, she said it was a pretty color; asked about my

new cologne when I visited preschool and laughed heartily at my wordplay-wisecrack – these seemingly insignificant remarks, comments, observations, etc. had huge impact on my psyche; built me up
  - ➢ Kids so respectful and in tune with me, incredible! Homemade sign language mixed with some ASL we had learned together before the whole schwannoma installment to our story a literal God-send when I returned to them with no voice
- ❖ Dealing with palsy and tremoring
- ❖ New appreciation for the elderly residents in nursing facility where the day care was set up for children of medical personnel ~ an connection built on understanding
- ❖ Dr. Zorick Spektor "fine-tuned" my new voice
  - Trusted him well
  - Explained to me what to expect
  - Revised previous scar from tracheostomy while at it
  - Awake during the surgery, with drape just below my chin to shield my eyes from my throat
- ❖ Running around dividing wall, through Lori's kitchen and dining room, and back to living room – more a hop, leg extension, plod! Hop, extend, plod!
- ❖ Our wedding in 1995
  - ➢ Perfect weather, no bugs (bugs bothered my eye and a few years earlier, my still healing scar); warm temp, but with slightest breeze (which kept bugs away)
  - ➢ So many friends, family, church family helping make it ideal
- ❖ Heart surgery the next year, so can safely bear children! God's presence everywhere throughout: finding out about murmer/ASD during routine exam by primary,

a cardiologist dr. Frazier (grandfathered in); referred to one of best Dr. John DiRossi at St. Francis Hospital... off the cuff question re scar – agreed to perform new procedure thru ribs <u>THANKFUL</u>

- ➤ Intubation/ extubating chipped front tooth could feel it for yrs with tongue but now worn even (a good thing or not?.. :D)

❖ Thorns in flesh = facial paralysis & varicose veins' and some other things to deal with, secondary to corrective surgeries. Answers always in scripture

❖ Thorns in flesh = facial paralysis & varicose veins' and some other

❖ *"My grace is all you need. My power works best in weakness." So now I am glad to boast about my weaknesses, so that the power of Christ can work through me. That's why I take pleasure in my weaknesses, and in the insults, hardships, persecutions, and troubles that I suffer for Christ. For when I am weak, then I am strong.* ~2 Cor 12:9-10 NLT

❖ *I have learned how to be content with whatever I have. I know how to live on almost nothing or with everything. I have learned the secret of living in every situation, whether it is with a full stomach or empty, with plenty or little. For I can do everything through Christ, who gives me strength.* ~Phil 4:11-13 NLT

Chapter 28

An Almighty God? Get Serious!

Paraplegic, quadriplegic comatose, or dead....
Those words imagined for me what my future could hold if science weren't enough to fix my health problem. But that was okay. Why?

Because *science never claimed to be the way, the truth, and the life*. True, people have claimed that FOR science, but science is a discipline – like math and communication are disciplines. Science is *humankind's systematic **study** of the physical structure of this natural world and the various ways its components behave. It's the study of mind and behavior. Of logic and mathematics.

Scientific studies have become more and more specifically focused over the course of our human history, especially over the last century or so, to the point that we now take them for granted...as if they have always existed. We call the different categories "branches of science," or "specialties," and we've given the branches names, like *biology, geology, physics, chemistry, psychology, economics*. But specialties emerge and develop as we need or want to understand more about the natural world we inhabit.

People who involve themselves in the science of things do it through *observing* the countless facets of the universe and by conducting *experiments* to gain more insight. If an experiment is done well, its outcome will support, disprove, or confirm the knowledgeable guess that someone has made about something.

This is the process we people use in order to learn about (and sometimes manipulate) our world, and that's it. Science is not almighty. In fact, science is a creation. Conceived of and developed by humans. I like science – very *much*, too. Science was used to save my life. How could I not be a fan?

But there's so much more to life than the physical. Sooooo much more!

Yes, we can learn many things about God by observing and experimenting with the natural world, but what's *really* important, is that we learn the things about God from His very own revelations about Himself–through His written word.

While I've always been thankful for the specifics of my situation, it wouldn't be until years later that I would grasp just how remarkable my recovery has been, or how exceptional it is that the *abilities I've been allowed to keep despite my surgery* **match up perfectly with my innermost ambitions!** I'm still amazed daily.

The most amazing thing about all of it, though, is that the Bible has given me everything I've needed for healing *(inside and out)*, for personal growth, for my relationships, for happiness *and* joy, for life *(both here and beyond)*, and for hope. Constantly correcting my path, God's word reminds me of who He is, and why I love and trust Him. In it I find help understanding my own value and purpose. The Bible takes me back to my source of strength and ability and encouragement – and it's addressed equally to everyone else.

2 Tim 3:16-17 (NLT) says it like this: *"All Scripture is inspired by God and is useful to teach us what is true and to make us*

realize what is wrong in our lives. It corrects us when we are wrong and teaches us to do what is right. God uses it to prepare and equip his people to do every good work."

What a precious gift.

We can trust the written word of God – it's living and active![300] Not only can it help us recognize what is wrong in our lives so we can discern what's true and then use truth to do what's right, but it tells us who we are, where we come from, and where we are going. To the person who wants to find God… to the seeker who looks for Him *wholeheartedly*, The Almighty promises He will be found.[301]

A word of caution, though, if I may… we have to be careful when reading Scripture. God stresses to us, through the same inspired Scripture, that <u>we are not free to change His Word as we see fit.</u>

"No prophecy of Scripture is of private interpretation," says the Almighty, "no prophecy ever came by the will of man: but holy men of God spoke, being moved by the Holy Spirit."[302] As if to highlight and underscore the significance of that reality, He mandates – in no uncertain terms – that <u>we are not to add or take away from what is written in His given Word.</u> I find it interesting, too, that these commands are placed in the *beginning*, *middle*, and *end* of the collection of writings we call *The Bible*.[303]

Do you, like some, wonder why God should command such a thing, as it might seem rather intolerant for a God who is supposed to be so loving and kind? Isn't guarding His words verbatim with a threat of punishment a bit over the edge?

This question may not be yours, but it's a question I've heard many people ask, so it deserves a reply. And while I do not profess to know everything about God (I'd be the first in line to call me a liar if I were to claim such a thing),[304] I do know some Bible scriptures which, having come to us through human writers by way of the Holy Spirit's guidance, can help us figure it out correctly. (Incredibly comforting, right?)

The first thing I remind myself of, when God's words don't make sense to me, is that God is God. He's my creator – THE Creator – and while He designed and activated His perfect plan for the earth and all that's on it and comprehends every single thing from beginning to end…I, on the other hand, am a creature – HIS created being – and I did not design nor put into effect my own or anyone else's existence. That means I don't get to make the rules.

Someone might jump in with, "But you don't know that! It's your belief system. It's not fair to expect me or anyone else to live by the same rules. You do you, and I'll do me."

I'd say, you're right, that my believing the Bible to be God's Word is by faith. Though, since I believe with all my heart that there is one God, who created all things, including me and every other person, I would be sinning if I didn't do what He says I must do. (Even if you privately reject an almighty God as worthy of my allegiance, wouldn't you agree that I'd be doing wrong – going against my own moral compass – by not sharing this? Somebody might say I wouldn't be staying *true to myself*.)

The Bible declares that God loved the world with such passion, He gave the only Son begotten directly of Himself, *"that whosoever believes in him should not perish, but have eternal life."*[305]

What do you think, should I keep what I'm convinced is great (and ESSENTIAL) news to myself? Could I be trustworthy, refusing to share it while believing earnestly that every one of us has sinned and fall short of the glory of God?[306] God's Word says our hope of salvation is found in Jesus Christ alone,[307] and this same Jesus specifically told his followers to share His message

An Almighty God? Get Serious!

of hope with everyone so *everyone* could have the opportunity to be reconciled to Almighty God. Shouldn't I share that?

The only begotten Son of God said it carefully: "All authority in heaven and on earth has been given to Me. Therefore go and make disciples of all nations, baptizing them in the name of the Father, and of the Son, and of the Holy Spirit, and teaching them to obey all that I have commanded you. And surely I am with you always, even to the end of the age."[308]

So here I am…relaying His command not to add or take away from the Word of The Almighty. He gave them to us precisely for a reason and will not tolerate our altering His message.

God is serious. Are we?

Well, here we are in the last chapter of this book. This is the end of my book…but not of my story. Just as, when you've finished reading this chapter and put the book on the shelf or whatever you do with it (could you share it with someone else?), you'll pick up your own story. Right where you left off. (Except now, having read this book will be a new part of your history. Every piece fits in there to make the whole!)

The staggering thing about your own story is that it started before you remember, has developed over time until it's where it is now, and will continue on forever.

You were created **in the image of** Almighty God, the one, true God who has no beginning or end, so clearly, we are more than our physical bodies. We all know that these bodies…these "earthen vessels" …will wear out eventually and go back to the natural surroundings from which they came. Our physical bodies are unique to us, as science shows us – individualized to each person (think DNA, fingerprints, personalities, family and medical histories, etc.). It's your **spirit** that has the image of Almighty God stamped on it. So please, if you're not already, get serious! Take care of your spirit.

Proverbs 4:20-23 (NIV): *"… pay attention to what I say; turn your ear to my words. Do not let them out of your sight, keep them within your heart; for they are life to those who find them and health to one's whole body. Above all else, guard your heart, for everything you do flows from it."*

See Psalm 36:2 (NLT): Open your eyes. *Don't be like the person who says there is no God, whose "blind conceit" keeps them from seeing "how wicked they really are."*

1Peter 4:17 (NLT): *"For the time has come for judgment, and it must begin with God's household. And if judgment begins with us, what terrible fate awaits those who have never obeyed God's Good News?"*

2 Thessalonians 1:8 (NIV): *"He will punish those who do not know God and do not obey the gospel of our Lord Jesus."*

2 Peter 3:9 (NKJV): *"The Lord is not slack concerning His promise, as some count slackness, but is longsuffering toward us, not willing that any should perish but that all should come to repentance."* [*slack* means "slow," or "negligent"]

Psalm 32:6 (ESV): *"Therefore let everyone who is godly offer prayer to you at a time when you may be found; surely in the rush of great waters, they shall not reach him."*

Jeremiah 29:13 (NASB): *"And you will seek Me and find Me when you search for Me with all your heart."*

Matthew 7:7 (ESV): *"Ask, and it will be given to you; seek, and you will find; knock, and it will be opened to you."*

Psalm 119:2 (WEB): *"Blessed are those who keep his statutes, who seek him with their whole heart."*

Jeremiah 24:7 (NIV): *"I will give them a heart to know me, that I am the LORD. They will be my people, and I will be their God, for they will return to me with all their heart."*

1John 5:1-5 (NKJV): *"Whoever believes that Jesus is the Christ is born of God, and everyone who loves Him who begot also loves him who is begotten of Him.*

By this we know that we love the children of God, when we love God and keep His commandments.

For this is the love of God, that we keep His commandments. And His commandments are not burdensome.

For whatever is born of God overcomes the world. And this is the victory that has overcome the world—our faith.

Who is he who overcomes the world, but he who believes that Jesus is the Son of God?"

Acts 2:36-47 (ESV): *"Let all the house of Israel therefore know for certain that God has made him both Lord and Christ, this Jesus whom you crucified."*

Now when they heard this they were cut to the heart, and said to Peter and the rest of the apostles, "Brothers, what shall we do?"

And Peter said to them, "Repent and be baptized every one of you in the name of Jesus Christ for the forgiveness of your sins, and you will receive the gift of the Holy Spirit.

For the promise is for you and for your children and for all who are far off, everyone whom the Lord our God calls to himself."

And with many other words he bore witness and continued to exhort them, saying, "Save yourselves from this crooked generation."

So those who received his word were baptized, and there were added that day about three thousand souls.

And they devoted themselves to the apostles' teaching and the fellowship, to the breaking of bread and the prayers.

And awed came upon every soul, and many wonders and signs were being done through the apostles.

And all who believed were together and had all things in common. And they were selling their possessions and belongings and distributing the proceeds to all, as any had need.

And day by day, attending the temple together and breaking bread in their homes, they received their food with glad and generous hearts, praising God and having favor with all the people. And the Lord added to their number day by day those who were being saved.

When Is a Seat Mate Better Than a Whetstone?

Early in 2020, one of my cousins got busy and brilliantly reconnected a bunch of our extended family members via a phone-text chat room. I say "brilliantly" because she successfully led the pack in overcoming an interesting assortment of obstacles due to outdated devices and various learning curves on phone software, etc.

Well, Brenda's diligence and forethought initiated the launch of what we lovingly call our "Chaos" – what started out as the meeting of maybe 19 or 20 minds dwindled over time to a core group of six pun-loving regulars. As it turns out, three are from her immediate childhood family, and three are from mine.

Our Chaos is small and cozy, "relatively" speaking, and from time to time a relative from the original group will enlarge our happiness with a visit! We enjoy one another as supportive enthusiasts, sounding boards, advisers, and quippy punsters, and we derive a great deal of pleasure from crafting new repartees – even if we're the only ones in the world who might find them amusing. Ahhhh, family!

In any event, soon after reuniting online, we made plans for a physical family mini-reunion, and it wasn't long at all before our two small tribes were eating together in Texas, where Brenda was now living. I tell you this because Brenda helped me and my daughter get our plane tickets there, and that fact plays a part in my meeting Karen (my coauthor-to-be) about two years later!

Fast-forward to 2022, when I began to wonder how I could combine my skills, talents, knowledge, and inclinations to create a new career for myself. Having an entrepreneurial spirit, a passion for learning, and experience in teaching, I wanted to help people flourish somehow in what has been an increasingly perplexing educational system.

As soon as I determined I would like to research and present meaningful information to teachers, to help them unravel their corner of the national befuddlement, I began to surf the Net for someone to hire or train me. Lo and behold, with unusual speed I discovered an organization of educators who endorsed close to the same ideals and vision I had, who was actively bringing about fruitful transformation in school rooms across the nation...and who was looking for people like me!

I excitedly put together the information they wanted to have from me, and I submitted an application, hoping to work with their organization. Within about a week, I received the acceptance letter I had hoped for, with an invitation to take part in their train-the-trainer course and become a certified associate trainer-consultant in classroom management. I could then branch out on my own and liberate that independent entrepreneur I've always felt was lingering inside me. It was a thrilling prospect. How perfect!

The next thing I knew, I was telling Chaos all about my new venture and making plans to fly to Florida, where I was to undergo training. Brenda messaged me, "Remember you and Beck still have tickets from when the airline bumped you from your flight two years ago...."

(Ohhhhhh yeah, that's right! It seems my dear cousin nabbed an extra dose of managerial smarticles from our genetic pool, and...hey, did she get mine?!)

I didn't have to be in Orlando until July 28th, and the round-trip ticket worked perfectly! I was able to fly out early and spend time with my father and sister (two of the other Chaosers) before driving the six hours to my Florida destination. My return flight was on August 1st, which was also the last day of the training. Leaving the event, I made it to the departing gate just a tad too late.... The airline I was using sent my replacement flight through its hub in Washington D.C., rather than the one in Charlotte, NC, where the plane I had just missed was to fly.

I did some speedwalking that day, and when I stepped across the threshold of my connecting flight just in the nick of time, I said a quick prayer of thanks!! With some momentum left from my gate race, and the zeal that comes with success, I steadied my hand-held carry-on behind my back and quickly made my way through the tight quarters toward my seat. I'm not sure how I managed to maintain equilibrium while I struggled to balance my luggage during my boarding pass search, but I never fell into anyone's lap or anything, and soon I knew which seat to set my attention on. Only there was a lady sitting on the aisle seat, looking up at me, and not moving aside.

Should I ask her to let me in? I knew she knew the general game plan, but what I didn't know until she spoke up, was that she had a temporary disability and couldn't stand up without difficulty. Okay, things made sense now, but I still didn't know how long the two or three people behind me would let me stand in the middle of that unspacious aisle without difficulty, so I somehow raised my carry-on into a free-throw pose, climbed over her knees, swiveled, and sat down. – all without doing harm to my seat mate or anyone else. So far this looked to be a good flight! Little did I know, it was only going to get better!

Okay, do you know the answer to *when is a seat mate better than a whetstone?* No? Read Proverbs 27:17 and the next page or two, and I bet you'll figure it out....

~Darlene

My Unsuspected Appointment

When I first booked my flight to visit my son and his family in Florida, I wondered, why in the world did I have to go from Kansas City, Missouri all the way north to Washington DC and then south to Pensacola? I didn't want to go to DC! I fussed about it for a day or two, and then the Lord, I believe, dropped into my spirit that maybe He had a reason for me to go all the way to DC! Why hadn't I thought about that? It would make perfect sense because it's my regular habit to pray in advance, before going on a trip, that the Lord would help me keep my eyes wide open for divine appointments as I go.

I quickly stopped whining and started to pray for direction. On the way there I didn't encounter any specific person to talk to or pray for, so I just walked around the airport looking out the windows and praying for the goings on in DC, the government, and the people of the United States. On the way back, as I got on the plane in Pensacola and into my seat, I was waiting for who that divine appointment might be. I was hoping God had arranged for someone to be my seatmate and then would make a way for conversation.

The seats were all so close together! Those little planes remind me of Volkswagens because it's so hard to get up and out of your seat once you're in it! When my seatmate did arrive and needed to get to the other side of me, I started fumbling, trying to figure out how to get up and let her in without pushing off on the arm rest or reaching to the seat in front of me to pull myself out. Both of those methods were not options because of restrictions placed on me, due to a recent surgery. I gave a quick explanation that I needed a moment to maneuver, but before I could execute my plan, this woman climbed over me and settled into her seat! She was very friendly and actually acknowledged me with some pleasantries without me having to initiate it. She didn't plug into her phone or ignore me by looking out the window. I wanted to discover if she knew the Lord and take it from there. I knew that He would give me words to speak because I had prayed for it!

It wasn't long before we determined that we were sisters in the Lord, and I started sharing parts of my testimony. Not necessarily the parts I would have chosen to share with a stranger, but the Holy Spirit was in charge, and it just came pouring out! She shared her amazing testimony with me also! At one point I noticed how rough the flight was with turbulence, but I was able to completely ignore it as we went on and on sharing the wonder of Christ in our lives. Somewhere in the conversation, after at least an hour of non-stop chatting, Darlene said that she was writing a book. I shared that I was also writing a book! We exchanged phone numbers and have talked, prayed, or texted together almost every day now for a year. We have only ever seen each other that one day on the plane! However, we have become dear friends and co-laborers for Christ. We have also encouraged and poked each other to finish our books so God can be glorified by our testimonies!

Little did I know that the appointment God had booked for me that day was the blessing of a dear friend and coauthor...and all through my Washington DC connection!

~Karen

Trophies of Grace

Karen Hanson

Acknowledgements

Thank you:

First and foremost, to the God of my salvation, who in His loving kindness, surrounded me with these amazing people.

To Alan, for gifting me a new laptop that made writing so much easier, and for living this amazing life with me.

To my Keys Connection sisters, many of whom walked me through my salvation and continue to be my cheering section and prayer warriors!

To my sister Kathy and beloved friends Michelle and Ellen.

To my editor Beck, who persevered through my horrific punctuation, and shared her wisdom!

To my daughter Jamie, who came to my rescue when I wrestled with my computer issues!

To my coauthor Darlene Lamoureux, who encouraged and coached me to completion.

May God be glorified in what we have accomplished!

Prelude

My life is a series
Of events to be told
You will see God's grace
As the story unfolds
A child was scared
Her death was planned
But the Father stepped in
And stretched out His hand
Our God got angry
From His heavenly place
He routed the enemy
And kissed her face
The pain was real
The scars were deep
But He took in His arms
The little sheep
With love and care
He wiped her tears
He has been her shepherd
Now for many years
The pain is gone
The scars are old
But the reason for
Her hope must be told

You see, she is only one
Of the many little sheep
Who the devil has
On his list to keep
Their eyes are glazed
Their minds deceived
As he wraps his talons
Around their little feet
My story brings hope
To a dying world
When Christ steps in
The devil is hurled
The bonds are broken
The enemy is bound
When love comes in
Little sheep are found
I owe my life
To our Heavenly King
His praise and glory
I loudly sing
I lift His name
So all can see
This trophy of grace
God gave to me

Table Of Contents

1. The Absolute Truth 175
2. I Am a Sneak, Beware of Me 179
3. What Was Determined as All My Fault 186
4. The Eighth Roommate 200
5. Nights in the Closet 210
6. Time for a Cool Change 217
7. Hundreds of Girls 224
8. The Night I Got Sick 231
9. My Salvation Story 238
10. The Fullness of Joy 264
11. For I Know the Plans I Have for You 275
12. A New Creation 283
13. The Child Soldiers of El Salvador 287
14. My Walk of Faith 295
15. A Miracle in Belarus 298
16. The Conclusion 302

Chapter 1

The Absolute Truth

I grew up in a small country township in central Pennsylvania. Our neighborhood was only one block big with the streets named 1, 2, 3, and 4. My family lived on 4th Street, the only one that was paved. 1st Street was more of a path, making 4th Street technically a dead end into a cow pasture. We had no Post Office, and The Sister's Inn was the only little store and gas station…located just out of the neighborhood, across the highway. The year was 1967, and I was nine years old.

I was hiding just around the corner of the kitchen wall as I listened to my mom talking to the doctor on the phone about taking me off my seizure medication. When I was just a few weeks old I was stung by a wasp on the soft spot of my head. I had a severe allergic reaction that was thought to have produced epilepsy. I was given phenobarbital, a highly addictive anticonvulsant drug.

Over the years, I had become dependent on this medicine. The doctor had determined that I had outgrown my epilepsy to a degree that I didn't need to take it any longer. Back then everyone believed what the Preacher and Doctor told them. They were the chief sources of information, and whatever they said was considered to be the absolute TRUTH.

As I listened to their conversation, I began to panic. That doctor didn't know how I felt! How could he determine what I needed? My mom hung up the phone and I followed stealthily behind her, watching through the partially closed bathroom door as she took my bottle out of the cabinet and hid it behind a stack of towels on the top shelf of the linen closet.

I wasn't weaned off, and no one had talked to me about how I might feel without the medicine. Without it, I couldn't sleep and would get nervous inside, jittery and very uncomfortable, my stomach would hurt, and sometimes I would throw up; I understand now that I was having withdrawal symptoms back then.

I sneaked into our linen closet, climbed up on the clothes basket, and retrieved the pills from behind the towels. I used them every day until they were gone. Then I took medicine from the cabinet above the bathroom sink, not knowing what any of it was. My mother had several prescription medications, creating an arbitrary smorgasbord of choices. I was a victim of circumstance. I didn't ask for an addiction, it wasn't a matter of juvenile rebellion; however, this situation created a residual effect for years to come.

When I was Kindergarten age, my brother, sister, and I were sitting at the kitchen table having egg salad sandwiches for lunch. Suddenly, my mom started to choke! Her face turned a dark purple and blood came running out of her mouth. We watched in horror as she grasped at her throat, unable to speak. My brother ran out the front door to the neighbor's house screaming and crying that my mom was bleeding and to please come help us. Of course, they came running, called an ambulance, and got her to the hospital. Apparently, a large shard of glass had broken off the bottom of the mayonnaise jar and had gotten in the egg salad. She swallowed it and it cut her throat severely. She was rushed into surgery in critical condition. Over the course of a few days, she had gotten a sepsis infection and was not expected to live. My dad took my brother, sister, and me to the hospital where we were ushered down a dull green hall and into a small room to kiss our mother goodbye.

She lived through her ordeal, but when she came home, she was addicted to morphine. No one realized it for quite some time because she needed ongoing wound care for the infection in her neck. Her doctor kept her on pain medication for a very long time.

It's funny how adults can overlook explaining things like, "Your mom is still sick but she's not dying anymore." No one ever thought to tell us she was no longer dying. A nurse would come to the house every day to change her bandages. Because of the heavy medication, sometimes my mother would fall asleep at the table during mealtime, and we would be told to go play in the basement because Mom needed to rest. This is why I thought she was still dying. It was a very long time and multiple surgeries before she fully recovered.

Over time, quite a bit of old, half-used medications had accumulated in our bathroom cabinet. It would turn out that the medicine I was taking from the cabinet were narcotics. When they ran out, I resorted to taking meds from other people's cabinets.

Being a victim of circumstance, for me, started changing to willful drug use after a period of time. It wasn't withdrawing that caused my inside jitters anymore, I had an emptiness, a sense of sadness, a lack of love. My lack was internal; there were these outside circumstances that contributed, but I had a dissatisfied spirit. By age eleven I was sniffing glue and trying other drugs that were showing up for sale at school. Had I known that such a thing existed, I would have said this was an empty hole in my spirit that I needed to fill.

Chapter 2

I Am a Sneak, Beware of Me!

When I was in the ninth grade, I had taken some barbiturates in school one day. It was Wednesday, Bible study and prayer meeting night at church. I didn't want to go. I was already deciding that God wasn't for me, but it was a rule in our house that everyone go to church, so there was no getting out of it. I decided that if I had to go, I would get high enough to last through the whole service. Just before it was time to leave the house, I sniffed some glue, then before we went out the door, I took another pill.

The members of the congregation were all settling down as the first hymn began to play. Afterwards, the preacher stood at the front and welcomed everyone to the service. When everyone sat down, I remained standing, mesmerized at the way his mouth was moving. It didn't seem normal, and it struck me as funny. I let out a laugh that was immediately followed by a gasping for breath. My Sunday school teacher was within reach and grabbed me and pushed me through a classroom door that was right beside us. She quickly realized that I was completely high and called for my parents to come. No one knew what to do so they threw me in the back seat of our car and headed for the emergency room. My mother and I were in the back seat as my dad drove us to the hospital. She was mad and hurt. I will never forget the look on her face as her distress turned into her own nervous breakdown.

I was admitted to the hospital with a drug overdose. My stay in the hospital turned into a month of intervention because my mother was admitted to the upper floor in the psychiatric ward, diagnosed with mental and emotional distress disorder.

I knew that it was my fault that my mother was sick. On top of everything that she already had to deal with, my situation just pushed her over the edge.

When I was finally released from the hospital, I was sent to live with my aunt and uncle in Florida. My cousin Joann was just a year older than me and was expected to be a good influence. Of course, she was. She had what I thought was the perfect life. She was an only child, a vibrant teenager, completely involved in school and she had a boyfriend that was constantly teasing and tickling her. She had plenty of friends and since her dad, my uncle Smokey, was the pastor of the local Methodist church, she was the ideal preacher's kid. My Aunt Peg and Uncle Smokey took me in like their own daughter. I completely enjoyed living with them and the special attention they gave my cousin and me. I really didn't know how to attract different kinds of friends in school. I didn't play sports or join any clubs. I still had the desire to use drugs and whenever the opportunity presented itself, I did. I also went to youth meetings with my cousin. One night there was an opportunity for people to get prayed for who wanted God to help them with their problems.

I didn't want to be a bad person. I wanted God to like me, and this night I was willing to see if He would. When I went for prayer, someone called my uncle to come and get me. I was told that it was ridiculous to claim that I had a drug problem. I came from a good family who loved me, and I just needed to stop

I Am a Sneak, Beware of Me!

pretending to be a "hippy," or whatever it was that I was associating myself with. They did everything they could to give me a stable environment to thrive in. What they didn't know was that the emptiness in me was real, and all the hugs and cookies in the world weren't going to fill my void.

After a few months, my parents came to Florida to bring me home and I started into the tenth grade. I wasn't home very long before my parents found some drugs in my room. They immediately took me to see a counselor, who wanted to send me to a drug and alcohol treatment center.

The night before I was to be admitted, my mom and dad refused to allow me into my room. My mother had put a few articles of clothing in a small suitcase with some toiletries for me to take to the rehab. Two camping cots were set up in the living room for my dad and me to sleep on, so he could keep an eye on me throughout the night. I could see that my dad was disappointed and ashamed of me. At the time, there was no understanding by anyone about how this whole process of drug abuse may have gotten started. It was just chalked up to me being rebellious. I knew that everything was my fault, but I couldn't seem to stop what was going on.

I was put in a drug and alcohol rehab with heroin addicts and alcoholics. There weren't and had never been any other thirteen-year-olds in the program. To a degree, the other patients resented me and the attention I received because of my age. My being there also got special attention from the President Director of the rehab. He decided he would oversee my treatment personally. He often showed up in the common areas to interrogate me to the point of humiliation in front of the others. He would demand that I confess that I was a liar, a sneak, and a good for nothing person, just in case I thought I was special for any reason.

I had my fourteenth birthday during my sixty-day stay there. My mother didn't know how to respond to me having my birthday in the rehab. She contacted one of the counselors asking if he could bring me a birthday cake.

When the President Director found out about it, he made me wear a sandwich sign that said, "I Am A Sneak, Beware Of Me!" Every hour I was required to stand on a chair and shout out this statement no matter where I was or what might be going on. If I didn't shout loud enough, the other patients were free to insult me and demand that I do it again. I also had to wear an old lady dress from the handout closet and proclaim at every meal that I was not a princess! Failure to do so the very first time resulted in community humiliation and an assignment to talk to three other patients every day about how I was a "liar" and a "sneak." After our chat they had to sign off on the back of my sandwich sign that I had spoken to them. I did not understand why the President Director thought I had done anything sneaky. I never talked to my mother, and I never got a birthday cake.

I may have been rebellious in my own life setting, but I did not fit in with these adult misfits. My level of sin and rebellion was far different from theirs. In this place, usually reserved for wayward adults, I was forced to grow up as I got a taste of these absurd adult consequences.

The language in the rehab community was always foul. I learned to cuss like a sailor, to roll cigarettes and smoke any time that I wanted to. The open rebellion at least made me feel like I was in control of something in my life!

What occasional interactions I had with the President Director were brief and confusing. He would often take notice of me when walking through a room. He would get really close, lock eyes for a moment, shake his head, and draw my name out: Karen… Karen…Karen… Then he would slightly shake his head and walk away. It made me uneasy, and afraid he might do something to turn the whole group against me again.

I wore the sandwich sign for two weeks. When I finally got it removed and was back to wearing my own clothes, I did my best not to draw any attention to myself. Whenever I entered a community room, I immediately scouted for an exit so I could slip out later on without being noticed. Most of all, I learned how to avoid the President Director.

When my sixty days were almost finished, I was approached by a counselor aid who told me they wanted to relocate me to a halfway house in town at the end of the week, instead of allowing me to return home. I didn't think my parents were going to go for that!

On the morning of the sixty-first day, my parents did not come to get me. I was loaded into a car with my small suitcase and taken to a house about half an hour from the rehab center, just outside of town. It was a neglected two-story wooden duplex with chipping white paint, trimmed in green. The house was nothing to be impressed about. Overgrown weeds and bushes were overtaking the narrow gravel driveway, and there was no yard to speak of. Four other girls had already been relocated to the house from the program.

When I arrived with the counselor, no one was home. The furniture was sparse and looked like it had come from a secondhand store. Nothing really matched. The house was uncomfortably chilly, and I couldn't help but notice the water-stained ceilings as I followed my escort upstairs. The bedroom was just one large room with five beds. I was directed to leave my suitcase on the bed the counselor said was mine, then I was shown the rest of the house.

I was expected to do my share of the chores, feed myself, and pay one-fifth of the household expenses. I had a two-week grace period to find a job so I could pay my way. I had never done anything to earn money before!

I could not find a regular job; I was only fourteen, and I looked it! I arranged to clean the house of an older lady in the program, and I offered to wash hard to reach windows for neighbors as well.

One weekend my brother Rick bought some chickens for me at a livestock auction. He got me a whole crate of live chickens thinking that I could sell them since I couldn't get a job! He put them on our back closed-in porch, with their feet tied together so they couldn't get away. The plan was for me to get up early in the morning and get rid of them by knocking on doors. This was a 16-year-old boy's bright idea of how I could get some money! I had never had to work for money before, so I supposed it was better than nothing.

The next morning, I was sitting at the kitchen table having coffee with the other girls. The oldest girl, Lisa, who had a rough disposition to begin with, said in a disgusted tone, "What the heck is that noise?"

Everybody listened but no one understood what she was talking about, so we all dismissed it. "There it is again!" she said. "Listen!" *Peck peck peck peck peck.* Something was tapping on the window between the porch and the kitchen! It suddenly dawned on me that I had completely forgotten about the chickens on the porch!

I jumped up and ran to the porch, confessing and apologizing while my new roommates were hollering at me and laughing as they all joined in trying to catch them! The chickens had gotten their feet untied and had pooped everywhere!

All dozen chickens had gotten loose, and one of them was up on the ledge pecking on the window.

Yvonne shouted out as she wrangled one of the chickens under her arm, "What the heck were you thinking, girl? What do you plan to do with these things?"

"My brother Rick got them at a livestock auction so that I could sell them to get my share of the rent."

Yvonne shouted back, "Sell them? In case you haven't noticed, these are not Girl Scout cookies! Where in the heck do you expect to sell them?"

Everyone had a good laugh and wondered just what it would look like for me to be carrying a crate of live chickens door-to-door to see who wanted to buy one!

To save face, I did in fact take the crate and go try to sell the chickens. What else was I going to do? I sold them for a dollar a piece to a sympathetic farmer down the road. He got me off the hook and bought the whole crate!

Needless to say, I never tried that entrepreneurial endeavor again! I went back to washing windows, cars, and cleaning houses.

Chapter 3

What Was Determined as All My Fault

I was at the halfway house for about five months when the President Director stopped by one evening. It was already dark. If he ever came for an inspection, it usually wasn't in the evening.

He walked through the door like he owned the place, without even the courtesy of knocking. Everyone all but jumped to attention at his presence, except Yvonne, that is! She saw right through him and wasn't shy about her opinion of what she saw. As he strolled through the kitchen, he spotted me over by the record player in the living room. Without looking directly at me, he instructed me to get my coat and come with him. Surprised and somehow honored, I dutifully got my jacket and followed him out to his car. I wondered where we were going but was afraid to ask. As I started to open the back door, he told me to sit in the front. I couldn't believe that he would ask me to go anywhere with him. It was clear that he didn't like me, although I really didn't know why. There were plenty of people more wretched than me at that rehab! I knew that the other girls must be jealous, especially because he didn't give them any extra attention at all.

Several of them were waiting for their turn to go up to the rehab and become a counselor aid. You were required to be clean a year before being considered for the job. I wasn't even close to a year clean of substances! They were probably all thinking that's what was going on. I was considered a "little princess" by them after all, in a jealous, snippy sort of way.

We had driven for about twenty minutes when he reached over and placed his hand on my leg. With a squeeze, he did what he had done in the rehab several times: he locked eyes with me and said in a drawn out tone, *"Karen...Karen...Karen..."*

I didn't know what to do!

The next thing I knew we were pulling down a long dirt road that led to a small garbage dump. He pulled around the other side of the dump, so we were hidden behind a stinking mound of trash bags. He put his hand on my leg again and proceeded to tell me what a nice-looking girl I was. He told me that what he was doing was for my own good and that I needed to know what to expect from a man. He also told me that I had to just keep this between us, or else.

He took me back to the halfway house and dropped me off in the driveway. I went into the house and ran upstairs to the bathroom. I couldn't believe what had just happened! I was bleeding from the assault, but worse than that was the guilt and remorse I felt because his wife was my therapist. She was like a second mother to me. I loved her and her husband knew it. He told me Charlotte would hate me forever if she ever found out what we had done. I knew nothing was my fault. I didn't ask for any of it, but the director had found a way to put the guilt all on me. I took the heavy burden onto myself, which preluded what would become years of shame and torturous dreams of his assaults.

Other than coincidental sightings, I didn't see or hear from the director for a long time after that night.

When I had been clean from substances for eight months the director called for me to come work at the rehab as a counselor aid. Because of my age, this was a directive, not a request. There were many people ahead of me and this was just one more incident to separate me from others in the program. I was the first person to be offered a counselor aid position at eight months of sobriety and certainly I had been the youngest. It was not a paid position, but I would be moving into a cabin at the rehab with only one roommate, and room and board was free.

It all happened very quickly. I was moved out of the halfway house and back up to the rehab by the same aid who had brought me to the house after my release as a patient.

My main duty as an aid was to sit with new women who came into the program and help them get over a variety of immediate physical, psychological, and emotional withdrawal symptoms. I held the puke bucket, stroked matted hair, held and rocked women suffering the shakes and DTs, and talked down heroin and other drug addicts who wanted to harm themselves as they were detoxing.

There was nothing easy about the job! Many times, I would stay up all night receiving a new girl. Sometimes the person in detox would throw items across the room and I would have to call for help. Sometimes the withdrawal was so violent that I had to call for a counselor to come and they would call an ambulance to assist. When my shift was over, I would retreat to my cabin, put my Carole King *Tapestry* album on the record player, and go to sleep. There may have been a day off here and there, but I can't remember them as anything more than chances to get a little more sleep.

I settled into my new job, and although it was emotionally exhausting, it was certainly better than hustling for a few bucks here and there doing odd jobs to pay rent.

After I had been at the rehab for a couple of months, I was summoned to the President Director's office by one of the counselors. I had never seen him in his office before. I was reluctant to go but it was in the middle of the day and other people were in the building. I cautiously made my way to the second floor and approached the only open door that I saw.

As I stepped into the doorway, I realized he was talking on the phone. He motioned for me to come in and have a seat, said his goodbye, and hung up the phone. Wordlessly, he got up, walked behind me, and shut and locked the door.

As he made his way back to the desk, he reached out and took some of my hair in his fingers. An alarm went off in my head, but I didn't know what to do. He continued around, to sit at his desk; opened one of the drawers and pulled out a document.

He looked at me directly, tapping the paper with his finger, and said, "I had a visit from your parents today."

Quickly, I shot back "I didn't see them, where are they? Why didn't you tell me they were here?"

"It was a private meeting, and I just wanted you to know that I am now your legal guardian. You know that you could not go back to your hometown, Karen. You are underage so I have taken responsibility for you. I am taking you under my wing as my own daughter. I am going to move you into my house and put you back in high school. After discussing your care with your parents, I have decided that this is the best thing to do. They have signed custody of you over to me. I just wanted you to see the document and remind you that it is important to keep our private life private. You are legally mine and I am your daddy."

I didn't leave that office without paying my dues. It felt like my world was closing in around me. I went down the stairs and left the building with hopelessness and sadness in my heart. No matter how many times the President Director told me I was special, even privileged to have his affections and direction, he didn't neglect to tell me that it was for my own good because I was so broken without him. It was my fault that he had to provide this type of guidance. It was my doing that I had to go behind Charlotte's back and deceive her.

This was the greatest torture for me. Somehow, he had poisoned my mind into believing that the fault was completely mine.

I was moved into the President Director's house and enrolled into the local high school at the tenth-grade level. I was given the bottom bunk in a bedroom with the President Director's daughter June. The children were young; Faith was four and June was eleven. I didn't have much interaction with them. It seemed they were always at school or at the babysitter's, except on weekends.

I didn't have very many personal items, just a few changes of clothes, a small boombox type radio, and my Carole King album. There wasn't anything in the bedroom to suggest that any of it was mine.

The President Director did not assault me for at least a month after I moved in.

Until one day when I was alone in the basement, tasked with the chore of doing laundry. I turned around and there he was, saying my name in that drawn out kind of way: *Karen...Karen... Karen...* With his family right upstairs, he turned off the light and took his pleasure at my expense.

I loved his wife Charlotte and was even grateful for opportunities to ride alone in the car with her to go for groceries. These were moments that I imagined that Charlotte was my real mother, giving me real affections with no strings attached.

One evening all the family members were in the living room, reading or playing quietly. I was lying on my stomach on the floor looking at a magazine close to Charlotte's chair. She reached down and put her hand affectionately on my back in a motherly way. It was like acid to my heart. I loved the simple gesture of affection but with it came a flood of guilt for what I knew was going on behind her back. My eyes started to tear, but I accidentally noticed the President Director looking at me. I couldn't risk any drama, so I lowered my head and with that movement Charlotte pulled back her hand and the affection I so desperately needed. I swallowed down my emotions and endless hours of mental anguish were added to the secret, that was determined as all my fault.

This was the second time I had started the tenth grade, but it didn't last very long. As a part of life after the rehab, I was expected to go to Narcotics Anonymous meetings several times a week. I was usually picked up by a friend who was older and taken to and from the meetings. The meetings were typically right in town at a church fifteen or twenty minutes from the house. This evening the topic at hand was Honesty, and then it was open for discussion. The nugget of the talk was that if you didn't want to go back to a life of drugs then you had to "clean your closet," and right your wrongs regarding relationships and things you might have done to other people. If you didn't, then these things would eat away at you and cause you to want to return to drugs.

I surely didn't know where I was going in life, but I didn't think I wanted to go backwards either! I wasn't certain if what I had experienced was addiction, compared to the stories I had heard from these adult addicts. My life was very juvenile and innocent compared to theirs. Either way, I could relate to guilt eating away at me and secrets that sucked away any hope of a normal life. I couldn't live with the deception any longer. I was tired of sleepless nights as the accusations of the President Director echoed in my mind over and over again. Every touch from Charlotte became an open wound of deceit for me to agonize over. After the NA meeting that night, I decided to confide in my friend Cindy what was going on. She was shocked at my story and didn't know if she should believe it. Cindy was a court reporter and so was used to hearing many shocking stories. She had also learned that most of them were true.

It was a school night and Charlotte was expecting me home shortly after the meeting was over. Cindy told me that I had to get out of that situation and that she would drive me anywhere I needed to go. I was still just a child, a fact that most of my acquaintances in this scenario seemed to forget. I had no place to go, and no resources to help me get there even if I did. Fear gripped every fiber of my being as I suddenly realized that my secret was out. Anyone with a sense of decency wouldn't let it go. The President Director was 43 and I had just turned 16. Mental and sexual abuse of this magnitude just couldn't be ignored. Especially by someone who was familiar with the law and sat in a courtroom every day.

I knew that the next thing I had to do was to tell Charlotte what was going on. I would have rather had my eyes gouged out, but there didn't seem to be a choice. I walked in through the kitchen door and Charlotte was right there to greet me. She smiled and asked how the meeting had been. Immediately she sensed that things were not right with me. The most common fear with people in the NA program is that they had a relapse and took some drugs. Charlotte was standing across the kitchen beside the phone hanging on the wall. I was on the other side of the kitchen table at the center of the room. She spoke right out and asked me if I had taken any drugs. I said no and saw a small measure of relief on Charlotte's face. Little did she know that the news I had was much worse!

I had only ever had one boyfriend in the ninth grade. I wasn't used to grown up relationships and I wasn't aware of anyone else in any similar situation. I didn't know the right words to say.

In the NA program there was a rule: no relationships within the program. Anyone caught dating someone in the program was forbidden to continue such a relationship. This was the only frame of reference I had to describe what was going on. As I spoke out the words, I knew that they weren't quite right, but the moment was too big to try to correct.

I told Charlotte, "Your husband and I are having a relationship. The meeting tonight was about honesty, and it really got to me. I can't keep the secret any longer."

It wasn't a relationship! It was rape! It was abuse! Only now as an adult do I have those words! I didn't know those words to reference at the time and I said it all wrong!

Charlotte's face contorted into something hateful and hurtful. When she found her voice she spit the words across the room. "Get out of my house!" At that very moment the phone on the wall rang. Charlotte picked it up then slammed it back on the hook. It registered to me that it had to have been the President Director. He would have guessed that something was terribly wrong and would head right home. Panic gripped me as I remembered his threats if anything like this were to happen. I was suddenly afraid for my life. Cindy was in the driveway waiting in her car. I opened the door and motioned for her to come quickly. Cindy helped me shove my few belongings in a bag and we ran for the door before the President Director had a chance to get home. The only problem was that I didn't have anywhere to go. I couldn't go to Cindy's place because if we got caught, she would suffer consequences as well. The only possibility was to go to where some of the former members of NA lived. There were four or five people who had fallen off the program and rented an apartment together in the next town over.

When we showed up at their door it was a mockery. Steve, a tall lanky 27-year-old, took a step back to assess the situation as the two of us stood on the doorstep. He shouted over his shoulder to his roommates in the other room, "Looky who's here guys! It's the princess." He turned back to face us with a puzzled look and asked, "What are you doing here? Are you selling cookies?" He laughed at his own joke, but at the same time was curious as to my real reasoning.

"Karen needs a place to hide from the President Director. We figured this was the last place he would look," offered Cindy.

"What's the matter, did you fall off the program and get Daddy mad at you?" The guy scoffed, but finally invited us in. I was relieved to be off the street, in case the President Director was out looking for me. The only way I imagined I could save myself would be to tell everyone what was going on. I gave them a two-line explanation of the problem just to see what their reaction would be. I didn't want to give any more ammunition for their ridicule. At this point there was no sympathy from them and immediately three of them agreed that I was probably lying, and maybe even there to report back what they were up to.

Cindy had to leave and get home so she could go to work in the morning. I sat there on the couch with my belongings in a bag at my feet. No one talked to me after Cindy left, and truthfully, they hadn't even said that I could stay! I was parched but didn't dare even ask for a glass of water. During the few minutes that I sat in the living room alone, Cheryl, an older female roommate, came quickly up to me and whispered rather loudly, "I believe you, he did the same thing to me!" Obviously, Cheryl didn't want the others to comment on her accusations either, because she left the room as quickly as she had come, and I didn't see her for the rest of the night. It was comforting to know that someone believed me, but the difference was that Cheryl was an adult and could defend herself; I was only a minor, and the President Director was my legal guardian!

I wasn't very welcome in this home. I fell asleep where I sat on the couch, and no one made any attempt to offer me another option. I woke up having to use the bathroom, and found it took a great deal of bravery to get up and find it. The house was quiet, and no one was in sight. I was hungry and thirsty but was afraid to help myself or move about. I spied a half full glass of dark liquid that had been left on the counter. I quickly took a big swig and put the glass back down like I had never touched it. It was soda, now warm and flat. The only good thing is that it was liquid, and I thought maybe the sugar would give me some energy to go on. Until this moment I had never experienced real hunger or a need that I had no way of resolving. I sat back down on the couch and closed my eyes, wanting to appear as though I hadn't been up to anyone who came out of their room. After some time had passed, I considered going into the kitchen and taking a piece of bread from a loaf I had seen on the counter. Again, I was afraid of getting caught and potentially thrown out. Anything was better than walking the streets with no place to go while the President Director was looking for me.

That evening Cindy came to pick me up and take me to a different house. It was the same situation: people who had dropped out of the program. They were equally shocked to see the "little princess" on their doorstep. I became more bold about shouting out that the President Director had abused me; I figured it was the only way to save my own life. He was very well-known in the community and had a lot of power to manipulate people's lives. When I had been working at the rehab, he once had me attend a court hearing where he recommended that a woman be placed in a mental institution for a sixty-day evaluation. The judge committed the woman without question, solely on the President Director's testimony. He'd wanted me to understand that he had power and that I had better respect it.

I was hoping that I hadn't made a big mistake doing all of this!

After two days of hiding out I went for a short walk close to the house, and Earl, the President Director's good friend, found me. He drove up beside me and told me to get into his car. There was no way I was going anywhere with him! I was pretty sure that he would take me straight to the President Director no matter what I told him, and then who knows what! I was hoping that if I told Earl I had been blabbing my story to anyone who would listen, he would just let me go.

He pulled his car over and got out. Dragging on his cigarette with an obvious attitude, he approached me. I was determined to keep my distance, although I didn't think he had the nerve to grab me.

"How are you doing, Karen? The President Director is wondering where you ran off to. How about getting in my car and I'll give you a ride back?"

"No thanks! I'm fine," I said, backing up a bit to emphasize my point. Earl withdrew his wallet from his back pocket and offered me some money for whatever I needed, but I refused it. I was sure it was a trick of some kind. When Earl got back in his car and drove away, I knew I couldn't stay in the same place another day.

I considered calling my parents and telling them what had happened, but I knew they were disappointed in me, and I was sure they wouldn't believe my story.

Cindy came back to see me with the news that the President Director had found out she was helping me, and that she'd been fired from her job. "I'm sorry Karen, but there is nothing I can do for you now. I'm heading home to live with my parents until I can figure out what to do next." She hugged me and drove away. I retrieved my small bag of belongings from the misfit house and walked out into the night. It was cold, though I can't remember what month it was. I needed a place to sleep. There was a small laundromat a couple of blocks away, so I went in, sat on a bench in the warmth, and fell asleep.

I woke up hungrier than I had ever been in my life! I went to a small sink in the corner of the laundromat and drank from the spigot. I didn't know where to go or what to do! For a couple of days, I went to the school and slept in the bathroom as best I could with my feet curled up on the toilet seat.

I hadn't been enrolled long enough to have made any friends, so that was neither a help nor a hindrance. For what little time I spent in the halls coming and going, no one knew that I no longer belonged there. I was sleepy and needed to stay warm and I blended in at the school just fine.

At night I was slinking around, walking aimlessly down the back streets, when I passed by a dentist office and saw a woman open the cellar door and go inside. I knew she didn't belong down there! I followed, opened the door, and walked down the few cement steps that led to the basement. She looked at me briefly, almost like she expected me to follow her, then disappeared into a room off to the left and shut the door.

I cautiously walked through and discovered another room and a bathroom. It was clear no one was staying there; it was empty except for an old couch, and it was warm! For now, unless someone kicked me out, I was staying put! There was no way that the President Director would find me here!

I discovered that the woman who lived in the other room had a small son. I occasionally saw her coming and going but we never engaged in conversation. Whatever her story was, I didn't need to know!

More than a week had passed since I'd last had any food. I drank water from the bathroom faucet when I was hungry, and just didn't know what to do about my situation. I was weak and sometimes dizzy from the lack of food. Finally, I figured the President Director probably thought I had left town.

Without any other choice, I decided to venture out to find something to eat. The only place I knew to go was a convenience store a few blocks away. I didn't want to steal, but I really had no choice. After spying out the store, I took the first thing I saw that looked safe to stick in my coat. As soon as the cashier was busy checking out other customers, I made my exit.

Once I was out of sight I pulled the box out of my coat. *Blast!* I clearly hadn't been paying attention to what I grabbed!

I had taken a pineapple upside-down cake mix! What was I going to do with that?!

I mixed the powder with snow and ate it right out of the box with a plastic spoon I had obtained at some point. It was delightful, and I was grateful for it. The sugar made me dizzy and was a bit too much for my stomach, but I managed to keep it down, and it gave me strength as the day went on.

I knew that I could not continue living like this. I was starving and needed to eat real food. After my encounter with Earl and then walking through the neighborhood without being stopped, I thought that maybe the President Director had stopped looking for me. Maybe he thought that I had gone home to my parents.

After finding some change on the floor at the laundromat, I called my ex-sponsor in the program who lived in Indiana. She had fallen off the program and returned to her hometown. She bought me a bus ticket to come and live with her.

As the Greyhound pulled away from the station and out of town I felt like I was finally escaping from the President Director. I guess it was an act of self-preservation to change my name to Roxanne and tell a whopper of a story to my seat partner about where I was going and why. I don't even remember what the story was, except that it wasn't true and somehow I felt protected by the lie.

My experience of staying in the dentist office basement and everything about the President Director was pushed down as a secret; never to be spoken about for years to come. I just simply got on the bus and rode away.

Chapter 4

The Eighth Roommate

The same day I arrived in Indiana, my friend Lisa was leaving on a road trip to Arizona to visit some friends. She said that it wouldn't make a difference at all if I came with her, so we jumped in her car and went on a two week vacation to Phoenix.

Lisa's friends all attended Arizona State University and lived together in a rented house off campus. They were all friendly and welcomed me as their guest. We had a wonderful two weeks of laughing, hiking in the desert, and sitting around visiting. Lisa paid for everything I needed and there was food to eat, a bed to sleep in, and fun to be had every day. By the time we left Phoenix I felt that I had made some new friends.

Back in Evansville, Indiana, my goal was to get a job and at least have some money to feed myself and figure out where my life was going. I was only sixteen and barely employable. I found a job at Arthur Treacher's fast food restaurant that was about a mile away.

Of course I didn't have the opportunity to learn to drive yet so I had to walk everywhere. It was still winter and though Indiana didn't usually get much snow, this year there was snow to traverse on my walk to work along the highway. I was grateful to work where I could get an employee discount and

The Eighth Roommate

eat enough food every day. I found that I enjoyed working. I was a good, reliable employee and learned the different stations of food preparation quickly. I even became friends with one of the employees that would chat and joke around with me while we were working.

Life at Lisa's house was fairly uneventful at first. Various people came and went frequently, mostly without engaging in conversation with me, and maybe not even noticing I was there. When I was at home, I watched T.V. in the living room while Lisa and her friends mostly visited in the dining room or secretively in the bathroom. Apparently they were hiding something, from me particularly. I didn't care and didn't want to know.

It all came to light one day when a woman named Wendy came in the door of the apartment out of breath and carrying a load of food and other new items. As she unloaded her plunder onto the couch Lisa came in from the kitchen smiling and asking what was going on.

"I barely got away this time!" Wendy said as she was still trying to unload and calm herself down. "This guy started after me just as I was going out the door and chased me all the way through the parking lot! It's a good thing that Brad was ready to pick me up! I got in the car just in time and we got away! I won't be able to go back there to shop for a while!" she said as she let out a loud exhaustive laugh.

I was watching with my mouth agape as Wendy started pulling steaks out of the pant legs of her jeans, and pork chops, chicken, and a box of candy from the sleeves and pockets of her coat! She also had some cassette tapes and, for goodness' sake, a pool stick down her other pant leg! She was laughing as she described not being able to pass up the pool stick, and how she stuffed it down her pants, and then about how difficult it was to jump in the car to get away! I never did understand how she ended up getting grocery items and a pool stick all at one store!

Anyway, the cat was out of the bag as I discovered that they were all involved in stealing items from stores! I remembered stealing the pineapple upside-down cake from the convenience store after I had gotten away from the President Director and couldn't imagine getting up the nerve to rob a store the way they were doing! I looked over my shoulder for at least an hour after stealing the cake mix and never felt comfortable doing such a thing.

Well here I was with all these stolen items in the apartment I lived in, and that made me an accomplice. Wendy did not live there but came and went frequently, often sharing her stolen goods with Lisa. Sometimes when Wendy came over they would disappear into the bathroom for hours. I tried not to pay attention, anyway, since I hadn't been invited to whatever it was they were doing.

One Friday evening after work my friend Debbie decided to come home with me to hang out. It was the first time I had even thought about inviting a friend over. I was a bit excited to be an adult and have an apartment to invite someone to. As soon as we got home it turned out that Lisa knew my friend Debbie and they started chatting like schoolgirls. I didn't even take off my coat before I decided to walk over to the market and get some snacks for the evening of movie-watching that we had planned. I had just gotten paid and although it was the day I was to pay Lisa rent, she was too busy in conversation, so I figured it could wait until later.

When I got back from the store, Lisa and Debbie were sitting quietly at the dining room table. As I approached I noticed that Lisa was asleep and so was Debbie! It took me a few minutes to figure out what I was looking at! Lisa had a needle hanging out of her arm and was not sleeping but passed out, high on heroin! And Debbie... I couldn't believe it; apparently she was also! Lisa opened her eyes for a second and muttered something I couldn't understand.

I had no idea where I was headed in life, but I knew for sure that it did not involve this!

I was still wearing my Arthur Treacher sailor type uniform, but I didn't care! I went into my room, put everything in my backpack, and walked out the door leaving Lisa and Debbie passed out at the table.

I walked for a while until I saw a pay phone. I called a Taxi to take me to the Greyhound bus station. Thank God that I had used some of my last paycheck to purchase a backpack! Everything that was mine fit into it. When I got to the bus station, I had no idea where to go! I reasoned that my only possible choice was to go back to Arizona and see if I could live with the girls I had met there. I was glad there hadn't been an opportunity to give Lisa my rent money earlier, because now I had enough to get to the bus station and buy a ticket. If I was careful with my money, I would be able to buy a meal a time or two along my journey, but without a doubt I would arrive in Phoenix with no money and no assurance that I had a place to live.

I didn't call the girls in Phoenix before I got on the bus. I reasoned that even if I couldn't live at their house, at least Phoenix was warmer than Evansville, and I could manage better on the street if it wasn't so blasted cold.

I was looking out the window as the bus pulled into the station. I was thinking about calling the girls but was afraid of what they might say about me just showing up. I went into the station, used the restroom, made myself presentable, and sat in the terminal for a while trying to work up the nerve to call.

When I had been here with Lisa months before, we went to Arizona State University, where all the girls in the house attended classes. I realized that on a college campus, it wasn't unusual to see people with backpacks just hanging out on the lawn or in the commons. A person could blend in and use the bathroom facilities without being recognized as someone who didn't belong there. This all gave me hope that Arizona was a good choice.

I fingered the paper I had with the girl's phone number until it was getting worn out from my worry. Finally I went to the pay phone and made the call.

"Hi Molly, this is Karen, Lisa's friend. How are you doing? Phoenix made an impression on me and guess what…I'm here at the bus station!" After a few awkward moments of exclamation and questions, I continued in a more serious tone. "I found myself in an awkward situation at Lisa's house a few days ago. I know that you all know about Lisa's problem with drugs a few years back. Well, I'm sorry to say she's doing it again. I came home from work on Friday, and she was passed out at the dining room table with a needle hanging out of her arm. I didn't know what to do, but Molly, I don't want any part of that life. I had just gotten paid, so I threw my stuff in a bag and walked out. I didn't have anywhere to go so I just got on a bus and came to the last place that I saw life was good. I was wondering if you all might have room for one more roommate?"

Molly assured me that they would make room for me and that I was welcome to come there. I became the eighth roommate in the house!

The Eighth Roommate

Without dwelling on it too much, my stay in Phoenix lasted four years. I grew up quite a bit in those few years. At first I walked the 11.4 miles to work at The ChuckBox restaurant right across from the college campus. It was an open pit hamburger joint with sawdust on the floor and beer kegs to sit on. It was a great place to work, and I fit in just fine. After a while I bought a bicycle to make the commute back and forth a little faster.

Donna was one of our roommates and one day she was complaining about not being able to find a job. I told her that was ridiculous, that if she really wanted a job, she could find one. When my job-search in Pennsylvania at age 14 was unsuccessful, I realized I could create my own jobs cleaning houses and washing cars; I knew that when times are desperate enough, you can try to overcome your situation with some ingenuity if nothing else! I told her that to prove my point, I would go out the next day and find a job. I really can't remember why I wasn't working at The ChuckBox at this point. Anyway, I was free to look for a job. Donna and I made a bet. If I couldn't find a job by the end of the day, I had to come up with a way to pay her part of the rent. If I did come home with a job then she had to come up with a way to pay my part of the rent.

I got up early in the morning, walked eleven miles into town, going into every single business along the way to ask if they were hiring. I didn't care what kind of business it was, if there was a job out there, I was going to get it! Well, call it a bad day! At the end of the day I started the walk home with no job. On my way, I noticed a building titled "Unemployment Office." I didn't know what that was, but unemployment sounded like my situation; so just to say I did, I went in. A lady on the other side of the desk immediately spoke to me," We close at 4:00. Take a number from the dispenser, you've got the last appointment of the day." I still didn't understand what appointment I had but, I was glad to have it. When my number was called I was ushered back to a small office with a woman sitting behind the desk. She was overweight and her space seemed too small and uncomfortable for her. She had an obvious attitude and when she looked up to see who had been ushered in she let out a sigh and said, "I'm sorry, I don't have any jobs for you, check back next week." I wasn't going to be dismissed that easily, especially since it seemed that I had gotten the last chance for someone to give me a job today! "How do you know that you don't have a job for me? You haven't even talked to me yet!" She was not happy that I challenged her authority, but I suppose she was obligated to go through the process. "Do you have any secretarial skills? Typing, answering phones, filing, or letter writing?" My answer was no. "Can you concrete or drywall?" Again, my answer was no. "Then I don't have a job for you, like I said."

I still wasn't going to go without pressing a little harder. I asked her to check over her list one more time. She wasn't in the mood to be challenged, so she answered with a patronizing tone, "Well, can you operate heavy equipment, specifically a forklift?" I didn't know if I could or not but since she didn't ask me if I already had experience at it, I said "Yes, I can do that." She smirked and said," You can drive a forklift?" I assured her that indeed I could, and she wrote me a slip of paper that gave me an interview at a construction site down the road. If I hurried I could get there before quitting time!

I was standing on a small porch built onto the construction manager's trailer at the site of a strip mall that was under construction. The manager was on the other side of the porch engaged in a heated discussion with a man with a complaint about something. He glanced over at me a couple of times, and when he finally sent the other guy on his way, he looked at me and said, "What do you want, girl?" I handed him my slip of paper and told him that I'd come for the equipment operator job. He laughed and asked me if I knew how to operate a forklift. Well, I had been standing there for what seemed like forever, waiting to talk to him, watching a guy operate a machine with forks on the front. I watched everything he did, and it didn't seem too hard to me.

"Yes, I can," I said, not quite confident enough to convince him.

He said, "I'm not going to give you a job as an operator, but you've got guts girl! If you can push a broom I'll give you a job cleaning up." That was good enough for me! Of course, having found a job, I went home the victor. My portion of the rent was only $45, so it wasn't a terrible loss for Donna. She ended up going to the same construction site a couple weeks later and also got hired on the cleanup crew!

The boss really liked me because I was a hard worker and could manage any job he asked me to do. Sometimes he would send me to the plumber who needed someone to run back and forth to the truck for supplies; I helped lay floor tile and I assisted the welders who needed someone to be on fire watch as they installed the ductwork for the air conditioning system. I was becoming acquainted with several types of construction jobs. I didn't really learn the main skills independently, but I was a good helper on the site.

The crew would most days go over to a Mexican restaurant next door for lunch. This day was a Friday, and the crewmen were anxious for the weekend and whatever plans they had. A few of them ordered beers with their lunch, which was overlooked only on Fridays, assuming there were no big jobs to accomplish before quitting time. We were in the finishing stages of the job and our afternoon consisted of planting some trees. The guy driving the forklift would scoop up the tree between his forks and lift the tree into a hole. A few others and I would fill dirt in around it then move on to the next one. There were men building a beautifying wall right behind us and we were instructed to be careful not to interfere with their work as we planted the trees. Just as the boss was walking past, the guy operating the forklift ran the front tire into the hole, swung the tree and knocked down part of the wall they had just finished! The boss was furious!

He shouted up at the guy because he knew he was one of the workers who had been drinking beer at lunch. "You idiot! You should have let somebody else drive the forklift! As a matter of fact, this girl can drive it better than you! Get down off of there, you're fired!" He looked at one of the other laborers and said, "Take this girl out back and teach her to drive this forklift." From that moment on I was a heavy equipment operator with a dollar-an-hour raise! I was nineteen at this point. I hadn't had the opportunity yet but now was my chance to get my first driver's license. I didn't have my own car, but my roommates taught me to drive and took me to take the test.

I worked as an equipment operator in Phoenix until the construction company moved out of the area and I didn't have a car to follow the work.

During the four years I lived in Arizona, I was introduced to hiking mountain ranges by my roommates. We went hiking and camping in the Superstitions, the North and South Mountains on the outskirts of Phoenix, Four Peaks, and, of course, the Grand Canyon. Those few years in Arizona were very good for me.

One year my roommates went together and got me a five week old, black German Shepherd puppy for my birthday. I reasoned, Tuesday wasn't Monday, and it was one day closer to Friday, so I named my dog Tuesday!

I loved working, hiking, and camping in the mountains with my roommates. I also took an art correspondence course, which was wonderful because there were periods of time in my life where personal pleasures were few and far between.

Anyway, once a month, an art instructor would come and meet with students at a local hotel conference room. It was clear to me that, while I had some artistic talent, I was nothing special. I learned some things, but like most things in my life by this point, I never got to finish the course. When I lost my construction job, I couldn't pay for the course any longer. Truthfully, I was satisfied to quit while I had some well-graded drawings to hold onto – as tokens to prove I had some kind of worth.

Chapter 5

Nights in the Closet

My roommates were starting to graduate from college, and one by one moved out of the house and on with their lives. When the walls around me began to crumble, everyone else went forward, and I went two steps behind. I didn't have a plan or career to move onto. So when the house split up, I found myself moving into a car with another girl who was also in an unfavorable circumstance. We drove around selling off her album collection at record stores and donating plasma twice a week in order to put gas in the car and eat every day.

After several years of staying drug- and alcohol-free, I was at a party one night and when a joint was passed to me, I smoked it without giving it a second thought. I don't think I behaved like an addict of anything, needing it every day, but the willingness to participate in alcohol and drug use was back whenever the opportunity presented itself. My life had no foundation to build on. My boundaries, if they even existed, weren't very clearly drawn. I was wandering aimlessly, trying whatever there was to try, and becoming more and more aware that there was an emptiness in me I couldn't seem to fill.

When I moved into the car, my possessions consisted of a backpack larger than the last one I'd been living out of, and a fully grown German Shepherd. Tuesday was very well-trained

Nights in the Closet

with hand signals and was an excellent watchdog. She would do anything I asked of her.

We lived in this car for a couple of months. The police would tap on the windows at least two or three times a week and demand that the car be moved because there was no overnight parking allowed. We washed up in public bathrooms and ate whenever we could. Many times it wasn't nearly enough, but eating every day was the main goal.

I was nineteen at this point, but I looked fourteen, which made it extremely hard to find a job. Not having an address and having a fully-grown dog were other details of my circumstances that kept us foraging for food on a daily basis. When the album collection ran out and we were too thin to make the necessary weight for donating plasma, it was typical for Linda and me to manage only a dollar or two a day for all of us to eat on. We would usually go to Burger King to get a Whopper to cut in half. It was the biggest bang for our buck. The only problem was that I had to split my half with my dog. On better days we could get five tacos for two dollars and eat our fill. Tuesday would scrounge the trash cans and eat what we couldn't. Then at five o'clock we would head to a nearby bar in hopes that someone would buy us a drink and feed us some food.

My car mate was in hard times but decided that she didn't want to compound her bad luck any longer by being responsible for me and my dog. One night without any warning, I got booted out of the car into the parking lot of a Denny's restaurant. Linda was ready to move on and didn't want any extra baggage. I stood in the parking lot with my backpack and my dog who was, by the way, pregnant and ready to give birth any day. I leaned on the trunk of an old Mercedes and looked up at the stars. They seemed to mock me. They never changed. No matter if I was hungry or fed, loved or unloved, lonely, or drunk; they stayed the same, looking down from afar, unsympathetic to me or my life.

I surveyed my surroundings in the darkness, trying to find somewhere to sleep for the night. I remembered having once stopped at a small apartment across the street with one of my friends. Her mother lived there. It was a while ago but, what the heck, I decided to go knock on the door and ask if I could spend the night. I stood on a single step that served as the entrance, knocked, and waited. I knocked again, harder this time, and heard movement inside. The woman cussed as she struggled to open the door. An obviously unhappy woman in a housecoat and slippers stared down at me for a moment, as if she were trying to focus.

I spoke up quickly before she could slam the door. "Hi, I was here with your daughter once. You told me that I was welcome to come back. Well, here I am. I was waiting for a friend to pick me up and take me to Phoenix, but she didn't show up, and I am stuck here. I was wondering if I could sleep the night here, until I can get a hold of my friend."

The woman looked at me like I had three heads! "I don't have any room here! This is just a one room apartment!" Though her words were hard and uncaring, I sensed a weakness in her. Maybe she wondered about her own daughter and where she might have been sleeping that night. She was clearly drunk and didn't want to be bothered.

But, maybe because of her own regrets, or just a moment of compassion, she changed her mind. "You can come in, but I really don't have any place for you to sleep. You can sleep in the closet if you can fit. You'll have to put your stuff and your dog in there with you. I don't want to trip over anything if I have to get up in the night. You'll have to be out when I go to work in the morning." She opened the door and immediately ushered me into the coat closet. I shoved my way in and turned on the light by a string hanging from the center of the ceiling. I parted the coats and clothes that were hanging in my face and shut the door. I couldn't imagine how I was going to do this, but I was off the street and was determined to make it work.

I put my backpack at one end of the closet where I imagined my head would go, then I bent down and started to stack the shoes that were on the floor into a pile at the other end. When there was enough floor space to sit down I settled into the spot and put my dog between my legs. Tuesday put her head on my leg and settled in with a grunt and a sigh. I leaned against my backpack and let out a sigh of my own. I couldn't believe that I was in a stranger's closet with everything I owned and a pregnant German Shepherd!

I knew that tomorrow would bring enough trouble of its own, so I tried to relax and drift off to sleep. I don't know how, but Tuesday and I both managed to sleep most of the night. At one point the sound of snoring was coming through the wall but strangely enough, it was a comfort to have another person close by.

We hadn't had anything to eat, and I sure could have used the bathroom. I tried not to dwell on it too much, but I couldn't help but to trace my present circumstance back to my dysfunctional beginnings and, of course, the President Director. When my thoughts got that far I remembered the look on Charlotte's face the last time I saw her. The President Director's accusing words came flooding back and the overwhelming feelings of guilt and shame flooded every cell of my being. I played the horrific scene over and over in my mind. I couldn't shut it off!

Then I played back every scene of his sneaky pursuits to catch me alone and off guard.

Finally, exhausted and extremely sad, I snuggled closer to my dog and willed myself back to sleep. The rest of the night was fitful, with dreams of the things that were eating me from the inside out. Things I couldn't do anything about.

The morning came with the woman opening the closet door and informing me that it was time to leave. I gathered up my stuff and went straight out the door, saying my thanks as the door was shutting behind me.

After finding a good patch of grass for Tuesday to relieve herself, I decided to go into Denny's. Tuesday would stay without complaint under a small tree by the parking lot and guard my backpack. I shook the crampy feeling out of my legs and raked my fingers through my hair, trying my best not to look like I had just crawled out of a closet. I grabbed my toothbrush from my backpack and crossed the street to Denny's.

The smell of food made my head spin. I blended in with some people at the food bar and took a warm plate from the stack. I chose some sausages and two plain pancakes. I didn't have time to mess with butter and syrup, the way I really liked them. I casually followed the person in front of me from the food bar to a table. I slid into the booth right behind them and shoved half of the food in my mouth as fast as I could. I tucked the rest of the food in a napkin and quickly moved toward the bathroom.

As soon as I was inside I rolled the pancake and sausage in a paper towel and put them in my pocket. I used the facilities and quickly ran my toothbrush over my teeth, rinsed, and was ready to go. I always tried to maintain a clean appearance so I could blend in with the crowd in restaurants, especially those with food bars! Before anyone had the chance to notice me, I could get something in my stomach and be on my way.

I opened the door of the bathroom a little and looked out into the restaurant. Everything looked normal. I walked out with the front door in sight and walked as casually as possible towards it. I looked over to the table where I left my plate and noticed that a couple of dirty plates had been stacked there by other people. Mission accomplished! I had blended in just fine. I didn't take time to taste the food I had eaten, but at least I knew that my stomach wouldn't hurt from hunger for a few hours.

I went back out to the parking lot and found Tuesday faithfully guarding my stuff where I had left her. I fed her the sausages and smashed pancake I had hidden in my pocket. She wolfed it down then sniffed my pocket for more. "Not now girl." I said as I scratched behind her ears.

I ended up staying in the closet a few nights. Tuesday and I didn't wander too far from the Denny's. If anyone had caught onto me and my schemes, they weren't doing anything about it. I chose the busiest times of the day to make my move, so I was coming in with different crews. For the few days I was there, no one seemed to notice.

Tuesday was clearly getting ready to have her puppies, and I tried to get her to nest under a boat behind the woman's apartment. Tuesday wasn't very happy with my suggestion, and when all was said and done, she delivered her puppies in the closet! Goodness, of course there had been no stopping it once it started, and the woman was a drunken irritation as each pup came out. In all, thirteen were born! Only two showed any signs of life. By the end of the night, all thirteen puppies were dead, and Tuesday was an emaciated mess! I guessed that the stress of not having enough food and water, along with our living conditions, was just too much. Not to mention that she may have gotten something in the trash bins to put her pregnancy at risk. I couldn't imagine how to deal with puppies in our situation, but the fact that they all died was very much a heartbreak for both of us. As each puppy was determined to be lifeless, the woman wrapped it in a paper towel and disposed of it in her big silver trash can outside. When it was obvious that the labor was over, the woman had me clean the closet, and then she booted us out!

Tuesday was too weak to walk, so I took her out back and crawled under the boat with her and held her while she slept in my arms. I gave her water out of a paper cup and fed her a small amount of food I had in my pocket from Denny's.

Chapter 6

Time for a Cool Change

The next morning Tuesday was doing quite a bit better, but I knew she needed more rest. I didn't want to leave her outside by herself while I went into Denny's, so we continued to rest under the boat until it was closer to happy hour. After brushing off the dried grass that was all over us and trying to look normal, we headed in the direction of the bar, about a mile away. We were halfway there when a red station wagon drove up beside me.

The driver was a woman, shouting out the window, "Karen, Karen! Hey, it's Toni." She pulled over and shouted my name again. I knew this woman a couple of years previously, and the last thing I had heard was that she had gone off to the Army. "Hey Toni, how are you doing? I thought you were in the Army." "I was, but I just got out! "I'm heading out to the Florida Keys tomorrow. What are you doing? Where are you going?"

I didn't want to tell her what I was doing or where I was going! I gave her some deflective answers, without telling her anything. "Why don't you go with me to Florida! Come on, it will be fun! Are you up for a road trip?"

I didn't know what to say or do. Just then a song came on the radio: "It's Time for a Cool Change." As the song repeated the phrase over and over, I made my decision to go. I told Toni that my dog had just had puppies and was not feeling well after losing every single one. She assured me that we could all stay at her apartment and rest for the night then head out early in the morning after she turned her keys into the office and got her deposit back. I told her that I really didn't have any money for traveling, and she said that it didn't matter because she had plenty of cash for the both of us. With the prospect of dinner and a place for Tuesday to get her legs back under her, we got in the car and took off.

Things went just as planned. When we got to Toni's apartment there was a soft couch to sit on, and she even put a bowl of water on the floor and made some scrambled eggs for Tuesday to eat. After a hot shower and a change of clothes, I could pretend that I hadn't just crawled out of a closet or up from under a stored boat. We left the next morning on the two-day trip to the Florida Keys.

Tuesday did not recover very quickly from having the puppies. She was weak and began throwing up as the day went on. I was using my clothing from my backpack to catch the mess, then I would throw them away when we got to a gas station. I didn't know what to do for her except hold her head in my lap and stroke her fur in a comforting way. We spent our first night in Texas in the back of the station wagon. It was very cold. Toni had an Army regulation sleeping bag and I had an old JC Penny nylon sleeping bag just big enough for one person. I was absolutely freezing and could not go to sleep. Toni was sound asleep and oblivious to the needs of me and my sick dog. I looked out the window into the dark starry night and again tried to sum up the value of life. Struggle, struggle, struggle! Was there anything else? What was the purpose of life anyway?

Time for a Cool Change

Once when I was in a grocery store, I saw a woman shopping with her kids; her cart was full, and every time the kids begged for something special, she'd put it in the cart for them. All I could think about was how she would get to take it all home and wouldn't have to split it in half because there wasn't enough. How could that woman or anyone else know that someone right next to them might be pretending to gather food in their cart, just to feel normal, only to then leave it abandoned and walk out of the store still hungry? No one had a clue. The world just went on, and I felt like an outsider looking in.

The stars were mocking me again this night as I looked up at the familiar sky. If there was a god up there, was this all just a game? As I understood it, if you sinned you would go to Hell, if you believed in God. I could not continue down that road of thinking since I knew stealing was a sin; not to mention my many other secrets! It was better for me to believe that he didn't exist and that sometimes life just didn't happen in our favor.

Toni didn't know anything about my circumstances. I don't remember what I told her, but it most assuredly was a lie. I reasoned with myself that I didn't have to tell her! I had no obligation to tell anybody anything. I decided right then that from that point on, I was going to try and be the best person I could be. I would learn what I could, find work where I could, and work hard. I would try my best to live a better life.

Just then I remembered something Toni had told me. She said that the rock and roll group, Three Dog Night, got their name from Australian hunters who would sleep with their dogs on cold nights, the coldest being called a "three dog night."

I was really worried about Tuesday. I was afraid she would die, and then what would I do? She was so thin, and she had been throwing up all day. Maybe she had an infection inside or something. I decided to do what the Australian hunters did; I unzipped my sleeping bag and shoved her in. Under normal conditions she would have protested but she was shivering and easily complied with my efforts to zip the bag around the two of us. We both slept deeply the rest of the night, comforted by each other's company and warmth. We woke up in the morning, feeling rested and all around better. Toni bought Tuesday a small bag of dog food and I hand fed her and gave her water little by little all day as we continued our trip. By the time we arrived in Florida, Tuesday was on her way to getting back to normal.

We were headed to Key Largo, the first and largest of the Florida Keys, where Toni's father and brother lived. The Keys, a chain of tropical islands, started at the southern end of Florida and went south 125 miles to Key West, the southernmost tip of the United States.

Florida was a wonderful and welcome change. The days and nights alike were warm and comfortable. Toni's plan was to stay with her dad. The only catch was that she hadn't said anything about bringing a friend, or a dog for that matter!

U.S. Highway 1 is the main road in and out of the Keys and runs from Miami the whole way to Key West. The islands are connected by 42 bridges. The location of the Islands and businesses on US 1 are referenced by their mile marker and bridges. It is 18 miles down the stretch from the mainland, then Key Largo is the first Key at Marker 107. Lower Matecumbe Key is a little less than halfway at Marker 75 and is connected by a seven-mile-long bridge. The Gulf of Mexico is on the west side of the road and the Atlantic Ocean is on the East side.

As we were getting close to the 18-mile stretch Toni said that she was nervous about showing up with Tuesday and me without clearing it with her dad. We agreed that I could manage on my own, so she dropped me off in Homestead, right before the stretch to the Keys. I was used to making do, finding food or going hungry, and looking for a place to sleep. I wandered around for a few days then finally hitchhiked my way down to Key Largo.

It wasn't hard to find the water's edge when I got to the Keys; everywhere you looked there was water! I got dropped off at a restaurant and bar called The Caribbean Club. There was some kind of event going on, and the place was packed with people, inside and out. There was a guy on the beach standing behind a big grill and condiment stand with a sign that read, "Free hot dogs," so it was obviously the right place for me! I got a hot dog for myself and Tuesday and found a place to sit down and experience the festivities. It turned out to be a speedboat racing event, which was very exciting for me because I had never seen anything like it! With no place to go and no schedule to keep, I stayed the rest of the day enjoying live music and free food.

When the sun started to slip below the horizon, the sky exploded with beautiful color, and I was mesmerized by the beauty. Yes, it was past time for a cool change, and this seemed like the perfect place to be. I realized that it was also time for me to grow up and do my best to be my best! Even though there were times that I would be overcome for days from nightmares about the situation I left behind in Pennsylvania, it was time for me to stop being a victim and move on with my life. I could be anything that I wanted to be. This was a chance to start with a clean slate. No one needed to know that less than a week ago I had crawled out of a closet. From now on, I was the master of my future. I was taking charge.

Well after the sun went down, Tuesday and I crossed the road and walked south on the bike path. After about two miles

I found the perfect place for us to spend the night: an old, covered wagon in the parking lot of a BBQ restaurant, obviously for the purpose of advertising. There were only a couple of cars left in the lot, so when the coast was clear, Tuesday and I climbed in and settled down for the night. It was kind of fun to imagine the pioneers going west and living out of wagons like this. As the restaurant closed for the night and the last of the cars pulled out of the lot, I felt relieved that we could finally relax and go to sleep.

The next morning, just after sunrise, we climbed down from the wagon and went across the road to Pennekamp state park. I was grateful that there was a public bathroom on the beach. After freshening up, Tuesday and I wandered down to the water. I took off my shoes and sunk my toes in the sand. The sound of the seagulls was therapeutic, and the sun was medicine to my mind, body, and soul. Tuesday enjoyed the sun and water just as much as I did. We drank water from the bathroom, and I rinsed off clothes and all in the outside shower. I even got some soap from the sink and rubbed it into my hair and clothes. Between the sun and the soft breeze, it was no time at all before my clothes were dry. After getting situated, I decided it was time to call Toni and see if I could join up with her again.

Toni's dad didn't have room for us in his small place, so instead I went to live in an apartment below her brother's house at Marker 107. It turned out that he was the manager of Fat Boy's BBQ, where I had stayed in the covered wagon! That was a secret that I decided to keep to myself! I began working at Fat Boy's, learning food prep, and waiting on tables. I loved to work, and by that time I could pretty much say that my life of going hungry and without a home was behind me.

Time for a Cool Change

Chapter 7

Hundreds of Girls

I got my first checking account, and eventually bought my first car. When it became clear that I didn't want to spend from sunup till sundown working inside the restaurant, I sought out a different job. With my heavy equipment experience, I got hired by Monroe County Public Works as a heavy equipment operator. I was the first woman ever hired by the county as an equipment operator. I got hired because the cocky old supervisor wanted to tick off the men who weren't pulling their weight on the job.

In spite of the disadvantage of being a pawn, with time, I earned respect among the men as a good operator. I really wasn't into women's liberation specifically, just a woman tired of working for minimum wage and willing to think outside of the box. This job paid twice as much as any other job I knew of, and I liked it most of the time. The boss liked me because I was easy on the equipment, unlike some of the men who liked to horse around. The only problem was that operating equipment wasn't something I could see myself doing as I got older. After four years working that job I decided it was time to set a plan in motion to get into the medical field.

As a child I was always nursing dolls, pets, and stray animals. As I grew older I still always had the first aid kit on hand and was willing to take control of any potential medical emergency situations. I could find solutions and treatments for things like broken fingers, sprains, strains, bee stings, cuts, and lacerations. It was something that I was a natural at. I decided I might as well learn how to do it properly and make money at it. But first I needed to become a High School equivalent.

I went to the Key Largo Library and studied basic Math, English, and History. After getting my GED diploma, I went to the Red Cross and took every course they offered to the public. In the end I was a First Responder and Red Cross certified CPR and First Aid Instructor.

In the Fall of 1984 I took the entrance exam to Valencia Community College, was accepted into the Respiratory Therapy program, and moved to Orlando. I rented a house, found a roommate, and got a job delivering pizza to pay my tuition and household expenses. I didn't know anything about grants, I thought that I had to figure out how to pay my own way, so I only took as many classes as I could afford at a time. My boss gave me permission to add a little entrepreneurial twist to my delivery job. I hired two boys to ride around town in the back of my truck for a couple of hours on Thursday evenings, jumping out at apartment complexes to put coupons on every door, and on cars in grocery store parking lots. I put my initials on the back of the coupons. Every order that came in with my initials on the coupon was given to me to deliver, and at the end of the week the boys got paid a quarter for every one. It worked out perfectly! I made enough money to pay for everything I needed, and the boys got a little cash in their pockets

My first day of college classes was surreal. As I walked into my auditorium class I felt like I was going to disappear with anxiety. I tried to convince myself that I belonged there as much as anyone. I pushed down my thoughts that people were staring at me and judging everything about me. I didn't want to do anything to embarrass myself, so I chose a seat in the back and tried to be as invisible as possible. I listened intently and took notes on everything the professor said.

I was so afraid of failing that I did every bit of extra credit work in all of my classes.

One afternoon right after class I was approached by a young man from Iran. "My name is Hassain, and I would like to talk to you," he said in a heavy middle eastern accent. He sat next to me in English 101, so when he suggested that we go have lunch together, I accepted.

In a small Italian restaurant over a salad and a plate of spaghetti, he started his talk.

"My father, my uncle, and I have been watching you for over a year. You are a very intelligent girl." He lifted his chin and spoke, as a matter of fact, "We have chosen you over hundreds of girls to be my wife."

I laughed and gasped at the same time, causing me to choke on my salad! Hassain jumped to his feet from across the table and offered me his napkin. "Your wife?" I asked, trying to regain control of my lunch.

"Yes," he said. "You and I can be surgeons together. My father will pay you, and he will pay for your university. Does this sound like a good offer to you?"

"You don't even know me!" I said, still in shock.

"I do know you. We have been watching you, and you have very good grades. We have chosen you over hundreds of girls."

I laughed a little to myself. Good grades! My goodness, this guy didn't know anything! I did get good grades, but I worked harder than anyone for them! He didn't know that I was a ninth grade dropout and that I had to study extra hard to get an A- or a B because I had fried important brain cells on drugs a few years earlier. He only ever saw my English papers! I had to pay to have them proofread because my spelling, punctuation, and grammar were so bad. I wrote some good papers, but they weren't the least bit acceptable until they were edited! He didn't know I had to study using color codes so I could remember things. My biggest problem was that without ever having taken algebra, chemistry, or biology in high school, it was impossible to understand my respiratory therapy classes. I found myself back in the library and hired a tutor so that I could stay two weeks ahead in order to understand how to do my assignments. What a joke! However, I decided to let this play out and see what else he had to say.

He continued as though I had asked him to. "My father will pay you a quarter of a million dollars if you agree to marry me. In addition, he will pay for your university, and we can have a practice together."

I cleared my throat and raised my brows as I asked, "Excuse me, you said that your dad will pay me $250,000!"

"Ah, yes, he is a very wealthy man. He and my uncle own oil fields in my country."

"Why don't you wait until you find a girl that you fall in love with?" I asked.

He blushed deeply and answered, "I am from the country of Iran. There are no good medical schools there. I want to be a heart surgeon, but I cannot get into the university in America unless I marry an American. I have applied in Germany, but there is a waiting list of three years. I do not want to wait because

I am young and very intelligent. I want to be a surgeon while I am young."

"I understand your position, but I am not sure that you have picked the right girl."

"My father, my uncle, and I have picked you out of hundreds of girls," he said.

Again, I laughed a little. "Yes, I know. You've said that already."

"My father will pay you a quarter of a million dollars, and we will pay for your university." He said this as if it were the only thing to consider!

"So, this is a business arrangement right? I mean, you're just looking to buy a wife on paper. You're not expecting us to fall in love and have babies, right?"

"Ah, yes, a business arrangement. We will have to get an apartment together so that immigration doesn't disagree. I have to prove that I am married to an American. You will have to answer questions about our life together. We will pay you a quarter of a million dollars."

" Yes, you've said that several times. When do you need my answer?"

"Of course you will say yes, as soon as possible!" He said with excitement of the possibility.

I pinched myself under the table to see if this was really happening. Oh my goodness, this was weird! Of all people, why on earth would he, or anyone else for that matter, pick me, over hundreds of girls? My thoughts went back to all the days that I didn't get enough to eat and the many nights with no place to sleep.

I have been in a lot of situations in my life. Why would this be any harder than what I had been through already! I was about ready for some of the good life. I loved medicine. Even if I couldn't make it through medical school, he would have his paper wife and I would have a hand up that could change my life forever.

The next few months were interesting indeed. I told my friends and family about Hassain, and they all treated it like a joke. My brother joked that after this guy got to know me, he would most likely take me back to his country and trade me for a camel! They didn't believe that I would actually marry a foreigner for money.

Although I couldn't imagine the reality of it myself, I accepted Hassain's business deal. We applied for a marriage license and started apartment hunting.

My life on campus changed immediately. Every time I turned a corner Hassain was there to greet me. It didn't take long to discover that whatever his father and uncle had in mind, he was determined to marry for love. I kept reminding him that this was a business deal and that I had no intentions of entertaining his fantasy of falling in love.

Multiple times, after my classes, I would go to the parking lot and find him sitting on the hood of my little Isuzu pickup waiting for me. Although I had never met his father or uncle, Hassain was constantly giving me gifts: a watch, a necklace, or perfume. I gave back the gifts each time, to make my point that I was not interested in a romantic relationship. However, the next day he would be there again, trying to offer me another token of his love.

As the end of a semester was approaching I started to get cold feet about this whole business deal. Hassain had grown anxious in his plan to make me fall for him. Though he didn't cross major boundaries, he was becoming more and more persistent. So far I had managed to avoid having him meet my friends and family. I never gave him my address or invited him to my house. I can't be sure that he didn't follow me, but it didn't seem like he had. He seemed like a good guy, but nonetheless, after my experience with the President Director, I wasn't the least bit interested in a relationship with any man. The fact that he was trying to force what was not coming naturally scared me.

At the end of the semester, I withdrew from all my classes, went home, packed all of my belongings on a Friday afternoon and drove back to the Keys! I felt bad about leaving Hassain without an explanation or a goodbye, but his insistence had caused me to panic, so I ran.

Chapter 8

The Night I Got Sick

I had already been contemplating getting out of Respiratory Therapy. Through more exposure to medical career options, I realized I was far more interested in Emergency Medicine. Although I had done it plenty of times at the rehab, I was not thinking that my calling was to siphon mucus from diseased lungs or deal with other body fluids that made my own stomach do flips. I could calmly deal with broken bones, gashes, and lacerations. I stayed calm in emergency situations and was even able to delegate assisted help as I assessed an entire emergency scene. If I was going to set myself up for a job I liked, it wasn't going to inevitably include a puke bucket!

After getting settled back in at Key Largo, I enrolled in the Emergency Medical Technician courses through Dade County Community College. I was neck and neck with another student, earning the top grades of the class. I loved working in emergency medicine, and I was good at it. I wasn't a great test taker so unfortunately usually ended up with an A- which put me one step behind my competition. I graduated second place in my EMT class.

However, the only position within the Ambulance Corps was with a volunteer service. I found a nice three-bedroom house with a fenced-in yard for a great price, but I needed a paying job.

When I was in Phoenix, for a short while, I worked as an animal handler and trainer at a guard dog service. Let's just say I may have exaggerated my qualifications a little during my interview for the animal shelter. But as it turned out, Monroe County needed to hire an officer immediately, so I got the job.

I worked at the Island Animal Shelter as an animal control supervisor. I supervised a small staff of officers and a couple of animal handlers. I worked at the animal shelter during the day and was on call with the ambulance service all night.

The county provided management courses for me and sent me to conferences and classes, which resulted in a class A pharmacy license for the purpose of medicating sick animals at the shelter. Things were going really well for me, except for the secrets of my past that would sneak up on me in my dreams… and then, of course, the night I got sick….

I took my pulse and tried to calm myself down. I was experiencing an incredible pain in my chest. As an EMT, I should have known what to do. My heart was racing, and my palms were sweating. I took a deep breath through my nose, held it for a few seconds and exhaled slowly, the way that I had instructed my patients to do hundreds of times.

I sat up straight and raked my fingers through my hair. I was hoping that I could just shake this thing off, but the pain was real, and I could not convince myself otherwise.

I made it to the kitchen table and into a chair. I felt like I was having a heart attack, but there were some factors missing from the diagnosis. I looked at the phone and thought about calling for help. I knew I should, but how in the world was I going to call the ambulance crew that I worked with to come and take me to the hospital? It was a fact that a large percentage of people who were taken to the emergency room were sent home to take a Tylenol and call their doctor in the morning. I didn't want to add to those statistics! I reasoned with myself that if I was sent out on an ambulance run tonight, then I would go get checked out in the emergency room.

I probably overreacted and allowed myself to suffer an anxiety attack when I first felt the pain. It was probably just a bad case of indigestion from eating too fast; everyone ate too fast when they were on call. You never knew if you would get to finish your meal, so you just wolfed it down and suffered the consequences later.

I always carried Tums in the pocket of my jumpsuit, like most of the other medics. I quickly chewed up four tablets hoping they would be a miracle answer to my situation. With my hand still to my chest I got up and went over to the refrigerator. I opened the door and took out a pitcher of cold water. Not wanting to take the time to get a glass, I drank right out of the pitcher. When I was putting it back my arm suddenly felt weak, and the pitcher slipped from my hand and crashed to the floor. The glass broke and water went everywhere. I simply could not deal with it at that moment, so I left it there and made my way into the living room.

If it were anyone else in this situation, I would advise them to immediately call the ambulance for help; however, I couldn't do it. I could not submit to the humiliation of having my coworkers come to rescue me. So I laid on the couch trying to convince myself that I would still be alive in the morning.

I eventually fell asleep still dressed in my jumpsuit and didn't wake up until 7:30 the next morning. At my first moment of consciousness I jolted awake, disoriented, and experiencing a new wave of pain. Clutching my chest, I tried to sit up to evaluate the situation. In an effort to deny the disabling pain, I tried to stand up, but after realizing there was no way I could function normally, I called in sick at my day job and made a doctor appointment for later in the day.

When this sickness came on me I had been back in the Keys a little more than two years. I had just spent those two years working with the district attorney to expose embezzlement by the organization that leased the animal shelter from the county. There had been a couple of older ladies in there who were not operating above board. When it was tipped off, the county asked me to document the proof.

The organization claimed to never put an animal to sleep. They begged the public for donations to save the animals, and people would give generously.

In truth, the ladies would ration the food donations, and it was suspected that they were pocketing the money that was donated. They covered themselves by using supplemental money that was being provided by the county.

They had numerous animals put to sleep after promising that they would be adopted out (for an appropriate donation given by the do-gooders who brought the animals to the shelter).

I was the officer on staff who maintained a class A pharmacy license for the purpose of medicating sick animals and administering lethal medicine for euthanasia. The animal organization never put the animals to sleep, themselves, but they ordered it done 10 to 15 times a week. It was the part of the job that I hated, and most of all I detested these ladies that dripped with promise as long as the cash was put in their hand! I would often load up my truck with animals to be euthanized and take them to another shelter to be adopted without the organization knowing about it.

After two years of documentation, showing incident after incident of mishandling donations and representing their business affairs falsely to the public, law enforcement moved in and shut the shelter down, charging the workers with embezzlement and fraudulent activities.

It had been three months since the shutdown. Having been appointed by the county administrator to serve as supervisor over the new shelter operations, I eagerly got things above board and operational within the first thirty days. I liked working with the local veterinarians and learning how to treat the animals. They would even call me to sit in on surgery when they had an interesting case. It all gave me the opportunity to increase many skills that my ambulance partners didn't have yet. The job was just a steppingstone. I expected to eventually work with a paid ambulance corps.

For now I was here, and I loved both of my jobs. At this point things were running smoothly enough at the shelter, and I was on a volunteer schedule with the ambulance corps. I should have no trouble taking a little time off to let this sickness, or whatever it was, pass.

After being seen by the doctor, I buttoned my shirt and went out of the examining room and into his consultation room. Doctor Whiting motioned for me to have a seat. "Do you think that you have been under any particular stress lately?" he asked.

"No more than usual, even though I catch wild animals by day and work on the ambulance team by night!" I laughed because it sounded absurd to me as I heard myself say it! I tried to answer honestly even though it was funny. "No, really, I love my jobs and seem to do them without any particular trouble." I wanted to resolve this quickly and get back to work!

Doctor Whiting was writing in my file as he continued. "I can't really find anything wrong with you. Your EKG seems to be normal. I think that you should take a few days off work and do something fun and relaxing. You are probably working too hard. In the meantime massage your shoulders and use some moist heat where you are having the pain and drink plenty of water. You are definitely a little dehydrated. If you don't see any improvements within two weeks, call for another appointment."

I got into my little pickup truck and backed out of the parking lot. I was glad that I hadn't called the ambulance last night! Whatever this thing was, at least it wasn't going to kill me!

The Night I Got Sick

Chapter 9

My Salvation Story

When I got home I made some phone calls and arranged a week off from both jobs. I gathered my heating pad, a cold drink, a joint, and the TV control before settling down on the couch. I lit the joint and with no responsibilities to think about. allowed myself to smoke more than half of it.

At first I welcomed the opportunity to just zone out and get stoned. However, the marijuana euphoria did not help the pain at all. As a matter of fact, if anything, it made it worse because I didn't have a clear mind to diagnose myself. The pain was not going away. I was in misery, and after burying my head in a pillow I gave in to the only comfort available and cried myself to sleep.

After a few days, I was embarrassed to tell my ambulance friends that this thing wasn't going away on its own, although the doctor basically gave me a clean bill of health.

I had regained a better long distance relationship with my parents; we had all accepted that life needed to go on. We didn't talk about my time at the rehab. I never told them about my struggles with homelessness, and they never knew about the President Director.

The year I had gone into the rehab, my mother was able to identify and recover from her dependence on prescription narcotics, and a few years earlier their move to Florida had served as my parents' own new start. I kept in better touch, but concerning this situation, I didn't want to worry them over nothing. I expected this problem to work itself out before long.

However, after just three days of suffering at home, I was back at the doctor's office. When Dr. Whiting saw me standing at the counter with a look of pain across my face he came over to speak to me. "How are you doing, Karen"? he asked.

"Well, I'm no better." I explained. "As a matter of fact, I think I'm worse. I can't figure it out, but I have this pain that seems to move from my chest to my back and down my arm. The strangest thing is that I cannot lift up my feet when I walk. I shuffle my feet because I can't pick them up!"

The doctor gave the desk nurse directions to take me back to a room.

An hour later I was leaving for home with orders to see a cardiologist. The earliest appointment available was in four days, so in the meantime I holed up in my house and tried to survive.

Because of my fear of death, that night I got to thinking about God. I remembered back to when I was a child attending church with my family. The preacher had spent himself on yet another soul-wrenching sermon on hell fire and damnation. "The end of the world is coming, and only a precious few will get into heaven!" Those were his words. He told the congregation over and over that only those of their particular church affiliation would pass through the narrow gates of heaven.

I remembered, as a child, looking around at the tiny church. Our number had grown to about a hundred, but surely heaven was bigger and God more forgiving than to only allow these few people into heaven! I couldn't help but imagine all the poor souls who would burn in the fires of hell.

Out of emotional and physical exhaustion, I fell asleep around midnight and dreamt, as I had recently been doing, that the end of the world had come; and I was lost in the middle of the destruction...

Smoke rose up from the earth. The ground cracked and shifted out of place like a planet that was about to self-destruct. I was in a panic to get somewhere, maybe home, but where was home? Earth looked like a dark, alien-invaded planet from a science fiction movie. The stench of sulfur seeped up from the lacerated soil, and all other signs of life were gone.

Alone and afraid, I cried out into the darkness. But even my own voice didn't come back to me. It went out, into what seemed like infinite darkness and was lost, along with everything else that was familiar. As I jumped from crag to mound, I was transported somehow into my own neighborhood. The danger seemed less imminent there. There were no people around, and the earth hadn't yet started to convulse. I walked down the middle of the street past the neighbor's house, looking to see anyone. Just another living, breathing person.

As the address on our mailbox came into view, I ran into the driveway and jumped inside my family's car. Though there was no one to be seen, I felt a presence.

I needed some time to look around and scout the house to see if it was safe. From my hiding place on the floor behind the driver's seat, I noticed several zipper baggies stapled to the sun visors. I reached between the seats and ripped them from their place.

The baggies held personal effects that belonged to my family. My dad's watch, my mother's ring, my brother's pocketknife, and my sister's doll.

Then, out of the corner of my eye, I saw a movement in the house! My heart quickened as I thought it might be my father. But what was his watch doing in the car, and where was everyone else?

Then I saw through the window that the movement was a stranger, looting the house!

Ignoring the danger, I ran towards the house, my blood pumping hot within my veins. I would demand to know where my family was, and I would throw the intruder out by the power of my own adrenaline!

I flung the door open, and the man turned around. His eyes were coal black as he laughed right in my face, giving evidence that evil had moved in, and my family had been kicked out!

I screamed and woke myself up. I was in incredible pain, and the effects of this dream invaded every cell of my body, as well.

I couldn't figure out why I kept having these dreams, anyway. As far as God and all the Heaven and Hell business went, well, I supposed that the ability to find God was something that you got from your parents, and I hadn't. Or maybe God chose certain people and showed himself to them so they could believe, and I just wasn't worthy. Whatever! I had tried God, and it didn't work out for me. I tried with all my heart at times, and it only lasted two weeks at the most.

No, God was on the shelf, and this sickness and these dreams only justified my position. If I had to live in fear of God, then I would just avoid him.

"Hi there. Hey, are you OK?" I opened my eyes to a young man rapping on my truck window. I tried to focus as I rolled down the window just enough to talk to him.

"Yeah, I'm fine," I replied.

The man raised his voice to be heard over the sound of a truck passing on U.S. Highway 1, behind us. "You've been here for quite a while. You probably ought to go home. Do you live around here?" the man asked in a patronizing tone.

"Yea, I live just around the corner. I came over here to get some stuff from the store." The reason I was there was coming back to me just as the words were coming out of my mouth.

"I guess you had a heck of a night last night, huh?" He laughed a little to himself.

"No, I just don't feel good right now. Don't worry, I'm going." The young man backed away from my truck shaking his head as I started the engine and put the truck in gear.

How long had I been there anyway? I remembered going to the Circle K store to get something to eat. There wasn't anything left in the house, so I had decided to venture out to get some lunch meat.

I reached over to the seat next to me and felt inside the brown paper bag with the lunch meat in it. It was room temperature. No telling how long I had been asleep in my truck. The sun was hot, and I was incredibly thirsty. I hoped that the lunch meat was still good. It was getting more and more difficult to go out and actually make it to where I was going, and then back home again. Many times I would just be incredibly tired or in pain and have to pull over. I would rest my head on the window of my truck and wake up hours later. Once I didn't wake up until the next day!

The Florida Keys is a very transient place, and most people don't think anything about someone asleep in their car. They just figured it was some poor soul who had partied too hardy the night before. I wished that was all I had to worry about!

I went to the cardiologist and wore a monitor for a week. The results were inconclusive. From there I was referred to a neurologist. I couldn't get in for two weeks, and it would cost $200 just to walk through the door! I had already spent $200 to see the cardiologist. It was a good thing that I was single and was able to save a good amount of my paycheck each week; I had around $800 in my account. The insurance company would reimburse me, but that would take some time, so for now I had to lay out the cash. At this point I didn't care how much it would cost! I just wanted this thing to end!

Each night I was afraid that I would die in my sleep, yet each morning I woke up to face another day. I still hadn't told my family what was going on. What good would that do anyway? Yes, they would be there for me, but I wasn't sure I wanted that. I left home at age thirteen because of uncontrollable circumstances and maintained a long-distance relationship with my mom and dad since then. My mother would want to take over my whole life if she knew how sick I had become. Even in this distressful state I realized that I had too many issues in my life that my mother wouldn't approve of, and I did not welcome the effort of having to cover up anything, especially now!

I got out of the truck and sighed heavily as I approached the flight of steps to my house. I lived in a stilt home on a canal in Lower Matecumbe Key. It was a very quiet island with a population of about 1,200. Most people were just passing through on their way to Key West. This was called paradise! I could wake up in the morning and have coffee on the terrace in my PJs, while fishing for fresh yellowtail over the banister. This morning however, I sat down on a step halfway up to catch my breath and regain my strength.

There were church bells ringing, coming from a little church across the canal. They could be heard on the whole island, as small as it was. I rested my head against the side of the house and let the warm sun bake my face. Though I didn't think much of church music, I found the bells comforting.

As the music ended I fought to maintain consciousness, knowing that I had to make it inside to get a drink before long. I was parched, and the sun was getting hotter as the day wore on.

From my usual spot on the couch, I stretched for the ringing phone that had somehow gotten knocked off the coffee table and was in the middle of the floor. I swore as the stretch caused a stabbing pain.

"Hi, Karen? This is Trisha. I heard that you were sick, and I just thought I'd call to check on you."

I ran the name Trisha through my memory banks until I came up with a face. "Yeah, hi, how are you doing?"

"The question is, how are you doing? Where have you been? I haven't seen you at a meeting in a while."

"Yeah, well, I've been kind of sick." Trisha was my upline in Amway. She was a very likable person, but a Christian. And since I was not, we were more acquaintances than friends.

"So what do the doctors say is wrong with you Karen? Are you okay?"

I really didn't want everyone to know that I was so sick, especially since I wasn't getting better! However, it was nice to have someone care. "Well, they don't know. I have a pain that seems to move around from my chest to my back and we can't figure out what it is. I'm sure it will eventually go away," I half-explained.

My Salvation Story

"I know that you have been spending a lot of time alone. You are probably a little scared, and I just want you to know that I am here for you."

There was an uncomfortable silence that followed. I liked Trisha but really did not know her that well. "Thanks," was all I could think to say.

"How would you like to go to church with me this Sunday? I could pick you up and then we could go out for lunch afterwards."

"No thanks, Trisha. It's nice of you to ask but I don't do church. I've tried all of that stuff and it's not for me. Besides, I can't really stay up that long. I get really tired and I'm sure I'd never make it, being away from home that long."

As a matter of fact, there was a time that I got stranded along the highway while trying to make it to the grocery store and ended up in the emergency room. The doctor ran tests and drugged me up with morphine to control my pain, but I could not be admitted to the hospital because my insurance wouldn't pay for it without a diagnosis. So for the most part I suffered alone at home. I went from specialist to specialist who could all see that something was terribly wrong but could not identify just what it was.

So, I didn't want to be rude, but church was the last thing I wanted to spend my energy on. It was all that I could do to keep food in the house and keep my clothes clean!

One afternoon I was sitting in scalding hot water in the bathtub, trying to control the pain, and I cried out, "God, if you are there I have to know! I am no different than anyone else! I don't know how some people can be so sure about you when I am so unsure! I don't know if you appear to people, or if you send angels, or what you do, but I have to know – pick me! My hand is up highest! Show me if you are there!" Tears were streaming down my face as I poured my heart out as best as I could. This was my moment of truth. I gave it my best shot. If in fact there was a God at all, how could he refuse such a plea?

I sat there waiting for the lights to flicker or an angel to appear, but nothing happened. Something died in me right then, as I realized that God was not an option for me, no matter how hard I tried. I could not have been more sincere. If my plea didn't elicit a response from Heaven, then nothing would.

The next afternoon, I pulled myself up from the couch and held on to the wall for support. I was on my way to the bathroom when the 700 Club came on the TV.

Goodness, I hated those Christian shows! It was all so fake, and it just made me sick! I wanted to turn the station but did not have the energy to go over to the TV and still make it to the bathroom. Just as I turned to go into the bathroom, a woman on the program named Sheila Walsh seemed to speak directly to me.

"The Lord is giving me a word of knowledge that someone who is watching is suffering a great deal of pain in her chest. The pain travels from your chest to your back and down your arm. The doctors are confounded and haven't been able to help you. You've been from specialist to specialist, but you have found no help. I want you to know that God hears you crying out, and he is reaching down right now. He is going to touch you, and you are going to be healed. Just receive it right now." I was standing there stupefied! I was clinging to the wall for support and tears were streaming down my face. When I realized what I was doing, that I was standing there shedding real tears over a TV program, I reasoned that it was probably that time of the month and dismissed it as being overly emotional. I had already tried the God thing, and it hadn't worked.

At 11:30 AM the next day, I looked up at the clock for the 15th time. I was expecting my friend Jenny to come and take me to my doctor's appointment in Miami. It was an hour and 15 minutes driving time, if traffic was good.

I had just turned on the TV for the lack of anything else to do when Jenny pulled up. I flicked the TV back off and stood to my feet. I didn't want her to see the effort I had to put in, just to walk around the house. As I headed to the door I noticed that I was taking real steps! My feet actually lifted up off the ground when I walked. It had been a month since I could pick up my feet to walk! I headed out the door before Jenny could even get out of her car.

Jenny had a Trans Am that was really hard to get into. I strategically got myself in and then wondered how the heck I was going to get out again! I actually got in a little easier than I thought I would, and although I anticipated it would initiate a painful attack, it did not.

Oh great, I thought, *here they are finally ready to diagnose what is wrong with me, and I start to feel better!*

Of course, it was only in the daylight hours that I ever felt better. It was in the middle of the night, when I was alone and afraid, that the pain would grip me and threaten to take my life. I wiggled in my seat, knowing that the pain that seemed to have subsided was just masking itself.

I wanted the doctors to have the benefit of the whole picture when diagnosing me! I wanted them to see the misery I had been in. It was too easy to send someone home with a heating pad and a Tylenol and dismiss what you could not see for yourself. But for the first time in over a month, I really did feel a little relief.

I entered the doctor's office and took a seat. After just a few minutes, the nurse called my name. I got to my feet better than I did at home and again cursed the way things happened like that. After the usual check in with the nurse, Dr. Sage knocked on the door as a signal that he was coming in.

"Hi, I'm Dr. Sage. How are you feeling, Karen?"

"Well, I have been having a pretty hard time. About a month ago I started having pain in my chest and back, and I know it sounds strange, but I couldn't pick up my feet when I walked."

"How about walking across the room for me," the doctor said.

I rolled my eyes. "Just this morning, right before I came, I picked up my feet for the first time since I got sick!"

I walked across the room as the doctor watched analytically. My doctor in the Keys was sure that this neurologist was the answer, to coming up with a diagnosis. He had me bend down and touch my toes while he felt my spine and tested my nerves in different points with a low-electric stimulator. I watched to see the look on his face, for any hint of what he was thinking.

As time went on, I grew more and more concerned as to what that diagnosis might be. He ordered an MRI, and when everything he had ordered was complete, Dr. Sage invited me into his office.

OH goodness, I thought, *now he's going to tell me what is killing me!*

By this time, I looked like something was sucking the life out of me. Pain was always written across my face; my eyes were drawn and my skin pale. The look of sickness was all over me.

"Have a seat," the doctor instructed. As I sat down, I felt a little faint from the fear and anxiety of what he might say. "Well, your tests are all negative. Your MRI shows some arthritis, but otherwise, normal. I am a little surprised considering the things that you have told me. However, your neurological test is also within normal range. We could do some more extensive tests, but unless there is something we've missed, I can't really see it is a benefit to you."

I was relieved and disappointed at the same time. "Why do you think I am so sick?" I asked the doctor. "I can't seem to function, yet no one can figure out what's wrong with me. What should I do next?" Tears were forming in my eyes against my will.

"Perhaps you should see a cardiologist," Dr. Sage suggested.

"I have already seen a cardiologist. That's who sent me to you! Isn't that in my file?" I was getting irritated with the lack of communication between the doctors. I was beginning to feel like a number instead of a person. It was becoming more and more apparent that I was on this boat alone and no one really gave a rip enough to go beyond their comfort zone to help me.

I gathered my things and went to the front counter to pay my bill. It cost me $200 for nothing! It wasn't bad enough that I was sick and maybe dying, they had to suck all of my money away also!

My friend Jenny was in the parking lot waiting for me when I came out of the office. The sun assaulted my eyes, and they involuntarily closed in response. I put on the sunglasses that were hanging around my neck and reached out to open the car door. The hot sun felt good, it was like medicine to my aching, distressed body.

"So, what did the doctor say?" asked Jenny, as I lowered myself into the passenger seat.

"Oh, they don't know what's wrong yet. They have to run some more tests." I didn't want to say one more time that they had found absolutely nothing. People would think that I was a hypochondriac or something! I was sick, and tired, and exasperated! I just wanted to go home. After exhausting every avenue I knew of to get help, I resigned myself to lying on my couch. If I died, then I died!

Nearly every night I would go to sleep knowing that I might not make it until morning. The only thing that had changed was that I could walk normally, and some days were a little better than others. Most of the time I had to buy food around the corner at the Circle K because a trip to the grocery store would leave me stranded on the side of the road, or in the emergency room, with no ride home. My friend Jenny paid all of my bills, and for that I was grateful. I had a lot of sick time and vacation time saved up at work. However, Jenny thought that it was one thing that she could do without having to hold a puke bucket or something to be of some help to me. The thought of seeing her friend wither away was something she couldn't handle. With the generous check her father sent her every month, she could help me without jeopardizing her own finances.

The doctors thought that I had a sudden onset of MS. They thought that the neurologist would validate that suspicion, but like all other tests, they came back negative. Everyone could see the life being sucked right out of me, but the cause remained evasive.

On a Monday afternoon almost two months after my sickness began, I received another call from my Amway friend Trisha. "Hi, listen, don't say anything until I'm done, okay?"

"Okay," I said with a chuckle.

"I know that you said you don't like going to church, but I also know you must be lonely, and I know for sure that your friends aren't coming over much anymore. They probably feel helpless because you aren't getting better, so it's just easier for them to stay away. I want you to say yes and go to church with me this Friday. It's a celebration service in Homestead and I think you will like it."

I usually put up walls at the mention of church, but I was tired of lying on the couch, and tired of being tired! The thought of getting out of the house appealed to me, but I didn't know how I would ever make it all the way to Homestead and back. Not to mention, having to sit in some kind of church service for who knows how long. Before the conversation was over, though, I had agreed to go. In my mind, I was sure that I would never make it anyway.

Friday came too fast, and I stood at the mirror trying to get something to look right on me. I looked sick, and no matter what I put on, it just didn't look right. Finally, I settled for a midnight blue pantsuit that had once been my favorite. My sister Kathy had given it to me for my birthday a year past. At the time, it was the perfect thing. Until now, of course; everything seemed to hang on me, and there was no luster in my face to bring out the beauty of anything I wore.

As I stood in front of my dresser mirror I noticed a small red New Testament lying there. I picked it up and opened it to the inside cover. The Bible was inscribed in my own youthful handwriting, to *Karen Ann Grieb, 1969*. I couldn't believe what I was seeing! This was the first Bible my parents had given me, when I was eleven years old. I had been away from home for 20 years at this point, and I had not seen this Bible for who knows how long!

At one point, all of my belongings had been in a storage room and because I missed payments, everything had been auctioned off. I lost everything I owned that wasn't in my backpack. *Everything* would include that Bible, though I couldn't recall even having it there to begin with!

Trophies of Grace

I opened the little Bible at random and landed on Matthew 13:20: *The one who received the seed that fell on rocky places is the man who hears the word and at once receives it with joy. But since he has no root, it lasted only a short time. When trouble or persecution comes because of the word he quickly falls away.*

I immediately felt condemned. I understood that God wasn't pleased with me, and at times, I would do my best to stop taking pills and drinking. I would purposely not lie and would count up all of my wrongs and attempt to turn over a new leaf. The problem was that I always failed. Being religious was too much of a burden. Even when I tried my hardest, it just wasn't good enough. I figured there was just too much sin in an average person's life to have to quit doing it all at once!

I felt sad and hopeless. I didn't see any point in going to church, but I was tired of being in the house, and truthfully didn't care if I got stranded on the stretch or not, at this point!

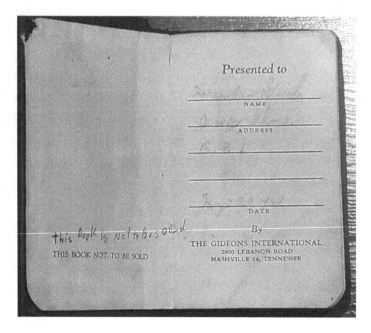

My Salvation Story

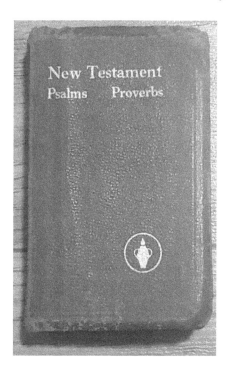

    I expected to feel worse than I did on my drive to the mainland. I had to drive about fifty miles one way. It was a beautiful drive up the Keys and onto the 18-mile stretch towards Homestead. The Gulf of Mexico was to my left and the Atlantic Ocean to my right. It was a perfectly beautiful day! Before I knew it I was on the mainland and pulling into the church parking lot. The palm trees were swaying in the breeze and the sun was hot on my skin. It felt good to be outside.

    I met up with Trisha and her family and followed them into the sanctuary of the church. It was a big Presbyterian Church with stained glass windows and high, beautifully ornate ceilings. On the back of the pew in front of me was a kneeling bench. I sincerely hoped that I would not be expected to get up-and-down on that thing!

The congregation sang a few songs accompanied by a man playing a guitar. Then the minister went up to deliver his sermon.

"Tonight I am going to talk to you about the Parable of The Sower." As the minister continued I recognized this as being the same thing that I'd read in my little Bible before coming to the service.

An usher passed out envelopes of tiny little seeds to everyone in the congregation, including me. There was a hole in my envelope and little seeds trickled out all over my lap. I brushed them on the floor so no one would notice. During the course of the service the seeds continued to fall on the pew, on my lap, and in my purse.

When the sermon was over and we were waiting for our turn to file through the door, Trisha made it a point to invite me to church again!.

"Karen, if you want to go to church on Sunday, I have a friend who said she would pick you up and take you to church with her."

"No, that's okay. I have a hard time staying up so long," I replied. I hoped that Trisha would leave it at that, but she didn't!

"I've thought about that," she said. "That's why I asked my friend Amy. She attends a church right there in Plantation Key. You really should agree to go. You need to get out of the house. She will pick you up and even take you to breakfast before church."

I was fuming inside! Give a Christian an inch and they'll take a mile! I said that I would go to church one time; I never said anything about being there every time the doors were open!

I was too polite to say those things out loud so I just said, "Okay." Trisha informed me that her friend Amy would call me by Wednesday to set things up. I decided not to contest it because I was sick, after all, and everyone knew it. I probably wouldn't be able to get out of bed on Sunday anyway. After saying my goodbyes I got in my truck and headed back to the Keys. I was surprised that I was doing so well. I couldn't believe that I had made it all the way to Homestead and sat through the whole service! I hoped that I could make it back home but I kind of doubted it.

I shoved the key in the door and made my way into the living room. My hands were full and I got really weak climbing the flight of stairs. I held that stupid envelope of seeds in my right hand along with my purse. The seeds were getting all over the place!

How many were in the blasted envelope anyway?

I went into my bedroom, turned on the light, and tossed my purse and the envelope on the bed. I couldn't wait to get out of my dress clothes. That's another reason I didn't like going to church; I didn't like having to dress up just to get in my AC-less pickup truck and drive with the windows down. By the time I got to where I was going I looked like heck anyway, and the clothes were uncomfortable!

When I finally decided to just throw the envelope in the trash, the floor and bed were littered with seeds, and some had even gotten on my dresser!

Wednesday came along and, sure enough, Trisha's friend called to ask me to go to church with her. I didn't want to go so I planned to say that I wasn't feeling well and simply wasn't going.

I picked up on the fifth ring thinking that maybe if it was Trisha's friend she would think I wasn't home and hang up. She didn't!

"Hi, this is Amy. Trisha asked me to call you. I'm glad that you want to go to church with me. I told my husband Dave that we have to be sure to go this Sunday so I can bring you. I will meet you at McDonald's at nine o'clock on Sunday morning. I will be by myself, and I'll be looking for you. I guess you will know who I am. Okay then, I'll see you Sunday. Goodbye!"

I was already irritated with this woman. She talked a mile a minute, never even giving me a chance to say I didn't want to go! The woman didn't let me say a word! The next thing I knew we were hanging up and I was going to church on Sunday!

I was mad! I felt I'd been set up, but for now I would let it slide. Who knew what would happen by Sunday; maybe I wouldn't make it until then anyway!

I woke up at 8:30 AM Sunday morning, swung my legs over the side of the bed, and tried my stability as I got to my feet. I made my way to the bathroom and looked in the mirror, forced to hold onto the sink as a wave of nausea threatened me. I had a feeling that it wasn't going to be one of my better days and was content enough to give in to it. What were these people thinking anyway? I slipped back under the sheets and resolved to go back to sleep. After a few minutes I pulled the pillow off my face and pitched it on the floor. I was too anxious to go back to sleep! I got back out of bed and went into the living room. I actually felt pretty good now that I was up. I wasn't the kind of person to just not show up if I committed to go somewhere. If I'd had the conscience to do so, I would have loved to blow it off.

I walked into McDonald's at 9:30 sharp. I spotted a young woman searching over the heads of people in line. I got a dreadful feeling that I shouldn't have come.

Amy was the kind of person that you just wanted to stop talking! I purposed not to encourage her by answering her questions with as few words as possible. At 10:15 we each got into our own vehicles and left McDonald's, heading to the church

My Salvation Story

a mile away. I laughed to myself as we pulled into the parking lot; I would never have guessed that this was a church. It looked more like a house with a big unpaved parking lot. Quite different from the big ornate Presbyterian church in Homestead!

We went inside and I followed Amy down a row of empty folded chairs and sat down. There were people scattered around the room saying their hellos and getting the microphones ready up front. No one spoke to us directly. Just before the service was about to begin, Amy looked at me and said, "My husband and I were having a disagreement before I left this morning and I told him that I was definitely coming to bring you to church, but I have to go now." With that, she got up, squeezed past me, and left.

It took a moment for me to process what had just happened. I could not believe that this woman got up and left! I had been shanghaied! This was the last place in the world that I wanted to be, yet I was stuck here for who knows how long!

I had a problem getting up and walking in front of people. I would usually figure out an exit plan upon entering a room so I could slip out without drawing attention to myself. If I didn't have that opportunity I would stay put until the room was nearly empty. I did not have an exit plan!

I was too self-conscious to get up and leave, but I threw a fit in my mind just the same. *What the heck am I doing here? I can't believe she did this to me! What am I doing here?*

Just then the Pastor got up and said to Jeff, the sound man who was preparing to tape the message, "The title of the sermon today is *What Are You Doing Here?*" I recognized the coincidence of the Pastor's words against my own thoughts, but that's all I remembered of the service.

As time went on it became harder to sit in my seat as the sickness claimed my strength. After the service I made my way to the back of the church so I could just get out of there and go home. I was approached by a woman named Janice who was asking if I wanted to be baptized, or something.

I had no ability to respond and mumbled that I had to get home as I continued toward the door. Before I made it out, the pastor's wife intercepted me. "Are you alright? You look like you don't feel well." I nodded and, without asking, Marian took my hand and started to pray for me right there by the door. A few minutes later I was in my truck and on my way to Lower Matecumbe toward home.

As I pulled into the driveway I had an incredible heaviness about going into the house. I just couldn't do it. With no further thought I put the truck in reverse and headed back up the Keys. With no place to go, I pulled into the now-empty church parking lot. I parked under a big shade tree, laid my head against the window of the truck, and immediately fell asleep.

I woke up to the sound of laughing voices as people were arriving for the Sunday evening service. I'd never thought anyone would be coming back! A woman named Sue came over as I opened my door and said "You came back! We are glad you are here, come on in."

I dutifully got out of the truck, wondering how in the heck I had gotten myself into this mess again! I did not have the energy that I'd had in the morning and faltered as I walked next to Sue in the parking lot. She took my arm and steadied me as we entered the church. It was obvious that I was unable to sit in the sanctuary, so Sue led me into the nursery and had me lie down on a couch. I stayed with Sue and the kids for the remainder of the service. At one point, Sue asked the children to come over and pray for me. About five of them laid their little hands on my arm and asked God to make me feel better. I'd never had anyone pray for me by touching me before, but it was cute, and it kind of made me feel cared for.

After the service I was unable to drive home, so Pastor Marlin and his wife took me to their house to spend the night. After answering a few questions about my sickness, Marian tucked me into their guest bed and settled into the living room with her husband to pray.

It was Thursday before Pastor Marlin and Marian decided to try and get me back to my house. I was not in good condition. I was experiencing such a heavy tiredness that I simply could not stay awake. After several hours at the Emergency Room, they drove me back to my house in Lower Matecumbe Key.

I woke up in my own bed. I recognized people from the church milling around the house praying. Occasionally I would wake to find someone sitting on my bed reading the Bible, or someone singing to me over the phone. I would fall asleep with the receiver at my ear and wake up who knows how much later to find them still there, singing songs to Jesus!

It was Saturday, in the middle of the night, that I woke up filled with pain and distress. Everyone had gone. I was hallucinating and seeing some things that people don't normally see, shadows and shadowy apparitions moving about. I felt a presence pushing me tight to the mattress. Although I wanted to get up, the force held me firm to the sheets. I thought that this must be my death. In a moment of resistance I forced myself up out of bed. I made my way to the bathroom and turned on the water in the tub. As I lowered myself into the near scalding water I cried out. I was not calling to God, but out of desperation or maybe simply, even cussing, I cried "Oh God!"

At that moment the pain in my body stopped. The hallucinations stopped and the voice of the Spirit of God spoke to me and said "REPENT." It was not an audible voice but a resounding from deep inside that could not be ignored. I understood the meaning of the word itself, but not quite how it related to me at that moment!

After a few minutes the pain returned, and I had that heaviness that I just couldn't stand. I got out of the tub and dressed in my blue pantsuit. If I died before morning, at least I would have my favorite suit on.

I climbed into my pickup truck at 4 AM and ended up in the parking lot of the little church. I pulled under the big shade tree and rested my head against the window of my truck. I slept until people started to arrive for the Sunday morning service. Once again I was escorted into the church by one of the people entering the building.

Three times before the service started someone came up to me and said, "You know it's okay to go up front." I knew what they meant. They wanted me to walk up in front of everyone at the end of the service so the pastor could pray for me, but I had absolutely no plans to walk up in front of any people for any reason. They managed to pray for me no matter where I was anyway.

At the end of the service, Pastor Marlin invited people to come up front. There were a couple of people already up there who would pray for whoever decided to go. I had no intentions of going forward, but before I knew it I was walking up the aisle. A woman named Sally put her hand on my shoulder and asked if I wanted to accept Christ into my heart. I didn't know what to say. I just expected that they would put their hands on me and pray for me to be healed again. I responded with, "I guess so." What else was I going to do? I was standing up there in front of everybody!

Sally started to have me repeat a prayer. I stopped after the first few words. I looked up at her and said, "I don't need another religious experience. If I'm supposed to be sorry for my life or if I am supposed to be having a big moment here, I am not having it. I don't want to just do an empty ceremony. I've had enough of those already." I didn't bother to explain that I had already tried to be a Christian and God wasn't interested in me. They should have figured it out already because they had prayed for me several times, and still nothing had happened.

Anyway, I turned and went back to my seat. Everyone in the service thought that I had become a Christian and they were clapping their approval. As I took my seat, I heard it again. The word repent. Not with my ears, but from deep within.

This time I understood what it meant. I understood that not only did I need forgiveness for my own sins, but I needed to be willing to forgive all the sins that had been committed against me. I had secrets about the President Director when I was fourteen and about my drug use. I'd had an entirely different life before I came to Florida that I had managed to stuff back into the recesses of my mind. They occasionally revisited me to terrorize my dreams and suck away my hope. There were many secrets I had that required abandonment if this God thing was ever going to work for me.

Without any further thought, I wrote a note and passed it up through the congregation to the pastor's wife. The note said, "If this is going to work at all for me, I have to talk to somebody today."

After church Pastor Marlin and Marian took me to lunch. I couldn't eat, and I hadn't eaten for three days already. By the time they had finished eating, I could barely sit in my chair without falling out of it. They took me to their house, and I sat on the sofa while I shared everything that stood between me and God. For some reason I was compelled not to leave anything out. I shared things that I could not imagine sharing with anyone. With each confession they prayed for deliverance and healing. After what I call my Royal Flush, they asked me to make a choice to forgive the perpetrators in my life. I didn't know how to put forgiveness next to what the President Director had done to me. Nevertheless, I said aloud that I chose to forgive the President Director and trust God to heal that offense in me. After that, I was able to ask Jesus to come into my life with the help of Pastor Marlin and Marian. I knew without a doubt that this was not just a religious experience, it was real, God was for real and I was truly set free!

Once again, I was so weak that I could not open my eyes. Pastor Marlin and Marian helped me to bed and went off to church for the Sunday night service.

By the time they came home from church I was able to sit up and have some tea and toast. Jesus had shown himself real to me and a new level of healing had begun.

My Salvation Story

Chapter 10

The Fullness Of Joy

One of the differences in my life from my first day as a Christian was a joy that seemed to just spill out of me! Yes, I was still sick, but this joy was different from feeling good physically, or happiness from something external. This was from that place that had been empty inside of me for a long time. It was a yearning for something I couldn't identify. Instead of the emptiness, I now felt satisfied and joyful!

Looking back, I can see that sharing my deepest secrets was so necessary and foundational for this joy I felt. People probably pay a lot of money for that kind of therapy! God knew that I had to unburden myself of my secrets in order to move forward in my life and to be able to recognize Him. Maybe it's not that way for everybody, but it sure was for me. I couldn't stay a victim forever! Sure, I would go maybe six months or even a year without nightmares about my assaults, but when they came they came with a vengeance and would consume my every thought, sometimes for two weeks at a time! I would go through all the emotions and guilt, as if it had just happened. I would agonize over deceiving Charlotte, and I would play the scenes over in my mind time and again. I would feel the weight of the abuse I suffered and would dream about his assaults. I would agonize and analyze what he said was my fault. There was no turning it off once it started!

To share all of this was the first step to my healing. I learned that all the possible negative outcomes I imagined if I ever shared these things were an unnecessary emotional burden. I came to understand that we are not meant to carry our burdens alone!

Marian gave me a Bible to read and highlighted some things that I might like to know as a new believer, such as 1 John 1:9: *If we confess our sins, He is faithful and just and will forgive us our sins and purify us from all unrighteousness.*

Even if what the President Director had said was true, I was forgiven. Along with dishonoring my parents and my family, ignoring God for years, stealing and lying and my anger and hate against the President Director; these were just some of my sins. My drug use and countless other ugly things about me that I would never even write down were all covered by this promise of God. Everything was wiped away and was not written in some secret book of God's to send me to hell!

Psalm 103:12: *As far as the east is from the west, so far has He removed our transgressions from us.*

The fact that God would choose not to remember all these things about me made me realize just how much He really did love me! My guilt was turning into gratitude, and my gratitude into love. "God loves you" wasn't just an irritating fairytale to me anymore! I was discovering that my understanding was wrong about all the *thou-shalt-not* rules of religion. As I actually read the Bible, I learned that these rules of character essential for believers were not to restrict us from enjoying life, but to allow us to develop better relationships with God and other people. I realized that living within the guidelines that God had designed initiated a life with much less stress, anxiety, and adversity. Okay, I could get on board with that!

I wanted to believe that God created me on purpose, for a purpose, like the Bible said.

I wanted to discover what plans He had for me. I started to believe and trust in His love. Maybe life wasn't just a roll of the dice after all! Who am I, and what could I possibly do with what I had, to live with a purpose determined by God Himself?

I had never seen value in the Bible before this! I thought that it was too boring and difficult to understand, so I never tried. Now I was discovering its value. There was nothing difficult at all about reading the Bible. As a matter of fact, I began to understand that all those times I thought God had been ignoring me, or was simply nonexistent, He was, in fact, leaving His fingerprints for me to discover that He had been there all along! As I started looking back over the things that had happened just since I'd gotten sick, I realized that God really was helping me. Back when Sheila Walsh spoke those things that seemed to be directed to me on the 700 Club; when I was able to pick up my feet as I walked, after my prayer in the tub; the Bible from my parents that inexplicably showed up on my dresser; that blasted envelope of seeds and the parable of the Sower; the persistence of Trisha to get me to church; the coincidence of Pastor Marlin's sermon, "What are you doing here?"; the people from the church who were willing to sing to me over the phone and pray at my house.

All of it started becoming real to me, the knowledge that God was there all along. I couldn't hear Him, and I didn't know that He was doing all those things, because my sin had separated me from Him. He did all of it so that, when I eventually asked for forgiveness, I would finally be able to see and understand. Reading the Bible became alive to me, and my life started to change pretty drastically when I saw how it was all personally directed toward me. "I was lost but now I'm found, I was blind but now I see" were not just empty words anymore, they became the song of my heart and my worship. When God started to make Himself known to me, I couldn't get enough! It was like falling in love and being consumed with joy and happiness. I couldn't wait to spend time praying, listening, and reading His Bible.

I still wasn't able to go back to work, but I began to have more good days. The ladies of the church spent time with me. We would go to the beach at America Outdoors Campground and hang out while their kids played. They answered many of my questions and prayed for me on the days my sickness seemed worse.

The evidence of God's presence became more and more real to me as I learned to pray and wait quietly afterward, to sense God in a personal way. I learned that to fear God *wasn't* to be afraid of Him, but to respect Him and to care about what He thinks about my life and my choices. The fear that I had grown up with was a plan of the devil's to keep me separated from God. I knew I was nothing special, that God should want to save me. But the fact that He did overwhelmed me every day and made me want to sing those blasted Christian songs that I used to hate! It made me want to pray and to know more about God.

A few weeks after all of this, my doctor arranged for me to fly to The Cleveland Clinic in Ohio to be examined by a team of specialists. Virginia, a lady from the church, had a daughter who lived in Cleveland, and she agreed to host me for my week of clinic appointments. Charles and Marjorie, some old friends of mine, also lived in Cleveland, and Marjorie agreed to pick me up and take me to and from the clinic every day.

Marlin and Marian drove me up to the airport in Miami and agreed to come get me upon my return. Everything was all taken care of. Marian gave me a book to read on the plane. She knew that I was afraid of flying and *Prayers That Avail Much* was a book of prayers for certain circumstances. She marked the page about fear and when I boarded the plane I read the prayer over and over to calm myself for the flight.

Of course, we got there without falling out of the sky, and my fears were relieved. I had appointments with some of the top doctors in the country and at the end of the week my final evaluation was with a cardiologist. Once again the fear and dread of hearing my diagnosis made me feel unsteady and surreal as I took my seat at the desk across from the doctor.

"Well, Karen, along with examinations from our team doctors, we have done several diagnostic tests this week to determine the cause of your sickness and pain. Unfortunately there are some things in medicine that we just can't explain, and yours seems to be one of them. All of your tests have come back negative, for Lupus, Cancer, MS, and Rheumatoid Arthritis. I can only suggest that you treat your symptoms as they present themselves and stay in touch with your family doctor if there are any changes. Do you have any questions?"

I was absolutely exasperated from all of the poking, probing, and testing that had once again resulted in nothing! I definitely was better than I had been when the whole sickness started, but it seemed to be on a day to day basis. It definitely wasn't over yet. Now what was I supposed to do?

I decided to tell the doctor about what had happened to me with the church. "This little church that I have been going to said they believe that God is healing me from whatever the problem is. I have gotten somewhat better since they started praying for me, but one day I'll be better, then the next day I won't. They said for me just to trust God, that my healing was apparently going to be a process. They gave me a Bible and this pamphlet about why they believe what they believe."

"That's very interesting," the doctor said, "Do you mind if I make a copy of your pamphlet?"

Of course, I agreed. He seemed genuinely interested to discover these possibilities.

I checked out of the clinic and flew back to the Keys with nothing to hold on to except a tiny bit of faith that God really might be healing me. On the plane there was a young woman sitting across the aisle from me. We exchanged hellos and comments about the balmy weather in Cleveland. She said something about being uneasy to fly and I noticed that she had the same book I did, *Prayers That Avail Much*!

"Hey, I have that same book!" I told her. "Turn to page 81. That's the prayer I prayed on my flight here! I hate flying!"

We laughed at the situation and settled in for the takeoff. It seemed too unreal that this would happen! I was becoming more and more convinced that these "coincidences" were indeed the fingerprints of God, making His presence known. It happened way too often, and the circumstances were far too specific to believe they were only coincidental!

With my willingness to lean into the Lord and lay down my past, God was able to begin a new work in me. When I say lean, I mean LEAN! I had the ability to accept the people from the church, I had a freedom and a joy that I couldn't explain in my own words yet, and I had a desire to go to church and read the Bible, something I had never done before! However, I had little understanding of what God wanted from me, and certainly no understanding of how I might go about forgiving the President Director! I simply yielded to listening to the sermons from Pastor Marlin, and I read my Bible like an instruction manual. I realized that there was a lot of reconstruction to do in my life.

Psalm 16:11: *You will show me the path of life: In your presence is fullness of joy; In your right hand there are pleasures forevermore.* I learned from this that my joy was because I had simply said yes to God and was spending my time praying and getting to know Him and His ways.

I had no idea how this Christian lifestyle was going to work for me, but I was going to try my hardest. Things that seemed ridiculous in the past became my lifeline. I read Psalm 119:11 that said that if I hid God's word in my heart then I wouldn't sin against Him. I took this scripture seriously. I was grateful that Jesus saved me and if it was possible, I didn't want to do anything to dishonor Him as a Christian. I memorized the scriptures that initiated changes in my belief system and character. 2 Corinthians 10:5: *Take every thought captive to the obedience of Christ.*

When the memories of the President Director tried to bring on an attack, I would say out loud, "I take that captive to the obedience of Christ! Nothing about that situation was my fault and I choose to forgive." Then I would start singing or anything to take the place of those thoughts. After just a few minutes I would be fine and move on.

Philippians 4:8: *Finally, brothers and sisters, whatever is true, whatever is honorable, whatever is right, whatever is pure, whatever is lovely, whatever is admirable—if anything is excellent or praiseworthy—think about such things.*

That was a whole new list of things to measure my thoughts against!

I did it like an assignment and God helped me start to align my preferences with His own. My character got better. Not in a snippy way, with a better-than-anyone kind of attitude. I reconsidered the things I liked to watch on TV, the music I listened to, and the people I hung out with. I measured the negative things I talked about and the gossip that came out of my mouth. My character started to change as I became aware of how I treated other people. I became more respectful and thoughtful of others and stopped judging them for their faults. I started praying for people and their struggles. I actually started to love people instead of dismissing them in irritation because of their faults.

At first, I didn't want to tell my parents about my decision to become a Christian. I didn't think they would believe me. It would have been more believable to them if I said I had joined a cult! I managed to avoid the issue for a month or so, but as my passion for the Lord grew, the fact that I needed to ask my parents for forgiveness for all the distress I had caused them became more and more apparent.

My healing increased weekly, and after about four months since the start of my sickness, I was back to work. There were still some days that I had to take off and most of the time I worked in my office and delegated the physical work. All in all, eight months passed before I stopped having any bad days.

I planned a weekend in Orlando to visit my mom and dad with the determination to tell them that I had become a Christian. I was nervous about talking to them and so I asked God again, just in case I could get out of it! I was standing in the kitchen waiting for the right moment as my mom buzzed around doing her chores. In my heart I was ready to bail out! The closer I got to my moment the more ready I was to run away from it. I went out to sit in my truck and I was actually nauseous as I tried to disobey what God was asking me to do! I kind of grabbed myself by the shirt collar and pulled myself back into the house.

As soon as I walked in my mom passed in front of me. I reached out and hugged her sweetly from behind and told her that I would like to talk to her in the bedroom alone. We sat down on her bed, and I started by asking for her forgiveness. I know that this was a dream come true for her and a lifelong answer to her prayers. I didn't make any excuses for my wrongs, and I didn't bring up anything that was attributed to them from the family dynamics. I simply said, "I'm sorry for all the heartache I have caused you and for dishonoring you and dad as my parents. Will you please forgive me and let me start with a clean slate?"

Her answer was "I will forgive you, if you forgive me."

There were no excuses, no blame, no rehashing, just forgiveness! We hugged, let a few tears slip out, then smiled sweetly at each other!

I told her that I had become a Christian and had asked Jesus to wash me clean.

I told her about my sickness and all the ways God had tried to reveal Himself to me. I shared about how the people from my church recognized me as a divine appointment and that they collectively scooped me up, walked me through my healing, and have been discipling me to be successful in my decision to follow Jesus.

When I was all talked out we heard movement at the bedroom window and turned to see that my dad had been there listening through the open window as I made my amends with my mother and declared my faith in Jesus! Another orchestration from God to restore my life and bring me back into a relationship with my family!

It wasn't too long after that when my sister confided that she had a problem she would like to talk to me about. I expected that I could be a listening ear and encourage her to look to Jesus for her help.

"So, what's up Kathy, what is your problem?"

"You!" she said

"Me?" I was shocked, "Okay, tell me." I had no idea what I could have done, but I was about to find out!

"When you left home I didn't know what to do. Mom was a mess, dad had to work, and Rick just stayed busy hunting and fishing. I felt like all the attention was on you, and my childhood got stolen. Mom was so fragile that I felt like I had to protect her from you. She couldn't take any more surprises. Dad and I had to take away her medicine so she could withdraw from it. That was a week of hell! I try not to let it bother me, but it does."

It had never dawned on me that my messed up life and bad choices had affected my sister so much! I was immediately filled with remorse and compassion for what she had gone through. I couldn't change anything that had happened, but I did ask her to forgive me, and we prayed together that God would heal Kathy's broken heart and give us a new chance to grow together as sisters.

Over the years since then, my sister and I have become best friends! We encourage each other almost every day as we talk on the phone and pray, each of us on our way to work in the morning! Kathy is iron sharpening iron to me and also a great example of a life redeemed and transformed through Jesus.

Trophies of Grace

Chapter 11

For I Know The Plans I Have For You...

I was moving forward, discovering what was broken and moving quickly to make amends where I could. The scriptures were alive to me, and I was seeing results!

I opened my heart and allowed God to shine light into all the corners of my life that were still in darkness. I laid all my secrets and sufferings at His feet and asked Him to heal me until I was brand new.

In addition to everything that He was already doing, I asked God to cleanse my mind so I could receive a fresh start concerning love. One morning as I was out walking my dog Sandie, I prayed, "Lord, I believe that you have forgiven me for my past. I know that my lifestyle wasn't pleasing to you, and I really want to be healthy in every way! I give you my complete understanding about love and relationships and ask that you put it in your safekeeping until I can be trusted with it again. Everything that I think and feel about love is so messed up and I do want to please you with everything in my life! Please heal me in my damaged places and make me new. In Jesus name I pray, Amen."

At the end of my prayer my dog Sandie started to run. I closed my eyes and held on to the leash. I ran, trusting to be led. It was exhilarating to run with my eyes closed. I hoped that I could trust my dog as much as I believed I could trust God!

I took my blind running experience as a sign that God was indeed leading me as I stretched out my faith once again to believe for the impossible.

I can't even tell you how it happened, but Eleanor, Pastor Marlin's mother, became one of my best friends after I got saved. I was 31 and she was 72. If you'd never seen us face to face, you would never guess by our conversations that our age difference was so great! We accepted Christ around the same time, and she was having as delightful a time getting to know the Lord as I was! We talked and prayed together and were so excited about what God was doing in our lives. We were like two kids!

Eleanor had a chocolate chip cookie ministry. If a new person or family moved into her neighborhood, she would bake a batch of her delicious cookies and go pay them a visit. A week or so later, she would go back with another dozen and start a friendship. Before long she was able to invite them to church or pray for any needs they might have.

I was also realizing that my joyful glow attracted people. I was having opportunities to share my faith and to share some of the wonderful things that were happening to me. I didn't know much, but I couldn't keep my mouth shut about what I was discovering day by day, and it seemed that people wanted to hear it!

Eleanor would ride her bike about 15 miles every Tuesday to America Outdoors Campground, where we would have lunch together at the little hamburger shack on the dock and share our excitement for the Lord.

Ellen, a young woman from the church, was also one of my dearest friends. We would go sit on a big rock out by the ocean together to pray and sing and sing and pray! I would go pick her up in the evening and we would drive around in my little Isuzu truck laughing, praying about everything we could think of, and singing to Jesus! We couldn't get enough! We have been faithful friends for about 34 years now and still can't wait to pray about everything and share what God is doing in our lives!

Right about eight months after I had gotten sick, I was experiencing my first week of complete healing. It was Sunday morning, and I was sitting near my friend Eleanor about three rows back on the left side of the church, waiting for the service to begin. Janice turned in her seat, putting her hand up to direct her words to me without everyone hearing. "Hey Karen, look at that cute guy over there, he looks like your type."

I did not look! I didn't have a type! I had already asked the church members to pray for me because I needed to figure out where I fit in the church and in ministry. I thought that I could never be a Sunday School teacher, and I definitely couldn't be a Pastor's wife, but I didn't know what else women did, and more specifically what I could possibly do! But when they mentioned missionary work I figured I could do that! Of course it was quite a while down the road before I understood what missionaries really did and what the requirements were. I thought that it was like being a Nun. I thought that you had to live a life only for the Lord, promise never to fall in love, and be willing to live in a tent in Zimbabwe! I figured I could do that! That's what I said yes to! I was already signed up with Youth With A Mission and was just waiting for whatever was to come next. I had no plans to meet a guy!

Sometime during the service that morning I caught a glimpse of the visitor. I remember accidentally looking and involuntarily doing a double take. He was a handsome man! He had a peaceful look about him and I thought that if I had a type of guy, he might be something like that. He was definitely easy on the eyes! I was resolute about being a missionary and with my understanding being what it was, I gave this new guy no further thought.

The second Sunday that this visitor came for service, my two friends, Janice and Debbie, came up to me after almost everyone had left the church and said, "The new guy put his visitor's card in the offering plate today and we're going to go get it out!" They each hooked arms with me and dragged me up to the offering plate to get his name and address off the card!

I laughed and protested, "I can't go up there and get into the offering plate, I'm new, someone might think I'm stealing!"

They were laughing saying, "We're going on a manhunt!"

Okay, it was funny! They didn't know anything about my past and they certainly didn't know that I wasn't interested in finding a man! Janice had twin babies that she usually drove around after church until they fell asleep. She had two other children also. We all piled into her van, went through McDonald's to get the kids some lunch, and then went looking for the address that Alan Hanson had put on his visitor's card. We found the address and it was in a subdivision less than a mile from the church. The address was a duplex and there were no cars in the driveway to identify which one might be his. After fooling around with my friends and joking about the possibilities of me getting a date, that was the end of our manhunt!

The following Sunday when the service was over I noticed that no one was talking to the new guy. I didn't know if he was a believer or not and was genuinely concerned that everyone was just talking to their friends and overlooking him. I introduced myself and found out that he was a believer. His mom asked him to come from Texas and help her and her husband Frank run a carpet cleaning business. He said he would come if there was a good church for him to go to. She said that she didn't know how good it was but there was one just a little way down the road. That's how Alan came into my life.

My friend Eleanor had a gleam in her eye about Alan and me from the get-go! I knew she was praying! The whole church was watching as God wrote our love story! I didn't agonize over anything concerning Alan. He loved God as much as I did and was determined to live life to please Him. He was very respectful to me and didn't show any signs of anything other than a wonderful human being that I was falling in love with.

We had a whirlwind romance! I prayed and prayed for God to stop me in my tracks if this was wrong for me! However, every day it was becoming more and more evident that Alan and I were meant to be together.

I had submitted myself to God's will and trusted Marian, the Pastor's wife, to counsel me on what to do. There were no flags, no adverse feelings, and no opposition to our relationship. Two months after we met, we went on our first date. He asked me to lunch after the Sunday service. We spent the rest of the day together driving to Key West with the windows down in his 1972 Mercedes. The day was beautiful and warm.

Every day I spent with Alan made me want a hundred more! We didn't go on very many dates, but we were in church together every time the doors were open and were always among the last ones to leave. Two months later, we were having a picnic dinner on the beach of Plantation Yacht Harbor when he asked me to be his wife. I couldn't believe this was real, but it was! Before we made any plans, we fasted and prayed together for a week. When we were certain that God was for us, we started to tell our family and friends!

Alan and I went to Orlando to visit my parents and ask for their blessing. They'd never thought they would see the day that I would get married, and certainly not to a wonderful man like Alan! They immediately loved him and gave us their blessings. It felt good to make them proud of me!

Alan and I were attending a pre-marriage course with Pastor Marlin and Marian. Goodness, here I was engaged, and I had never even mentioned that my doctor told me I could probably never have children! At this point the only possible opposition we had come up with between us was that I liked animals and had almost always had a dog, and Alan had no desire or plans to ever own a pet! He grew up in a very large family and had had all the pets he'd ever cared to have.

I had never entertained the idea of having children, so I never even thought to tell him about that! I did not accept the anxiety that was knocking at my door about it! I prayed for God to lead me through it and completely put it in His hands! After I told Alan, he gave me a sweet hug and a kiss and told me that it made no difference to him whatsoever. Having grown up in a large family he had no great desire to have kids. How about that!

Two months later on September 8th we were married! I had asked Eleanor to be one of my bridesmaids! At first she said," Oh, you don't want an old lady like me!"

I told her," Eleanor, you are one of my very best friends! You prayed me into Alan's arms for goodness' sake! I couldn't imagine you not being in my wedding!" I knew that she was tickled and excited that I asked her! I wouldn't have had it any other way. She was just as beautiful as could be and fit into my wedding party just right.

My wedding day was one of the best days of my life! I'll never forget what it was like to have my father walk me down the aisle. It was a proud day for both of us and something I had never dreamed of for myself. There Alan Hanson stood at the altar, tall, thin, dark hair, brown eyes, and a smile that made my knees weak! He was the most wonderful man I had ever met! When my father released me to Alan's side, we joined hands, exchanged our vows, and promised to love each other forever.

We had a really nice wedding. Several of Alan's brothers and sisters came from Missouri and New York to attend and be part of the wedding. Our reception was on the dock of America Outdoors Campground down by the water's edge, on the Gulf of Mexico. This is the same place where, less than a year earlier, I had been baptized! This is where I met Eleanor every Tuesday for lunch, and as Alan and I became an obvious item, Eleanor and I would pray fervently for God's will concerning it.

On our wedding day our families came together to celebrate our love. My brother Rick, who was a butcher, brought the meat and everyone from the church came together bringing their favorite covered dish to the reception. Alan and I were planning on joining Youth With A Mission as full-time missionaries after our honeymoon. In light of this, everyone who knew and loved us came together for a family style reception. My Uncle Smokey announced us as Mr. and Mrs. Alan Hanson for the Bridal Waltz. So began the "until death do us part" journey of my life as Karen Hanson.

Trophies of Grace

Chapter 12

A New Creation

2 Corinthians 5:7 "Therefore, if anyone is in Christ, he is a new creation. The old has passed away, behold, the new has come."

As I yielded my life to God's care and direction, by His grace, He took the sufferings of my past, redirected my passions, and gave me hope for my future!

Married life was easy for Alan and me. It seemed like it should have always been. After a few honeymoon days in the Bahamas, we spent one night together at his house in Key Largo then off we went to *Youth With a Mission* as missionary students.

As newlyweds, we were in a dorm building called *The Ark* with eight other missionaries. Every morning a little four year old girl named Gracie would jam her face against the two inch crack at the bottom of our door and shout, "Halan, Halan, wake up! Halan, are you awake?" She was enamored with Alan and couldn't wait until he was up and ready to play!

We were still newlyweds, and to find our privacy while living in a dorm, we would wait until everyone was asleep in The Ark and drive our camping gear out to the field behind the administration building. We gazed up at the stars, thanking God for placing us in ministry together in such a wonderful place.

Our first phase of missionary discipleship training was about discovering our passions and our part in following Jesus, in light of God's purpose for the world. Our focus was also on identifying whatever stood between us and the Lord. We walked through forgiving people and letting go of hurtful situations from our past, having a clean heart before God, learning how to minister as a team, and increasing our personal support base.

We were in the classroom for a couple of weeks, then we would travel by bus to minister in the home churches of various teammates. I was so grateful that my friends at *Spirit and Truth Ministries* discipled me so well, having already addressed all of these personal issues. For me, this phase of training was just confirmation of what the Holy Spirit was already helping me with, and that Alan and I were on the same page and walking right with God. We were able to still give attention to each other as newlyweds and enjoy our new lives together without the heavy emotional stuff that can naturally come with soul searching.

While we were at a training seminar, I learned that I was pregnant! What the doctors said was nearly impossible had become a reality. I hadn't thought that I wanted kids until I became pregnant! I had never even entertained the idea of being a mother! Much to my surprise, it was an absolute joy being pregnant! Well, other than the fact that I craved BLTs for breakfast, lunch, and dinner, and that I couldn't begin to tolerate the smell of pancakes, which was Alan's favorite food!

I was fourteen weeks pregnant, and I was doing really good. Alan was the main bus driver for our team as we headed out on a seven-week mission tour. Our team went to twenty-two cities, towns, and villages throughout the U.S. and Mexico.

We were ministering in a church in Spring, Texas on Valentine's weekend before crossing into Mexico, and Alan and I were invited as guests into the home of one of the church members. They were a wonderful couple with an amazing house! Our very first night, strangers in their home, they made a wonderful steak dinner, set a romantic table for us, then they left the house and gave us the evening to ourselves to enjoy and celebrate Valentine's Day!

What a nice surprise! Our baby was kicking like crazy, and it was so fun for Alan and me to marvel over.

On our second day there I started to have cramps and light bleeding. We decided that it wasn't wise for me, at that point, to go to an indigenous village in Mexico, so I flew home to Orlando to stay with my parents and get checked out. Alan was the bus driver and had to continue on with the team.

After the outreach in Mexico he came to Orlando to be with me through one of the most difficult times of our lives. At twenty weeks I had a greater complication and gave birth four months early to our son, Joshua Alan. He lived about fifteen minutes. We kissed him, kissed each other, held him close, then prayed for grace as we gave him back to God. All I can say is that the Lord gave us the strength and peace we needed to get through it.

I really did believe that nothing got past God concerning me. I trusted Him, and though I didn't understand why He didn't save my baby, I didn't allow myself to go down that dark hole. I reasoned, He doesn't create disasters to teach us lessons, but as we go through hardships in this messed up world, He will not waste our sufferings. I knew that God was present because the thing that I couldn't deny was a peace I had, to not demand an answer to the question "why?"

Jeremiah 29:11 says, *"For I know the plans I have for you, declares the Lord, plans to prosper you and not harm you, plans to give you a hope and a future."* This verse is so much deeper than it appears, as I discovered during this very sad situation. God did not say that all our struggles would be over as Christians and that life would be a bed of roses. This scripture revealing God's nature proved true to me, that no matter what situation I am in, I know that I am not alone. God is always with me and will never leave me.

Someone once explained it to me like this: We can hold our child by the hand and walk beside him, and he can still trip and fall. We pick him up, kiss his hurts, and help him to continue on. We carry him if need be. That's what God did for Alan and me. We trusted Him with our lives, and with Joshua's also. We didn't know why, but somehow we had enough grace not to even ask. Being pregnant with Joshua was a gift, and I will always remember his hiccups, his powerful kicks, and his beautiful heartbeat!

Chapter 13

The Child Soldiers of El Salvador

After a few weeks of healing with my family, Alan and I went back to the mission base to continue twenty weeks in *The School of Evangelism*.

In our second phase of training Alan became a licensed and ordained minister through Ecclesia Bible College at YWAM. Our focus was to learn the needs of people, how to sit where they sit without judgment, and how to introduce them to Father God as they gave us permission. We prepared to live without a home for a while, to respect other cultures and live without the conveniences and comforts we were used to. We prayed together for divine appointments with people who were needing and searching to fill the void in their lives.

We resigned to the fact that we may be facing possible dangers by going into the streets and potentially uncivilized villages of other countries. We prayed for wisdom, that we might not take unnecessary risks. We learned leadership skills, how to lead small groups and teams. Most of all we learned the importance of waiting and depending on God through intercession and corporate prayer.

God had a perfect place for me to learn and live out my Christian lifestyle. I thank Him over and over again for allowing Alan and me to start our lives together in this magnificent way.

Our mission assignment was to El Salvador. When we arrived at the airport, just before we touched down, we realized there was a great military presence camouflaged beneath the trees. After everyone went through customs, our luggage was thrown on top of a couple of buses, and we started to travel toward *Campamento de la Iglesia de Cristo*, located in Santa Tecla, near San Salvador. It was dusk, and just before the sun slipped below the horizon, the driver turned off the headlights and we drove in the dark. We passed several small towns and, likewise, there were no lights turned on from what we could see. El Salvador was in a civil war. Our team was not a target, but a bomb went off about a mile from our camp within the first hour of our arrival and knocked out the water and electricity for a day or two.

Maybe the situation was just too surreal, but we had no fear. The entire camp was enclosed with a high stone wall. The top of the wall had cemented-in broken bottles to discourage anyone from climbing over.

Our room was a plain empty cement room with a bathroom and a shower that was all open, with no door. We had a cement floor, but some of the dorm rooms on the ground floor had dirt floors and bunk beds. We had a double size air mattress, and everyone brought sleeping bags. Our cooking facility was an outdoor open fire pit, with an area having a couple of stone prep tables and a double sink. The dining area had a cement floor, with plenty of cement tables and benches.

Everyone on the team had jobs. I was the cook and team medic, and Alan was the fire builder and purchaser of food.

Together we served our team of 73 students and staff: breakfast, sack lunches, and a cooked dinner over the open fire. On our first day at the camp, Alan found a large, flat piece of metal in an alley that was just perfect for making a griddle over the fire. God knew exactly what we needed, and He provided it!

One of the first things we noticed was that everything was creepily silent. There were no bug noises, no birds to be seen or heard, no animals, no stray dogs or cats, no wild or domesticated animals anywhere. There was only silence. In war they either flee or have been eaten as food for people caught in bad circumstances.

Another thing, so unlike the United States, is that there were child soldiers everywhere. Boys that looked as young as 13 to 17 years old were on the street corners carrying rifles that seemed too big for them. We were told that during the day people went on with their lives, gathering food and running their shops at the market and such. But at night, in the hills outside of town, the war continued.

Alan and I went to sleep at night, clearly hearing gunshots in the not-too-far distance. Most days, after breakfast, men from the local churches and some interpreters would come to the camp. We would break into a few smaller groups and go into the nearby towns to distribute food, hand out Bibles, and try to see whom God had for us to share His good news with.

One of the things I remember most about this trip was hiking up the mountain with a group of these soldiers on their way to battle. Many were child soldiers with a meal wrapped in cloth, tied to the end of their gun. We had interpreters that helped us communicate as we prayed for their salvation and protection and offered them small New Testaments for their shirt pockets.

Reaching an unseen line drawn where we could go no further, we turned around and hiked back down the mountain, stopping at houses along the path, talking with children and parents about Jesus. The residents were very polite and receptive. They seemed to enjoy our attention to them and their needs.

We all had to be back at the camp behind the protection of the wall by 4:00 PM.

Some afternoons Alan and I would not go with the team so we could go into the market with our interpreter and find the food necessary to feed our large group. We made a connection with some local women, who would provide chickens for us to cook. The first time they brought them, the heads and feet were still attached! I didn't know what to think about that, and the women giggled to themselves about my reaction.

Come to find out, they didn't waste anything in processing and cooking a chicken. The heads and feet were coveted parts of the bird. Alan made an arrangement to give the women all the heads and feet to take home to their families. They were very happy with this arrangement, and so was I! From thereon out, those parts were already removed by the time they arrived at the camp. Yeah Alan!

At one point we were advised that our food budget had to be reduced to $1.50 per day, per person, because we needed to purchase more Spanish Bibles. Every day a few of our teammates had the task of going to the bakery and bringing back 100-150 individual-sized bolillos. This is a French bread, locally called pan, baked in a stone oven. They would also get handmade tortillas and pupusas. Along with black beans and rice, these were the staples of El Salvadorian cuisine. With the help of our dear friend Olga who taught me how to cook black beans the right way, we ate simple but excellent food on this trip for $1.50 per person, per day!

Alan and I were approached by our leaders and asked if we would separate from our team for two weeks and join up with a medical team who needed more help. This was a dream come true for me! I loved being an Emergency Medical Technician. I really felt like God had wanted me to put that aside after my salvation so that I could devote my time to getting settled in my new lifestyle. I was eager to do everything asked of me and I obeyed His prompting quickly. I'd had no idea that was going to mean getting married and becoming a missionary!

Now, I couldn't believe that I was being asked as a missionary to join a medical outreach! Our first day, my job was to dress up like a clown nurse and play with the kids waiting to see the doctor. I had an oversized stethoscope and helped the kids with their nervous jitters by playing and showing them exaggerated versions of the equipment the doctor might use to treat them. It was really fun. Alan was holding an umbrella to keep the sun off the sickest ones in line, and he kept things flowing well at the door of the makeshift clinic.

The second day I was asked to take a position helping to examine the patients, provide any treatments, and prescribe medication that we might have in our team pharmacy. I was told that I would have a doctor in the room on my right and a nurse in the room on my left. If I had any questions or needed help, I could call on them to help me.

We sat up in the evenings discussing the most common cases like burns from campfires, intestinal parasites, gastrointestinal problems and malnourishment in babies and children. The doctor and nurse did a wonderful job instructing me, and I learned as much as I could. I was amazed that God would allow me to be part of the team. I always thought that if life would have been different for me when I was younger, I probably would have gone to medical school and become a doctor.

Although my present training was an EMT, I always read whatever I could to learn more. Working at the animal shelter and on the ambulance corps gave me a lot of practical experience.

On my very first day, my very first patient, an older woman, carried a younger woman into the clinic on her shoulder like a plank of wood. She leaned her against my chair, and because her body couldn't conform to the chair, we laid her on the examining table.

The only moving part of this woman was her eyes. Her wrists and legs were small like a child's, and she was as thin as a reed. The woman who carried her explained that her condition had continued worsening in the past couple of weeks. She had complained of muscle spasms, trouble eating and swallowing, and now, her muscles were all stiff. I had never seen anything like it. I deduced that it was an extreme case of tetanus. I had no idea what to do.

I asked the Doctor for assistance, and he confirmed that my tetanus diagnosis was correct. He said that he couldn't believe that she was still alive, considering how progressed her disease was. There were no treatments, pills, or vaccinations that could save her. He told me to explain that we had limited resources to treat such an illness, and that she should be taken to the hospital in San Salvador. We had no means to take her, so the older woman picked her up and started to carry her away.

Right then, it seemed the Lord prompted me, "Do what they did for you." I immediately knew what He meant. During my sickness before my salvation, the members of my church cared for me. They put their hands on me and prayed for my healing, they sang to me and asked me if I wanted to receive Christ.

I went after the woman and asked her to come back. We laid her back on the table and with the help of the interpreter I gently and kindly explained that God loved her and is offering her hope through Jesus to spend eternity with Him. Even through the examination earlier, the young woman was able to answer yes and no questions reasonably by blinking her eyes. I can't be absolutely sure, but we believed that she asked Jesus into her heart. When the woman carried her off the second time they stopped at the receiving area where other missionaries continued to minister to them both.

Some day when I'm around the throne of God singing with all the saints, I expect to see this woman! I see myself standing up, pointing to her, and saying, "There you are! Look at you, there you are!"

I had the most amazing opportunity to be God's doctor for two weeks on this trip. I couldn't thank Him enough as he fulfilled my dreams and redeemed many opportunities it seemed I had missed due to the circumstances of my past.

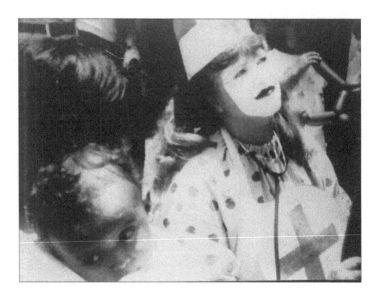

Chapter 14

My Walk Of Faith

After we graduated from *The School of Evangelism*, we accepted a full time position at the mission base in Elm Springs, Arkansas. We were full-time missionaries for a total of seven years. We had many adventures, working with people from around the world to help people see their need for Jesus. Alan and I both drove old Greyhound buses that were donated to the base. He was a main driver, and I was a backup driver. I had the qualifications because I had been an ambulance driver and heavy equipment operator earlier in my life.

I worked as the cook and medic at the base. Alan worked in maintenance and was a member of the Pastoral Council. As often as possible, we would help lead short term mission trips and also work with the new students that came for their missionary schooling.

I remember one time when we were still in classes, a guest speaker came to talk to us about walking the walk of faith with our finances. He talked about how he and his whole family were in full time missions, depending on donations from churches, friends, and family to pay their bills and be able to travel. He said that as they trusted God, He provided everything they needed. I was amazed at his stories, but I couldn't imagine anything like that ever happening to me.

While working with one of the training schools, Alan and I had an opportunity to go back to El Salvador. The war was over, the crickets were plentiful and noisy, birds were visible and singing, and we even saw some stray dogs and cats, and plenty of lizards! It was a completely different atmosphere.

For Alan and me, personally, it was a different kind of trip because our ministry wasn't on the street. Our mission was to take care of the team and their needs. Together we cooked their meals, Alan drove the bus for their times of ministry, and I nursed those who got sick. Although I was a little disappointed that I didn't get to go ministering with the team very often, the Lord reminded me that the team was part of His royal army. It didn't take me long to accept my responsibilities and get to work. Everyday Alan and I had reasons to praise Jesus for His faithfulness. We saw provision time and time again while trying to feed the team. There were at least four or five times when, after preparing a meal, we realized there wasn't enough to go around. Don't think for a second that Jesus is done feeding the 5000, because our kitchen help prayed over the food, and not only was there enough to go around, but there was even food left over! Day after day, time after time, the Lord showed Himself true to us.

While we were there one of our teammates got sick. Again, it was insight from the Lord that helped me diagnose a possible appendicitis. The doctor confirmed that we had gotten the girl to the hospital in time to avoid a rupture of her appendix. She had a successful surgery, but four days after the surgery she contracted a virus, and we had to take her back to the emergency room. The hospital was in San Salvador, about forty minutes away from our camp. Another person and I took the sick girl out on the street, to try and get a taxi. I'm sure that she doesn't want to remember that taxi ride! It was hot and bumpy and seemed to take forever.

Anyway, she was treated with shots and pills and the bill took up our taxi money to get back. We were standing in the Emergency Room praising God anyway and affirming to each other that God would be faithful. At that time I looked up through the glass wall to see a woman looking at me and walking briskly down the steps from the upper floor. She came into the Emergency Room, walked right up to me, and said, "God told me to come give you some money, do you need some money?" She was a Christian; I think she said from Italy. She handed me a fistful of bills and walked away as fast as she came!

We all stood in the Emergency Room amazed and crying with gratitude for God's provision. We got back to the camp with change in our pockets and another testimony to cheer us on in our walk of faith!

Luke 12:24 *"Consider the ravens: They do not sow or reap, they have no storeroom or barn; yet God feeds them. And how much more valuable you are than birds!"*

Chapter 15:

A Miracle In Belarus

Alan and I traveled as missionaries for seven years with Youth With A Mission. We had such a wonderful time experiencing different cultures and getting to know people and their needs in so many different places. Now, I'd like to give God the glory for a miracle that took place in Belarus, Former Soviet Union.

During our first visit to Belarus, we visited a children's hospital in the town of Maladzyechna. Our team members went from room to room, praying and ministering to the children, using puppets. We were walking from ward to ward, and as I opened one of the doors to go in, the nurse stopped me and said, "No, don't go in there, those are the forgotten children."

I asked, "What do you mean, they are forgotten?" She told me that these children had long term diseases that were too difficult for the families to care for at home, so they had been left at the hospital. They were well looked after, but there was little hope for their recovery. I said, "These are exactly the children we would like to see!" Then she opened the door and let us in.

The room was small, like a walk in closet. There was a crib against each of three walls, and one of the cribs had two babies, one at each end. The first child that we prayed for was a five year old girl named Oksana. She had been diagnosed with Rheumatoid Arthritis. She was completely crippled and couldn't walk. She was also going blind because of her condition. As we prayed, we felt that the Lord wanted to heal her right then and there. Believing with faith, we asked the nurse to hold her up and put her feet against the bed to see if there was any strength in her legs. Nothing appeared to be changed. There was no evidence of her healing at that time. The nurse explained that no medicine was available to control the pain and inflammation of Oksana's joints. Our team was scheduled to come back to Belarus in three months, so I asked for some specific information about Oksana's diagnosis and shared about the possibility of us bringing medications back from the United States.

When we came back three months later, we went back to the hospital to minister to the children and to deliver the medicine for Oksana. I spoke to the doctor about the girl, but he said that she was no longer in the hospital.

He said that her family lived about half an hour away and that they did not know her address. He thought that there was probably no phone at all in that town and that it could be very difficult to contact them. At that point my interpreter and I planned to take a bus to that town the next day and knock on doors until we found Oksana and her family.

As we were leaving the hotel the next morning, we saw a young man in the hallway looking lost. He said that his name was Yuri and that he was Oksana's father! We were so surprised and overwhelmed that God had brought him to us and allowed us to participate in His plan!

As we invited Yuri to come in and have a seat, I noticed that tears were welling up in his eyes. He said that a nurse from the hospital lived in his town and went knocking on doors the night before until she found him. She told him to go pick up the medicine at the hospital and to come see the Americans at the Hotel Maladzyechna.

He said that he didn't know that anyone prayed for his daughter or cared anything about his family. His eyes teared up again as he said with a broken voice, "My daughter is now walking!"

God did heal her! He did it in His own timing and in His very personal way so her mother and father could see and believe. It was almost too much for Yuri to take in as he learned all the details that had led to this moment and to the healing of his daughter! We didn't get to see Oksana on this trip because, as Yuri explained, she was out in the fields with her mother picking strawberries and vegetables to can for the winter! How about that!

In Belarus everyone is given a plot of land in the country to grow their fruits and vegetables. They have to take a train and stay for several days to harvest their produce. Typically they sleep in hammocks in a little cabin located near their plot.

Her father came back to the hotel the next day with a bouquet of flowers and a giant smile on his face. My interpreter and I sat down with him to answer his questions about who we were exactly and what we were doing at the children's hospital when we met his daughter. We had the opportunity to share the love of God with him for about three hours! He didn't know anything about Jesus, salvation, or the forgiveness of sins. He didn't know that God would spend time thinking about him or that He would go to such lengths to get his attention and help his family.

We left Yuri with a Bible, a connection to other believers in Maladzyechna, and a lot to think about. I believe that we left him with hope!

A Miracle In Belarus

My interpreter kept in touch with the family and reported to me that they had all come to accept Jesus and were worshiping with other believers. She also sent me a photo of Yuri and Oksana to keep as a testimony.

Chapter 16

In Conclusion

How could I possibly write about all that has happened in the years since I asked Jesus into my life? How can I tell of all of God's wonders, the things He has taught me, the way He has changed me, and shown Himself to be true, loving, faithful, merciful, and great! There is no way to fit it in the binder of a book.

Alan and I have had some great challenges in our lives, but with God, it's been worth every minute. Two years after we lost our son Joshua, I gave birth to another boy, Jonathan Alan.

His name means "God's gift." He had his first birthday during a mission trip to Belarus and his fourth birthday in Acapulco, Mexico.

Today he serves God, his family, and his country with honor and strength. He is extremely intelligent and a hard worker. He has an amazing wife, Shandi, and three wonderful children who call us Grandma and Pap.

Three years later we had a daughter, Melissa Mercedes. We named her Mercedes after our first date when we took a drive through the Florida Keys in Alan's 72 Mercedes. Her name means "diligent worker of mercy." This absolutely fits her personality. She has grown up to be a leader and diligent worker.

Melissa would give the shirt off her back to help someone. She is also a great lover of dogs and shows no interest in giving us grandchildren that don't bark!

Then the Lord blessed us with Jamie Marie. Her name means I love.

We named her after a musician friend who is just an amazing person. Jamie is smart, brave, talented, adventurous, thoughtful, and kind. Did I mention adventurous? Jamie puts feet to her dreams, and she is a very diverse and courageous person. She is a great blessing to her father and me.

I could talk all day about our children, which by the way, the doctors said I most likely would never have! I have determined that doctors really are practicing physicians, and God gets the final word!

Why me? Why did God save me? I'm no different than anybody else. That's my point here! John 3:16 says, For God so loved the world, that he gave his only begotten Son, that whosoever believeth in him should not perish, but have everlasting life. (KJV). I am a whosoever! You are a whosoever! Everyone is included, no matter who you are, rich or poor, seemingly successful, or just a hot mess! God made us in His image, with a spirit, so that we could communicate and have a vibrant relationship with Him. When we don't have that relationship, there is a void in our undeveloped spirit! That's the emptiness we can't seem to fill! That's the absence of peace and hope that makes us question the value of life and what truth really is.

I had to know what the truth was, and I simply said, "God, I need to know!" He put people in my path to lead me directly to

Trophies of Grace

Him. I accepted Jesus as my Lord and Savior, and He breathed new life into me. I am nobody, that He should have saved me, but the fact that He did causes me to praise Him with every breath!

I am a whosoever, just like you, and I have discovered that eternal life with God started the minute I believed. As I accepted God's direction on how to live this life successfully, I truly am healed, restored, and fulfilled!

I had to tell my story because there are many people who are weary, beaten down, abused, and forgotten. So many who want everything but are satisfied with nothing. Some who have recognized a void that can't seem to be filled, and some that have completely lost hope.

My encouragement, if this is you, is to simply ask God to show you who He is. Invite Jesus into your life and allow Him to speak to your tired, weary spirit, and to infuse you with hope, life, and love.

Matthew 11:28
"Come to me, all you who are weary and burdened,
and I will give you rest."

In Conclusion

Endnotes

1. 1 Samuel 17:45 (NIV)
2. 1 Samuel 17:45-47 (NASB)
3. Calucchia, Christie. Oct 11, 2019. Retrieved February 25, 2020, from https://www.mydomaine.com/how-to-do-transcendental-meditation
4. Genesis 1:27; Colossians 3:10
5. Lamentations 3:22
6. Ephesians 4:18
7. John 3:16; John 12:27-33; 2 Peter 3:9
8. 1 John 4:7-12; 1 Corinthians 7:15; Galatians 5:22; Colossians 3:15-17; Matthew 5:9
9. Genesis 1:1-2:3; Ecclesiastes 3:11
10. Exodus 2:1-10; 2 Samuel 4:1; Acts 9:36-39; Job 16:20; Proverbs 17:17; James 2:23
11. Matthew 6:26; Psalm 104:14
12. Ephesians 3:17-20
13. 1 Corinthians 9:19-23; Galatians 4:12
14. Acts 17:22-31
15. John 14:27 and 16:33; Philippians 4:4-7; Colossians 3:15-16
16. Luke 18:29-30; 1 John 5:20
17. 1 Corinthians 13:12
18. Acts 17:22-31 (BSB), emphases mine
19. Luke 24:27; Hebrews 1:1
20. Mark 12:29
21. Genesis 35:11; Revelation 21:22
22. John 3:13-18
23. John 10:10; Ephesians 3:14-21
24. John 1:14
25. John 1:14
26. John 3:16

27. Titus 3:2-4; Romans 6:6, 12; Romans 3:9
28. John 3:16
29. Isaiah 53:1-12; John 19:28-30, 33; Matthew 27:45-56
30. 2 Timothy 2:8
31. Luke 24:26, 46-48
32. Romans 6:5; John 11:23-26; John 5:29
33. Mark 15:42-47; John 19:38-42
34. Matthew 28:6; Luke 24:1-7
35. 1 Corinthians 15:1-8
36. Mark 16:11-14; Luke 24:13-42
37. 1 Corinthians 15:6; Matthew 28:7 (an angel's instruction), 28:10 (Jesus's instruction)
38. Luke 24:6-7
39. 1 Corinthians 15:12-19 (WEB)
40. 2 Corinthians 11:24-26
41. 1 Thessalonians 2:2
42. 2 Timothy 2:8-10
43. Mark 12:30-31
44. According to an insightful Rabbi, David Wolpe, "Love should be seen not as a feeling but as an enacted emotion. To love is to feel and act lovingly." https://time.com/4225777/meaning-of-love/
45. An enacted emotion. This is a spot-on definition of love, though the emotion in pure love stems from and is directed toward God, Himself. Our love for Him compels us to behave lovingly toward others, even those we do not like.
46. Matthew 5:44; Exodus 23:5
47. 2 Peter 2:1; Matthew 10:33; 1 John 2:22
48. Romans 3:23; 1 John 4:12-15
49. Romans 3:24-26; John 19:1-3; Luke 23:33; Matthew 27:46; Hebrews 2:17-18
50. Romans 1:16
51. 2 Timothy 3:16-17; Job 2:10; Matthew 5:45
52. Vermes, G., https://archive.org/details/jesusjew00gzav; Matthew 15:6 and 22:31; Mark 7:13
53. John 14:6
54. Goldberg, p. 4
55. Matthew 14:14; Mark 5:21-43; 6:13
56. Luke 7:11-17; 8:49-56; John 11:17-44*

Endnotes

57. Luke 7:11-17; 8:49-56; John 11:1-4
58. Mark 5:1-20
59. Matthew 14:31-33; Mark 4:38-40
60. Luke 9:10-17
61. Mark 6:47-49
62. Matthew 9:4; 12:25; 22:18; Mark 12:15; Luke 9:47; 11:17
63. John 8:31-32
64. Ephesians 3:20
65. 1 Peter 5:7
66. https://en.wikipedia.org/wiki/Cerebrospinal_fluid
67. https://www.healthline.com/health/ventriculoperitoneal-shunt#risks
68. Philippians 4:7
69. John 16:33
70. Galatians 3:26
71. Isaiah 29:16 and 64:8; Jeremiah 18:1-
72. Job 38:4 (NLT)
73. Job 38:19-21 (NLT)
74. Philippians 4:6
75. 1 John 5:14-15
76. John 3:16-17
77. John 1:12-13
78. Romans 5:1
79. 2 Corinthians 4:7
80. Psalm 17:15; Genesis 1:26; Romans 8:10-11; Titus 3:4-7
81. Ecclesiastes 12:7; Luke 23:46; Acts 7:59
82. 1 John 2:24-28; 1 Thessalonians 4:16-17
83. Psalm 139:14
84. John 10:10
85. Galatians 5:22-23; 1 Timothy 1:14; 2 Corinthians 1:5; 9:8; Matthew 25:35-36; James 1:27
86. (2 Timothy 3:16); Matthew 14:14; Mark 1:32-34; Luke 5:17; John 6:2; James 5:14-17; 2 Chronicles 32:24; Proverbs 13:12; 2 Kings 5:1-14
87. Psalm 65:9; Genesis 24:35; Proverbs 10:22; Psalm 68:10, 132:15; Numbers 11:18; Job 42:10
88. 1 Timothy 1:13-15; Ephesians 3:19-20; Isaiah 55:7; Hebrews 6:17
89. 2 Corinthians 4:5-18 (ESV)

90. Philippians 4:11-13 (GWT)
91. 2 Corinthians 1:3-4
92. Lamentations 3:18-26 NLT
93. Hebrews 12:2; Philippians 4:13
94. Psalm 119:11
95. Jeremiah 17:9
96. Romans 8:28
97. 2 Corinthians 1:3-4; Hebrews 2:18 (here are some practical examples of empathy in action – sometimes the helper's suffering is inferred: James 2:16; Matthew 14:15-16 and 25:35-36; 1 John 3:17)
98. In fact, Freda and her husband Boyd had been instrumental in bringing Ruth to Christ many moons before this!
99. Romans 8:28 (Human eyes just don't see it sometimes…)
100. And I mean, precisely. Everything I needed; nothing I didn't.
101. https://en.wikipedia.org/wiki/History_of_Haiti
102. https://www.soc.mil/ARSOF_History/articles/v11n1_true_force_page_2.html
103. James 2:14-17
104. Romans 6:23; 1 Timothy 6:12; John 3:36, 4:14, 5:13 & 20, 10:27-28; 14:6; Jude 20-23
105. John 3:15-17; Romans 6:4; Proverbs 16:24
106. Matthew 28:18-20; 2 Timothy 1:7-9; Romans 1:15-17; Mark 8:38
107. Luke 14:27-28
108. Colossians 3:17; 1 Thessalonians 5:8-11
109. Mark 16:15-16; Acts 2:38; Matthew 7:21; Romans 10:9-10; Hebrews 5:8-9 and 11:6; 2 Timothy 2:4; Revelation 2:10
110. 1 Corinthians 13:1-8 and 15:58; 2 Timothy 2:2, 21, and 4:2; Romans 10:14 and 12:1-11; Ephesians 2:10; Galatians 5:13 and 6:10; John 13:35 James 1:27; 1 John 4:16; Matthew 28:18-20; Matthew 5:44; etc., etc., etc.
111. Romans 11:33-34; Galatians 3:27-29; 1 Corinthians 2:7; Ephesians 1:23; Matthew 11:25-26
112. Ephesians 3:10-11 (NIV)
113. http://haitianchristianfoundation.org/wp/index.php/history-of-the-hcf/; https://haitianchristianfoundation.org/wp/center-for-biblical-training/
114. Matthew 28:20

Endnotes

115 John 8:28; 12:32; 18:32
116 2 Corinthians 5:16-21 (NLT)
117 Current travel in Haiti might be somewhat (or a lot) different than what my experience illustrates. Keep in mind, this was 1994....
118 If you don't know what your tootsies are – or if you didn't even know you have some – visit a preschool, become a parent, babysit in Texas, or look it up.
119 Hmmm, what existed already that could cause this? Not at all suggesting that God might have, but what else could, if nothing existed? Have you stopped to wonder?
120 My biggest problem with extrapolating from the (observably limited) natural selection process is that the official cosmology's *Theory of Evolution* is an unnecessary proposition, since the premises upon which it's built are not dependable. I mean that, for a hypothesis about the natural world to hold legitimate value, it needs to lead to deductions that can be tested, and the Big Bang hypothesis is faulty at its core. No one can test the spontaneous combustion of nothing, so why use such an idea for the **foundation** of any scientific theory? This theory, then, has no true supporting evidence and is not science. It's a belief system requiring faith.
121 Matthew 5:16 (ESV); see also Isaiah 60
122 Matthew 19:26; Mark 10:27
123 Matthew 5:45 (NIV), emphases mine
124 Psalm 40:8; Job 23:12
125 Matthew 5:44-46
126 Philippians 3:9; Romans 1:17 and 10:3; James 2:23
127 Matthew 6:12-15 and 18:21-35; Mark 11:26; Luke 11:4 and 23:34; 2 Corinthians 2:7; Ephesians 4:32; Colossians 3:13; 1 John 1:9
128 Hebrews 11:1-3, 6; John 3:11 and 4:48 and 6:36 and 12:37 and 20:29
129 2 Peter 1:9
130 1 Corinthians 2:7; Matthew 13:35; Colossians 2:3; Mark 4:22; 2 Corinthians 3:13-17
131 1 John 4:19
132 Romans 8:28

An ALMIGHTY God? Get Serious!

133. Luke 6:21-23; 1 Peter 4:14; Matthew 5:10-12
134. James 1:12; Matthew 10:22; 2 Timothy 1:8; Acts 14:22
135. Acts 9:16; Matthew 10:18, 22, 39
136. John 15:19-21; 2 Timothy 3:12; Ezekiel 3:7
137. 2 Thessalonians 2:16-17; James 1:2-4; 2 Corinthians 7:10; Romans 8:18-25
138. Philippians 4:4; Galatians 5:22
139. Psalm 28:7 and 91:1-6
140. Philippians 4:6-7
141. 2 Corinthians 7:10 and 12:8-1
142. James 1:2 (NKJV)
143. 2 Thessalonians 2:16-17 [Now may our Lord Jesus Christ Himself and God our Father, who by grace has loved us and given us eternal comfort and good hope, encourage your hearts and strengthen you in every good word and deed. (BSB)
144. Hebrews 13:21
145. Acts 17:26; Jeremiah 29:11; Psalm 23 and 139
146. https://www.healthline.com/human-body-maps/frontal-lobe#1
147. Just for the record, I would have been delighted to help them out with their research, had I, meanwhile, been encouraged to make (observable) strides toward my physical recovery.
148. Lamentations 3:21-26 (ESV). [I added some italics for emphasis and converted double quotation marks to single, for clarity.
149. Mark 9:23b (NIV)
150. Revelation 22:1-4 (BSB)
151. Revelation 22:12-16 (BSB) [I highlighted some words with bold print and some by underlining.
152. Titus 1:1 (NIV). I placed "our" in brackets, as a reminder about whom "their" is there for.... :
153. Ephesians 4:4-6
154. John 14:6
155. Jude 1:17-19
156. 2 Timothy 3:1-7
157. Matthew 12:36; 1 Peter 4:5; Jude 1:14-15; Hebrews 4:13
158. 1 Thessalonians 5:1-10
159. 1 John 5:11-13
160. Titus 1:2-3
161. Romans 10:13-14 (NLT)

Endnotes

162 Matthew 28:18-20
163 1Peter 3:15
164 2 Timothy 4:2 (GOD'S WORD® Translation)
165 Revelation 22:17
166 Acts 4:12
167 2 Corinthians 11:2
168 Matthew 16:18
169 John 3:29; Revelation 19:7-8
170 Ephesians 5:27
171 John 2:13-17; Jeremiah 32:26-35; Matthew 11:20-24
172 Acts 2:38 and 3:19; 2 Chronicles 32:26; Joel 2:13; Jonah 3:10; 2 Corinthians 7:10
173 Romans 8:9-11, 14-16, 20-21, 26-28, 31-34; Genesis 6:6; Mark 3:5; John 11:35; Matthew 23:37
174 1 Peter 5:7
175 Matthew 4:4; Deuteronomy 8:3
176 To beget means to bring forth. While we say the female "gives birth to," we say the male (father) "begets." It is a different process to beget, or bring forth from your very self, than it is to create by fashioning.
177 Genesis 2:1-22 and 3:1-23; Exodus 9:30; 2 Samuel 7:22-25; 1 Chronicles 17:16-17 and 22:19 and 28:20
178 Matthew 28:19; 1 John 5:6-10; Colossians 2:9
179 John 1:1-3, 14 and 14:26 and 15:26 and 16:15; Ephesians 1:17 and 2:18; Galatians 4:6 and 5:1-26 (NLT is smooth reading); Luke 10:21 and 23:46; Acts 2:33; Matthew 28:19 and 10:20; Romans 8:15 and 5:2; 1 Peter 1:3-21; Hebrews 13:15
180 Romans 1:20
181 1 Corinthians 13:12
182 Hebrews 12:22-24; John 6:40
183 Colossians 2:2-3
184 Deuteronomy 29:29
185 Mark 13:32
186 Matthew 24:36
187 John 3:16-17; Hebrews 1:1-3; Ephesians 4:11-13, 30; Hebrews 4:12, 15; 1 John 2:2 and 4:10; Romans 3:20-26; Matthew 25
188 Galatians 3:28; Philippians 2:1

[189] 1 Thessalonians 4:17 and 5:10; John 14:3; Psalm 16:11 and 73:24; Hebrews 4:8-10
[190] 2 Peter 1:21; 2 Timothy 3:16; Acts 3:18
[191] Jeremiah 29:13; 1 Chronicles 28:9; 2 Chronicles 15:2; Matthew 7:7-8; Psalm 34:4; Luke 11:9-11
[192] Romans 7:4; 2 Corinthians 11:2; John 3:29; Matthew 25:1-13
[193] Isaiah 54:5; Jeremiah 3:14; Hosea 2:19 and 3:1
[194] John 1:1-5, 9-14; Philippians 2:5-7; Hebrews 1:1-4
[195] Isaiah 62:2-5, 12; 1 Peter 2:9-10
[196] Ephesians 5:25
[197] John 1:1-4
[198] Romans 1:25
[199] 1 Corinthians 14:33; Titus 1:5
[200] Isaiah 29:13 (NASB) I uncapitalized a few letters for readability's sake.; Matthew 15:8-9; Mark 7:6-7
[201] Romans 1:19-20
[202] Romans 3:23
[203] Psalm 23:1
[204] Matthew 6:19-20 and 19:21; 1 Corinthians 2:9; James 1:17
[205] Romans 1:28 and 7:7-24; Hebrews 12:1-3
[206] Genesis 3:1-19; Matthew 11:6 and 13:20-21; Mark 4:17; 2 Corinthians 11:3; 1 Timothy 6:10; Hebrews 6:5-6
[207] That bold font is mine...
[208] Jeremiah 30:12; Hosea 5:13; Micah 1:9; Matthew 9:36; Mark 6:34; Ephesians 2:12; Romans 3:22-24
[209] Isaiah 59:1
[210] 1 Corinthians 10:13
[211] 1 Timothy 4:7-8 and 6:6; 2 Timothy 3:15-17; Hebrews 4:12
[212] 1 Corinthians 3:21-23; Romans 4:25 and 8:32; John 3:16-17; Matthew 7:11; Psalm 84:11
[213] 2 Peter 1:1-4 (NLT)
[214] 2 Peter 1:5-8 [Again, bold print is my doing, for emphasis]
[215] John 1:1-18
[216] 1 Corinthians 6:19
[217] Luke 11:13; Ezekiel 11:19 and 36:26-27
[218] Romans 8:1-2; 1 Corinthians 2:12 and 3:16 and 6:17-19; Galatians 4:6
[219] Romans 8:11; 2 Timothy 1:14; 1 John 3:24 and 4:13

Endnotes

[220] Romans 8:9; John 14:17, 23
[221] Galatians 5:22-23
[222] 1 Corinthians 13:4-8, 13; Romans 13:10; Mark 12:33
[223] James 1:2-3; 2 Corinthians 8:2; Philemon 1:7; Nehemiah 8:10; Luke 10:21
[224] Philippians 1:19; 2 Thessalonians 3:16; 2 Corinthians 13:11; James 3:18; John 14:27; Ephesians 2:17-18
[225] Philippians 4:7
[226] James 1:3 and 5:10; Colossians 1:11; Hebrews 6:12; 2 Corinthians 6:6; 2 Timothy 4:2; Ecclesiastes 7:8
[227] 2 Corinthians 3:6 and 6:6; Titus 3:3-5; Colossians 3:12
[228] 1 Corinthians 12:13; James 2:8; Galatians 5:14
[229] Galatians 6:8-9; Matthew 5:16; Psalm 25:7-9; 1 Timothy 3:7, 5:24-25 and Proverbs 10:9 and Revelation 14:13
[230] 1 Corinthians 12:13; Romans 6:3-5; Galatians 3:27; Acts 2:38
[231] 1 Peter 4:9-11 and 5:12; 1 Corinthians 4:1; Luke 12:35-48; 1 Timothy 3:15, 4:10; 2 Timothy 2:19; Hebrews 3:2-6
[232] Ephesians 4:2; Philippians 4:5; Colossians 3:12-13; 1 Peter 3:8-9; Psalm 138:6; 2 Corinthians 10:1; Matthew 21:5
[233] 1 Corinthians 9:24-27; Romans 13:14; 1 Thessalonians 4:10-12 and 5:6-8; Ephesians 5:17-18; Colossians 3:5, 17
[234] Galatians 5:16-26; 2 Peter 1:3-11; Colossians 3:1-3
[235] 2 Peter 1:3
[236] 2 Peter 1:4
[237] 2 Peter 1:5-8
[238] Ephesians 5:28
[239] Ephesians 5:25; Romans 12:1-2
[240] Genesis 2:18-20 and Matthew 19:4-6
[241] Ephesians 5:22
[242] Genesis 1:27 and 5:2; Matthew 19:4
[243] 1 Corinthians 11:11-12
[244] Ephesians 5:20-21
[245] Genesis 2:24; 1 Corinthians 7:12-14, 33-34
[246] 1 Corinthians 7:1-5; Ephesians 5:30-31; Romans 12:5
[247] 2 Corinthians 6:14-16
[248] 1 Peter 4:1; Romans 14:18 and 15:1-5; Colossians 3:1-15
[249] Ephesians 5:25
[250] Romans 10:15 (NLT)

[251] Galatians 6:2
[252] Galatians 3:27
[253] 1 Corinthians 10:13 (NIV)
[254] Romans 8:35-39 (BSB)
[255] Matthew 16:24-25 (NLT); see also Mark 8:34-35 and Luke 9:23-26; Matthew 10:39; Esther 4:14, 16; Matthew 16:26; John 12:25
[256] James 1:17 (ESV)
[257] James 1:2 (NIV)
[258] John 8:58 (WEB)
[259] James 1:3-4 (NIV)
[260] Philippians 4:19
[261] Psalm 23
[262] Colossians 1:15
[263] Acts 2:33 and 7:56; Hebrews 1:13
[264] Luke 23:34
[265] Mark 14:36
[266] Hebrews 12:2 (NLT)
[267] Hebrews 12:1-3 (NASB) I did the underlining and letter bolding...
[268] Hebrews 10:32-37 (NLT) I again emphasized some pertinent text with bold font
[269] Philippians 4:13
[270] 1 John 1:9
[271] 2 Corinthians 11:21-33
[272] 1 Peter 5:7
[273] Praise God From Whom All Blessings Flow - Acapella Trio - Cover by the Cerna Siblings (youtube.com)
[274] Psalm 40:5
[275] James 1:2-3
[276] Jeremiah 29:11
[277] Genesis 1:14
[278] Matthew 5:45
[279] Philippians 4:4
[280] Matthew 6:10
[281] Romans 8:18; Revelation 21:4
[282] 1 Peter 5:8
[283] Jude 25
[284] Ephesians 6:11-18

[285] Romans 12:2
[286] John 17:17
[287] Romans 1:16
[288] 2 Peter 1:4
[289] Revelation 12:10
[290] 2 Timothy 2:15
[291] Hebrews 4:12
[292] 1 John 4:1
[293] 2 Peter 1:2
[294] Philippians 4:8
[295] Ephesians 5:1
[296] Mark 12:30-31
[297] Matthew 19:26; Luke 18:27; Mark 10:27; Acts 2:24
[298] Philippians 4:13
[299] Ephesians 1:22
[300] Hebrews 4:12
[301] Jeremiah 29:13-14; Isaiah 55:6-8; Matthew 7:7-11; Luke 11:9-13
[302] 2 Peter 1:20-21
[303] Deuteronomy 4:2; Jeremiah 14:14-15; Revelation 22:18-19
[304] Isaiah 55:8; Deuteronomy 29:29; Romans 3:4
[305] John 3:16
[306] Romans 3:23
[307] Acts 4:12
[308] Matthew 28:18-20